BOOKS BY TERRY PRATCHETT

The Discworld® series

——————— **Other books about Discworld** ———————

THE COMPLEAT ANKH-MORPORK
(with the Discworld Emporium)

THE STREETS OF ANKH-MORPORK
(with Stephen Briggs, painted by Stephen Player)

THE DISCWORLD MAPP
(with Stephen Briggs, painted by Stephen Player)

A TOURIST GUIDE TO LANCRE – A DISCWORLD MAPP
(with Stephen Briggs, illustrated by Paul Kidby)

DEATH'S DOMAIN (with Paul Kidby)

A complete list of Terry Pratchett ebooks and audio books as well as other
books based on the Discworld series – illustrated screenplays, graphic
novels, comics and plays – can be found on **www.terrypratchett.co.uk**

––––––––––––––––––– **Shorter Writing** –––––––––––––––––––
A BLINK OF THE SCREEN
A SLIP OF THE KEYBOARD

––––––––––––––––– **Non-Discworld books** –––––––––––––––––
THE DARK SIDE OF THE SUN
STRATA
THE UNADULTERATED CAT (illustrated by Gray Jolliffe)
GOOD OMENS (with Neil Gaiman)

––––––––––––––––– **With Stephen Baxter** –––––––––––––––––
THE LONG EARTH
THE LONG WAR
THE LONG MARS
THE LONG UTOPIA

––––––––––– **Non-Discworld books for young adults** –––––––––––
THE CARPET PEOPLE
TRUCKERS
DIGGERS
WINGS
ONLY YOU CAN SAVE MANKIND
JOHNNY AND THE DEAD
JOHNNY AND THE BOMB
NATION
DODGER
JACK DODGER'S GUIDE TO LONDON
DRAGONS AT CRUMBLING CASTLE

Terry Pratchett was the acclaimed creator of the global bestselling Discworld series, the first of which, *The Colour of Magic*, was published in 1983. His fortieth Discworld novel, *Raising Steam*, was published in 2013. His books have been widely adapted for stage and screen, and he was the winner of multiple prizes, including the Carnegie Medal, as well as being awarded a knighthood for services to literature. He died in March 2015.

www.terrypratchett.co.uk

A Slip of the Keyboard

Collected Non-Fiction

Terry Pratchett

CORGI BOOKS

TRANSWORLD PUBLISHERS
61–63 Uxbridge Road, London W5 5SA
www.transworldbooks.co.uk

Transworld is part of the Penguin Random House group of companies
whose addresses can be found at global.penguinrandomhouse.com

Penguin
Random House
UK

First published in Great Britain in 2014 by Doubleday
an imprint of Transworld Publishers
Corgi edition published 2015

A CIP catalogue record for this book
is available from the British Library.

ISBN
9780552167741 (A format)
9780552167727 (B format)

Typeset in 11/15pt Adobe Caslon by Falcon Oast Graphic Art Ltd.
Printed and bound by CPI Group (UK) Ltd, Croydon, CR0 4YY.

Penguin Random House is committed to a sustainable
future for our business, our readers and our planet. This book is made
from Forest Stewardship Council® certified paper.

MIX
Paper from
responsible sources
FSC® C018179

1 3 5 7 9 10 8 6 4 2

Dedication

You have in your hands a book of words that cover my entire career and therefore it is only right that I should dedicate it to those delightful souls who have either collaborated or assisted me in myriad helpful ways* over many, many years.

To single out and to name just a few: my esteemed publishers Colin Smythe, Larry Finlay, Marianne Velmans, Philippa Dickinson, Suzanne Bridson, Malcolm Edwards and Patrick Janson-Smith. My wranglers of words Katrina Whone, Sue Cook and Elizabeth Dobson. My cherished editors Simon Taylor, Di Pearson, Kirsten Armstrong, Jennifer Brehl and Anne Hoppe. My ever-buoyant and ever-capable publicists Sally Wray and Lynsey Dalladay. Lord of the Über Fans Dr Pat Harkin. My friends Neil Gaiman, Professor David Lloyd and the scoundrel that is Mister Bernard Pearson. The Managing Director of Narrativia and even bigger scoundrel Rod Brown. My partners in writing Steve Baxter, Jacqueline Simpson, Jack Cohen, Ian Stewart and my personal cartographer/playwright/wearer of tights and Man of a Thousand Voices† Stephen Briggs. My artists

---

* Well, intended helpfulness and almost always with excruciating cheerfulness.
† As long as they're all Welsh.

Paul Kidby, Josh Kirby and Stephen Player and my enchanting enablers Sandra and Jo Kidby. Jason Anthony for *Discworld Monthly*, Elizabeth Alway for the Guild of Fans and Disciples, and Steve Dean for his most prestigious *Wizard's Knob*.

A special mention has to go to the Head of the Thieves' Guild, and man-who-can, Mister Josiah Boggis/Dave Ward* And to the Queen's Head, and their pickled eggs and most magnificent bubble and squeak.

And to anyone who has ever served or survived the mayhem that is a Discworld Convention as an attendee or part of the organizing committee, especially the founder and man responsible, Paul Kruzycki.

And to anyone else who has helped and not hindered me along the way, but most especially to Rob, who quietly gets on with it, and without whom . . .

Thank you, one and all. Thank you.

* Delete as applicable.

Contents

A Twit and a Dreamer

Days of Rage

And finally . . .

Foreword
by Neil Gaiman

I want to tell you about my friend Terry Pratchett, and it's not easy. I'm going to tell you something you may not know.

Some people have encountered an affable man with a beard and a hat. They believe they have met Sir Terry Pratchett. They have not.

Science fiction conventions often give you someone to look after you, to make sure you get from place to place without getting lost. Some years ago I ran into someone who had once been Terry's handler at a convention in Texas. His eyes misted over at the memory of getting Terry from his panel to the book-dealers' room and back. 'What a jolly old elf Sir Terry is,' he said.

And I thought, *No. No, he's not.*

Back in February 1991, Terry and I were on a book signing tour for *Good Omens*, a book we had written together. We can tell you dozens of not-only-funny-but-also-true stories about the things that happened on that tour. Terry alludes to a few of them in this book. This story is true, but it is not one of the stories we tell.

We were in San Francisco. We had just done a stock signing in a bookshop, signing the dozen or so copies of our book they had ordered. Terry looked at the itinerary. Next stop was a radio station: we were due to have an hour-long interview on live radio. 'From the address, it's just down the street from here,' said Terry. 'And we've got half an hour. Let's walk it.'

This was a long time ago, best beloved, in the days before GPS systems and mobile phones and taxi-summoning apps and suchlike useful things that would have told us in moments that no, it would not be a few blocks to the radio station. It would be several miles, all uphill and mostly through a park.

We called the radio station as we went, whenever we passed a payphone, to tell them that we knew we were now late for a live broadcast, and that we were, promise cross our sweaty hearts, walking as fast as we could.

I would try and say cheerful, optimistic things as we walked. Terry said nothing, in a way that made it very clear that anything I could say would probably just make things worse. I did not ever say, at any point on that walk, that all of this would have been avoided if we had just got the book-shop to call us a taxi. There are things you can never unsay, that you cannot say and still remain friends, and that would have been one of them.

We reached the radio station at the top of the hill, a very long way from anywhere, about 40 minutes into our hour-long live interview. We arrived all sweaty and out of breath, and they were broadcasting the breaking news. A man had just started shooting people in a local McDonald's, which is not the kind of thing you want to have as your lead-in when you are now meant to talk about a funny book you've written about the end of the world and how we're all going to die.

The radio people were angry with us, too, and understandably so: it's no fun having to improvise when your guests are late. I don't think that our fifteen minutes on the air were very funny.

(I was later told that Terry and I had both been blacklisted by that San Franciscan radio station for several years, because leaving a show's hosts to burble into the dead air for 40 minutes is something the Powers of Radio do not easily forget or forgive.)

Still, by the top of the hour it was all over. We went back to our hotel, and this time we took a taxi.

Terry was silently furious: with himself, mostly, I suspect, and with the world that had not told him that the distance from the bookshop to the radio station was much further than it had looked on our itinerary. He sat in the back of the cab beside me white with anger, a non-directional ball of fury. I said something hoping to placate him. Perhaps I said that ah well, it had all worked out in the end, and it hadn't been the end of the world, and suggested it was time to not be angry any more.

Terry looked at me. He said, 'Do not underestimate this anger. This anger was the engine that powered *Good Omens*.'

I thought of the driven way that Terry wrote, and of the way that he drove the rest of us with him, and I knew that he was right.

There is a fury to Terry Pratchett's writing. It's the fury that was the engine that powered Discworld, and you will discover it here: it's the anger at the headmaster who would decide that six-year-old Terry Pratchett would never be smart enough for the 11-plus; anger at pompous critics, and at those who think that serious is the opposite of funny; anger at his early American publishers who could not bring his books out successfully.

The anger is always there, an engine that drives. By the time this book enters its final act, and Terry learns he has a rare, early onset form of Alzheimer's, the targets of his fury change: now he is angry with his brain and his genetics and, more than these, furious at a country that will not permit him (or others in a similarly intolerable situation) to choose the manner and the time of their passing.

And that anger, it seems to me, is about Terry's underlying sense of what is fair and what is not.

It is that sense of fairness that underlies Terry's work and his writing, and it's what drove him from school to journalism to the press office of the SouthWestern Electricity Board to the position of being one of the best-loved and bestselling writers in the world.

It's the same sense of fairness that means that in this book, sometimes in the cracks, while talking of other things, he takes time to punctiliously acknowledge his influences – Alan Coren, for example, who pioneered so many of the techniques of short humour that Terry and I have filched over the years; or the glorious overstuffed heady thing that is *Brewer's Dictionary of Phrase and Fable* and its compiler, the

Reverend E. Cobham Brewer, that most serendipitious of authors. Terry's *Brewer's* introduction made me smile – we would call each other up in delight whenever we discovered a book by Brewer we had not seen before ("'Ere! Have you already got a copy of Brewer's *A Dictionary of Miracles: Imitative, Realistic and Dogmatic*?")

The pieces selected here cover Terry's entire writing career, from schoolboy to Knight of the Realm of Letters, and are still of a piece. Nothing has dated, save perhaps for the references to specific items of computer hardware. (I suspect that, if he has not by now donated it to a charity or a museum, Terry could tell you exactly where his Atari Portfolio is, and just how much he paid for the hand-crafted add-on memory card that took its memory up to an impossibly huge one megabyte.) The authorial voice in these essays is always Terry's: genial, informed, sensible, drily amused. I suppose that, if you look quickly and are not paying attention, you might, perhaps, mistake it for jolly.

But beneath any jollity there is a foundation of fury. Terry Pratchett is not one to go gentle into any night, good or otherwise. He will rage, as he leaves, against so many things: stupidity, injustice, human foolishness and shortsightedness, not just the dying of the light, although that's here too. And, hand in hand with the anger, like an angel and a demon walking hand in hand into the sunset, there is love: for human beings, in all our fallibility; for treasured objects; for stories; and ultimately and in all things, love for human dignity.

Or to put it another way, anger is the engine that drives him, but it is the greatness of spirit that deploys that anger on the side of the angels, or better yet for all of us, the orangutans.

Terry Pratchett is not a jolly old elf at all. Not even close. He's so much more than that.

As Terry walks into the darkness much too soon, I find myself raging too: at the injustice that deprives us of – what? Another twenty or thirty books? Another shelf-full of ideas and glorious phrases and old friends and new, of stories in which people do what they really do do best, which is use their heads to get themselves out of the trouble they got into by not thinking? Another book or two like this, of journalism and agitprop and even the occasional introduction? But truly, the loss of these things does not anger me as it should. It saddens me, but I, who have seen some of them being built close up, understand that any Terry Pratchett book is a small miracle, and we already have more than might be reasonable, and it does not behoove any of us to be greedy.

I rage at the imminent loss of my friend.

And I think, 'What would Terry do with this anger?'

Then I pick up my pen, and I start to write.

NG
New York, June 2014

A Scribbling Intruder

*On bookshops, dragons, fan mail, sandwiches, tools
of the trade, waxing wroth and all the business
of being a Professional Writer*

Thought Progress

20/20 Magazine, May 1989

A bit of writing about writing. Careful readers will spot that Small Gods *had been on my mind at the time.*

It's a pretty accurate description of the creative process at work . . .

Get up, have breakfast, switch on word processor, stare at screen.

Stare at screen some more.

Carry on staring at screen, but cock ear for sounds of postman. With any luck it will be large bag of post, leading to a busy morning's work. Last novel just gone off to publisher. Got nothing to do. Huge vacuum in centre of world.

Post arrives. One letter on Holly Hobbie notepaper, asking for a signed photograph.

All right, all right, let's do some research. What we need

to know for the purposes of the next Discworld plot is something about tortoises. Got vague idea that a talking tortoise is essential part of the action. Don't know why; tortoises just surfaced from racial unconsciousness. Possibly prompted by own tortoises surfacing from hibernation and currently doing Bertrand Russell impersonations in the greenhouse.

Find book on tortoises in box in spare room.

Will definitely get bookcases rebuilt any day now (clever idea was to prefabricate bookcase in garage, everything neatly cut, used setsquares and everything, two coats varnish, then all bits brought inside, assembled with proper dowels and glue, hundreds of books in neat array. Interesting science experiment: what happens to wood that has spent weeks in cold damp garage when suddenly brought into warm dry room? At 3 a.m., learned that every bit suddenly shrinks by one eighth of an inch).

Interesting footnote in tortoise book reminds us that most famous tortoise in history must be the one that got dropped on the head of famous Greek philosopher . . . what's the bugger's name? Very famous man, wherever the tortoise-dropping set get together. Sudden pressing desire to explore this whole issue, including what the tortoise thought about it all. Keep thinking it was Zeno, but am sure it wasn't.

Finding out that it was Aeschylus occupies twenty minutes. Not philosopher, but playwright. In his hands, early drama took on a high-religious purpose, serving as a forum for resolving profound moral conflicts and expressing a grandeur of thought and language. And then a high-pitched whistling noise and goodnight. Look up Zeno out of interest.

Ah, he was the one who said that, logically, you couldn't catch a tortoise.

Should have told Aeschylus.

Also read up on prayer wheels and, for no obvious reason, William Blake. While so doing, lady phones up to ask if we're the dentist's.

Definitely getting some work done now. The creative mainspring is definitely winding up.

Bound into action and press on with some serious disk backing-up. That's the beautiful thing about word processors. In the bad old typewriter days all you had to occupy yourself with when creativity flagged was sharpening the pencils and cleaning out the e with a pin. But with the word processor there're endless opportunities for fiddling, creative writing of macros, meticulous resetting of the real-time clock and so forth: all good honest work.

Sitting in front of a keyboard and a screen is work. Thousands of offices operate on this very principle.

Stare at screen.

Wonder why the eagle dropped the bloody thing on the playwright. It couldn't have been to smash it open, like the book says. Eagles not daft. Greece is all rock, how come eagle with all Greece to choose from manages pinpoint precision on bald head of Aeschylus? How do you pronounce Aeschylus, anyway?

Pronunciation dictionary in box in loft.

Stepladder in garage.

Car needs a wash.

Lunch.

Solid morning's work, really.

Back in front of screen.

Stare at screen.

Another lady phones to ask if this is Paradise. (Motel up the road apparently has a phone number one digit different from ours.) Give humorous rejoinder number three.

Stare at screen.

Start wondering, perhaps not eagle's fault after all, it just had job to do, it had been flying too many missions, jeez, you get thrown out of eagle air force if you start worrying about the innocent philosophers you're dropping your tortoises on. Hatch-22. No.

Stare at screen.

No. It was obviously tortoise's idea all along. Had grudge against playwright, perhaps tortoises had been insulted in latest play, perhaps offended at speed-ist jokes, perhaps had seen tortoiseshell spectacles: you dirty rat, you got my brother. So hijacked eagle, hanging on to desperate bird's legs like the tortoise in the old Friends of the Earth logo, giving directions in muffled voice, vector 19, beepbeepbeep, Geronimooooo . . .

Stare at screen.

Wonder if eagle has anything else a desperate tortoise could hang on to.

Look up biology of birds in encyclopedia in box on stairs. Gosh.

Supper.

Stare at screen. Turn ideas over and over. Tortoises, bald

head, eagles. Hmm. No, can't be playwright, what sort of person would tortoises instantly dislike?

Midnight . . .

Stare at screen. Vaguely aware right hand has hit keys to open new file. Start breathing very slowly.

Write 1,943 words.

Bed.

For a day there, thought we weren't going to make it.

Palmtop

Independent, 9 July 1993

You think of these kinds of computer as portable, but they aren't really – you could anchor a ship with my old Olivetti. Mine probably still work – I took good care of them – and although I have no particular need of them, I can't bring myself to throw away what is now vintage technology.

I remember my first portable computer. It weighed 15lb. The power supply was separate and in many ways resembled a small brick. The damn thing nearly killed me.

The next one was a mere 8lb, although there was still a (smaller) brick. I thought that was light until I had to run across an airport carrying it.

It dawned on me what was wrong. The important thing about portable computers, the common element, the nub or crux of the whole ethos, as it were, is that you're supposed to be able to carry them. What's the good of a machine that won't fit inside a briefcase *along with all the other things you want to carry in there*? Even 8lb isn't portable. Eight pounds is an item of luggage.

It always puzzled me why the weight of portable machines wasn't the first thing mentioned in any review. It tends to be in the small print even now, way down the page. This is because reviewers get hypnotized by shiny disks and glittery screens. Let them carry them around for a day, say I. Let them hoick them around so they can get on with their work in studio green rooms and hotels and the backs of cabs.

I grew up reading science fiction and there were always these guys carrying pocket computers which could talk and keep track of their diary and run whole planets. They never got hernias carrying the things. I didn't see why I should either. I was suffering from the opposite of future shock, whatever that is. Future suction? I don't want arms reaching to my knees, but I like to have a computer around.

I entered the palmtop world.

Jargon crops up everywhere. Once there were big machines that sat on desks, and there were portables (more or less). Now there are ultraportables and sub-notebooks and personal digital assistants and palmtops and pocketbooks. They're all very loosely defined by size and weight and the whim of the person describing them. Basically, they're all small and light.

They all occupy the twilight zone between laptops (the aforesaid portables, although now the bulk of new machines do quite a lot more than the ones I've had and weigh in at around 6lb plus quite a small brick) and small calculators.

The first acquisition was the Atari Portfolio, several years ago. It weighed in at about a pound, and came with its own built-in software including the usual 'electronic Filofax' yuppie bait of simple word processor, calculator, spreadsheet and phonebook. The word processor wasn't too bad; I typed tens of thousands of words on it, admittedly not very fast. But it wasn't perfect.

Rule Number One is: Weight is important. Rule Two is: What else do you need to buy?

Sir Clive Sinclair was able to sell the first sub-£99 computer by redefining what a computer was. It didn't need a dedicated monitor, or internal mass storage of data or a standard communications port, or a keyboard fit for steady typing – not if you were prepared to hook it into the TV, store programs on a normal tape recorder and type very slooowly and carefully. It didn't *need* more than 1kb of memory. So it didn't get it.

Since then I've always been wary of machines that need extra bits before they start becoming more than a useful toy. The Portfolio needed an add-on module if you wanted to increase memory to something closer to an acceptable amount. It needed a comparatively large plug-in module before it could print, and another one if you wanted a serial port. Without them, everything stayed locked in.

The theory was these bits stayed at home. But I do a lot of typing when I'm away from home for long periods, and you get very nervous if you can't print out or dump stuff on to another machine.

They also caused trouble at airport security. Security men could accept the basic machine, but the box full of mysterious plastic prolapses upset them. 'Show us this working,' they said. 'Certainly,' I said, 'please get me a power point and a laser printer.'

I found too many small, light machines that had the word '(optional)' in their descriptions. (Optional) means you're going to have to pay to do what you want . . .

After two years of looking, I ended up with, and indeed am typing this on, the Olivetti Quaderno. It cost me almost £600 and must have been one of the first on sale last year (pioneers are penalized; my agent bought one a few months later and they threw in a free add-on disk drive, and now there's been a sizeable further price cut amid reports of a new souped-up model). What it is, simply is this: it's the desktop PC I bought in 1987, shrunk to A5 size, one inch thick and weighing a little over 2lb. I've never weighed the little power supply and battery charger – I've never really noticed it weighing anything very much. It certainly fits in my brief-case. I can *lose* it in my briefcase. But most importantly, it runs all my software, accumulated over years of trial and error.

It runs memory resident programs like Sidekick and the incomparable Info Select. It runs WordPerfect 4.2 (the classic version). I don't have to look at a screen like a letterbox, or be forced to use someone else's idea of the 'right' software. It's got a 20-megabyte hard disk, which means you can write a novel on it and have it all there, all in one go. There's half of one on it now.

People say: yes, but what about the *keyboard*? Well, it's better than any other similar-sized one I tried – Hewlett-Packard's H-P 95LZ, an otherwise interesting machine, practically had calculator buttons – and I can touch-type on it.

People say: ah, but can it run Windows? Not in any way that a committed Windows user would accept. Windows demands high-resolution screens and a 386 processor and a fair amount of RAM and a user who is on a salary so that they can pass away those lengthy office hours by fiddling with the colours or selecting super new icons. I don't need that. And the Quad's screen is murky – there's no backlight, so lighting has to be reasonably good.

But it's real and it's here now. It's not a toy. I can carry around work in progress and my diary *and* the spreadsheet, all versions I'm familiar with and which gently move like a tide between the Quad and the office machine. The screen, apart from the touch of murk, looks like a smaller version of the one I'm familiar with. If I really had to, I could use it all the time.

Goodbye bricks. This one is *portable*.

I didn't actually use it on Ayers Rock. But I jolly well could have done, if I'd wanted to.

The Choice Word

Contribution for *The Word*, London's Festival of Literature, 2000

Oh lord, who keeps track of this stuff? In the UK, once an author has reached a certain level of availability, requests to write something 'which will only take a few minutes of your time' sleet in endlessly from newspapers. They're known in the business as 'My Favourite Spoon' items, and someone somewhere thinks they are good publicity. But a light-hearted survey to find the nation's favourite word was part of the hype for a large British literary festival a few years ago, and this was mine.*

I like the fortuitous onomatopoeia of words for soundless things. Gleam, glint, glitter, glisten . . . they all sound exactly

---

* I managed to get it on the first page of *The Wee Free Men*, too. I can't remember what the nation's favourite word turned out to be. It was probably 'Beckham'.

as the light would sound if it made a noise. Glint is sharp and quick, it glints, and if an oily surface made a noise it would go glisten. And bliss sounds like a soft meringue melting on a warm plate.

But I'll plump for:

SUSURRATION

. . . from the Latin *susurrus*, whisper or rustling, which is exactly what it sounds like. It's a hushed noise. But it hints of plots and secrets and people turning to one another in surprise. It's the noise, in fact, made just after the sword is withdrawn from the stone and just before the cheering starts.

How to be a Professional Boxer

Foreword to *Writers' & Artists' Yearbook 2006*

I bought my first copy of the *W&AYB* (second-hand) when I was about thirteen or fourteen. Sorry. But I'd just spent ten shillings on a very good second-hand copy of *Brewer's Dictionary of Phrase and Fable*, which was a big bite out of available funds. In some dimly understood way, I felt it was one of the things you had to have in order to be a writer, and that somehow professionalism would leak from it and be painlessly absorbed by me.

I read it solemnly.

Was it useful? Well, yes – but I have to say that some of the basics had already entered my life via science fiction fandom. Most writers in the field were fans once; many fans aspire to be writers one day. And so, at a major science fiction convention (and long before literary festivals became the new rock'n'roll) you'd find established authors, there at their own expense, explaining the basics to a hall full of hopefuls. The process is known as 'paying forward'.

I took notes. I've never had occasion to use one magnificent tip from a well-known author, but I pass it on anyway: 'Keep an eye on the trade press. When an editor moves on, *immediately* send your precious MS to his or her office, with a covering letter addressed to said departed editor. Say, in the tones of one engaged in a cooperative effort, something like this: "Dear X, I was very pleased to receive your encouraging letter indicating your interest in my book, and I have made all the changes you asked for . . ." Of course they won't find the letter. Publishers can never find anything. But at least someone might panic enough to read the MS.'

Having read and listened to all the good advice, I then handed over the MS of my first novel to a local small press publisher, just because I met him one day and he seemed a decent type. He liked it. I was totally unknown and he'd never published fiction before, so it didn't make much money. Nor did the next two. The fourth title was the first book in the Discworld series. It didn't exactly walk out of the shops, but it crawled quite briskly and with every sign that it was determined to make it to its feet. Transworld hesitated, and then published it in paperback. A few years later, I hired my former publisher as my agent, and life became rather crowded.

I was lucky. Incredibly so, when I think of all the ways things could have gone. But when the floppy-eared Spaniel of Luck sniffs at your turn-ups it helps if you have a collar and piece of string in your pocket. In my case, it was a sequel.

I get asked all the time, in letters and emails and questions from the floor: 'Can you give me a few tips about being a writer?' And you sense that gleam in the eye, that hope that somehow, this time, you'll drop your guard and hand over the map to the Holy Grail or, preferably, its URL. I detect, now, a slightly worrying edge to all this, a hint of indignation that grammar, spelling and punctuation have a part to play ('Don't publishers have people to do all that?' was one response) and that the universe is remiss in not making allowance for the fact that you don't have the time.

So, instead, I give tips on how to be a professional boxer. A good diet is essential, of course, as is a daily regime of exercise. Pay attention to your footwork, it will often get you out of trouble. Go down to the gym every day – every day of your life that finds you waking up capable of standing. Take every opportunity to watch a good professional fight. In fact watch as many bouts as you can, because you can even learn something from the fighters who get it wrong. Don't listen to what they say, watch what they do. And don't forget the diet and the exercise and the roadwork.

Got it? Well, becoming a writer is basically exactly the same thing, except that it isn't about boxing.

It's as simple as that.

Brewer's Boy

Foreword to *Brewer's Dictionary of Phrase and Fable* Millennium Edition, 1999

I guess we all have our measures of success. Being asked to write this was one of mine. It somehow completed a circle. I now have shelves of editions of Brewer's, *new and old, that have been acquired since that first one.*

The Revd Ebenezer Cobham Brewer wanted to tell people things; among his other works were A Guide to Knowledge, *a dictionary of miracles and* The Reader's Handbook of Allusions, References, Plots and Stories. *But it's the* Phrase and Fable *dictionary that has made him immortal. The book is – well, see below.*

I've checked. My copy is still right next to the dictionary. Now read on.

I was a *Brewer's* boy. I first grasped the spine of my

second-hand copy when I was twelve. It's still in amazing condition, considering the work I've made it do.

It was my introduction to mythology and ancient history and a lot more, too, because *Brewer's* is a serendipitous (see page 1063) book. In other words, you might not find what you're looking for, but you will find three completely unexpected things that are probably more interesting. Reading one item in *Brewer's* is like eating one peanut. It's practically impossible. There are plenty of other useful books. But you start with *Brewer's*.

Nevertheless, the book is hard to describe. You could call it a compendium (I didn't find this in my ancient edition, but I did find 'Complutensian Polyglot', so the effort was not wasted) of myth, legend, quotation, historical byways, and slang, but that would still miss out quite a lot of it. A better description would be 'an education', in the truest sense. *Brewer's* flowered in those pre-Trivial Pursuit days when people believed that if you patiently accumulated a knowledge of small things a knowledge of big things would automatically evolve, and you would become a better person.

Brewer's has been updated for this Millennium edition. It includes Gandalf as well as Attila the Hun (and why shouldn't it?). Some of the duller nymphs and more obscure Classical items have been dropped to make space for such additions to the language as 'hit the ground running' and 'all dressed up and nowhere to go'. To be considered obscure by *Brewer's* is a real badge of obscurity, and it is sad to see them go; but the serious Brewerite can only hope that Cassell might one day be persuaded to release a 'preservative' edition, so that this detritus of myth and legend is not forever lost.

But today is tomorrow's past. One day the Fab Four (ask your dad) will be one with . . . oh, some of the things that no one cares about any more. Given the speed of change, they're already well on their way. It's an education in itself, seeing them take their place with old Roman senators and mythological fauna, and watching the dust settle. We're the next millennium's ancients . . .

Brewer's Dictionary of Phrase and Fable is the first book to turn to when questions arise and the final desperate volume when the lesser reference books have failed. No bookshelf, no WORLD is complete without it. It's as simple as that.

Paperback Writer

Guardian, 6 December 2003

*Maybe it's the influence of the net, but people talk about writing
in terms of 'getting'. Where do you get your ideas/your characters/
the time? The unspoken words are: show me the coordinates
of the Holy Grail.*

*And, at best, you throw up a barrage of clichés, which have
become clichés because . . .well, they're true, and they work. I've
heard lots of authors talk on the subject and we all, in our
various ways, come out with the same half a dozen or so clichés.
And you get the sense that this isn't exactly what's wanted, but
people go on asking, in the hope that one day you'll forget and
pass on the real secret.*

Still, this newspaper paid. That's one of the tips, by the way.

When I was thirteen, I went to my first science fiction
convention. How long ago was that? So long ago that

everyone wore sports jackets, except for Mike Moorcock.

Most science fiction writers were once fans. There's a habit they have, not of paying back, but of paying forward; I know of no other branch of literature where the established 'names' so keenly encourage wannabe writers to become their competitors.

I came back from that event determined to be a writer. After all, I'd shaken hands with Arthur C. Clarke, so now it was just a matter of hard work . . .

The first thing I do when I finish writing a book is start a new one. This was a course of action suggested, I believe, by the late Douglas Adams, although regrettably he famously failed to follow his own advice.

The last few months of a book are taxing. Emails zip back and forth, the overtones of the English word 'cacky' are explained to the US editor who soberly agrees that 'poop' is no substitute, the author stares at text he's read so often that he's lost all grasp of it as a narrative, and rewrites and tinkers and then hits Send –

– and it's gone, in these modern times, without even the therapy of printing it out. One minute you're a writer, next minute you have written. And that's the time, just at that point when the warm rosy glow of having finished a book is about to give way to the black pit of post-natal despair at having finished a book, that you start again. It also means you have an excuse for not tidying away your reference books, a consideration not to be lightly cast aside in this office, where books are used as bookmarks for other books.

The next title is not a book yet. It's a possible intro, a

possible name, maybe some sketches that could become scenes, a conversation, some newspaper clippings, a few bookmarks in an old history book, perhaps even ten thousand words typed to try things out. You are not a bum. You are now back in the game. You are working on a book.

You are also fiddling with your internal radio. Once you're tuned in on the next book, research comes and kicks your door down. Something is casually mentioned on TV. A book about something else entirely throws out a historical fact that, right at this moment, you really need to know. You sit down to dinner next to an ambassador who is happy to chat about the legal questions that arise when a murder is committed in an embassy and the murderer flees outside, i.e., technically into another country, and the plot gulps down this tidbit.

People are magnificent research, almost the best there is. An old copper will tell you more about policing than a textbook ever will. An old lady is happy to talk about life as a midwife in the 1930s, a long way from any doctor, while your blood runs cold. A retired postman tells you it's not just the front end of dogs that can make early-morning deliveries so fraught ...

Undirected research goes on all the time, of course. There's no research like the research you're doing when you think you're just enjoying yourself. In Hay-on-Wye, under the very noses of other authors, I picked up that not-very-famous work *The Cyclopedia of Commercial and Business ANECDOTES; comprising INTERESTING REMINIS-CENCES AND FACTS, Remarkable Traits and Humours* (and so on, for 64 words). There are obvious nuggets on almost every page: Preserved Fish was a famous New York financier. Then there is what I might call secondary discovery, as in, for example, the dark delight of the Victorian author, when writing about a famous German family of financiers, in coming up with sentences like 'soon there were rich Fuggers throughout Lower Saxony'. And finally there was the building up of some insight into the minds of the people for whom money was not the means to an end, or even the means to more money, but what the sea is for little fishes.

I've learned one or two things over the years. One is that the best time to work out a book is in bed, just after you've woken up. I think my brain is on time-share to a better author overnight. A notebook is vital at this point. So is actually being fully awake. If I had been fully awake I probably would have written a fuller note than 'MegaPED:' on the back of a card by my bed the other day. It's probably the key to a plot idea, but don't ask me, I only wrote it down.

And if you think you have a book evolving, now is the time to write the flap copy. The blurb, in fact. An author should never be too proud to write their own flap copy. Getting the heart and soul of a book into fewer than a hundred words helps you focus. More than half the skill of writing lies in tricking the book out of your own head.

Advice to Booksellers

July 1999

This was written not for publication but for the use of the worthy people at Ottakar's bookshops. They have since disappeared, unfortunately, but the advice is still valid fifteen years on.

Let's start with this: on the face of it there is not a lot for the author in a signing tour, and the more popular the author the less there is. If it's going well, it's exhausting; if it's going badly, it's exhausting and frustrating and a lesson in humility. I'm not certain it sells that many extra books; it simply means that books sold in that town will be sold mostly at this one shop. It doesn't hugely affect the bestseller list – Bookwatch, for example, 'adjusts' returns from shops that have held signings to ensure these don't distort the national figure, and a very successful author will have to work very hard to influence their position on the list. Meals happen at odd times or not at all. You live out of a suitcase. The world blurs.

Of course there are pluses, but these tend to be for the shop (if it sells a lot of nice shiny books) and the publisher (who consolidates a relationship with the shop or the chain). What the author gets, mostly, is indigestion.

We do it sometimes because we're bullied, we're vain, we've always done it, we have a vague sense that it's the right thing to do, a few of us just like it in some strange way, and − to borrow from another branch of the entertainment industry − we feel that however much work you do in the recording studio, it's not rock'n'roll until you take it on the road.

What you should expect from an author

To be on time, to be polite to staff (you may need to modify this requirement in the case of one or two authors) and friendly towards the customers, and to stay to the end of the advertised time.

Then immediately you get into the grey area. Should the author sign backlist titles? Write a dedication in every book? Sign all the telephone orders? And orders for other shops in the chain? And, in the case of a successful signing, stay beyond the advertised time to send all the queue away happy?

My feeling is that the default answer should be 'Yes', but signing tours can be crowded, taxing, and generally designed to be the most unhealthy way of spending a few weeks outside the Lard-eating Olympics. So those areas have to be matters of gentle discussion with the publicist beforehand.

What should the author expect from the shop?

In the last eleven years I've spent fifteen months 'on the road'; and here are the little notes I've collected:

Before the event

Are there books? Don't laugh. Sometimes there aren't – or, at least, aren't enough. You still run across the unreconstructed shop who thinks a good order for a signing is about twenty-five extra copies.

It's nice if the shop staff knows who the author is and why they are there.

A guest should get something further up the scale upon arrival than 'Wait here and I'll go and find someone' or, possibly, 'Oh, was it today?' Remember: an author, no matter how successful, is under that cool exterior as twitchy as a shaved monkey, and will be pathetically grateful for a friendly smile and (assuming that they've been good and arrived well in time for the event) a swift stroll to . . .

. . . a chair in some office, preferably, rather than a stool in the stock room, where they have . . .

. . . a nice cup of tea and can loosen up a bit. I generally use this time to sign orders and stock, and listen to any scurrilous gossip. Authors will always appreciate hearing how much worse other authors' signings went. (But if devilment overcomes you and you praise a known rival, you can actually see certain muscles in the author's face freeze up. This is great fun. But don't do it.)

I personally don't dedicate books ordered by phone except in special circumstances, simply because of pressure on time, but it's worth finding out from the publicist in advance how an author feels about this. The sensible mantra is 'We cannot promise a dedication on pre-orders because there may not be time' but I prefer to say 'no' right from the start if we know it's going to be a crowded tour – it saves raising and dashing hopes. Incidentally, the desire to get books signed for other shops in the chain is a natural one, but don't force it – most authors will be happy enough to do this if there is time, but don't get insistent and don't pretend that all 600 are really just stock for your own shop. It's been tried. Play fair.

If the local paper/radio/cable station contact you for an interview, for heaven's sake let the publicist know as soon as possible. It's best to pass the request straight to them. They may be able to arrange the day to fit it in, but that depends on knowing in advance. It makes for a tricky situation if they simply turn up unbeknownst to the author (mumbling something on the lines of 'we spoke to someone') and expect a twenty-minute interview while the queue waits. That's bad manners.

It's a good idea to make sure advertising for the event takes place before the event. I wish I didn't have to say this.

The event

Is there a table and chair? I wish I was joking, too. One shop once forgot these completely, and elsewhere I've sat on, at or around various strange items of bookshop furniture. It should be a real table and a real chair, not a stool in front of a shelf unit with no room for the knees. Try to put together something you would be comfortable sitting and writing at for several hours.

Give some thought to where the signing table is. I prefer to have my back to something – a wall, shelves, whatever. That means the kid with the blue anorak and one blocked nostril can't stare over my shoulder for two hours, which is off-putting (there's always one . . .).

Some shops like to put the author near the doors. This is a problem on winter tours – I've frozen before now, so try to put the table out of the worst of the icy blast. Shops in malls sometimes get the author to sign out in the mall. This is probably fine for a 'media' author or an author who can definitely draw a big queue, but it's hell on wheels for the rest. Besides, it's always too noisy and you get a Greek chorus of Uzis – the little old ladies who stand around glaring at the luckless author and muttering 'Uzi? Uzi den? Izeeonnatelly? Uzi?'

Vase of flowers on the table? That's nice, but someone will knock it over, so take it away when the signing starts.

A lot of authors travel with their own pens, but it's a good idea to have a few available, including a marker that will take on a shiny surface. Try to avoid Biros with chewed ends – they lack that certain something. The author may require – or at least haughtily expect – help with opening books at the right page and so on, although in my experience most are quite happy to get on with the event and require nothing more than that staff keep a lookout for the mad axeman.

Give some thought to the queue itself. Try not to make it stand out in the rain. Some bookshops appear to think of queues as a nuisance to be punished rather than a long line of customers, whereas I will definitely go back to the shop which, having been forced to make the queue stand outside their (small) premises on a cold November day, went to the bakery across the road and got a really good deal on 250 hot mince pies. That was style, and probably good business, too.

Ladies with small yet terminally loud children should be ushered to the front while everyone still has their eardrums. I've learned that people in wheelchairs are usually happy (even determined) to wait their turn – as one said to me, 'After all, at least I'm sitting down.' It's worth tactfully policing a long queue, though, for those who will clearly suffer during a long wait.

If you have got a TV personality promoting something with a title like 'The Whoops-Where-Did-That-One-Go? Christmas Fun Book' don't pass comment if they spend a lot of time reading their book while they're in the shop. It may be the first time they've seen it. Do not offer to help them with the longer words.

Hardly anyone turned up? If it's absolutely no one then something has gone really wrong, especially if you've done a decent promotion. It's probably not your fault. Don't leave the author alone but chat to them, keep knives away from them and tell them stories about how even this is good compared to what happened when Miss X did a signing here.

Have loads of people turned up? In the wash of relief, most authors will at the very least sign for everyone who was present in the queue by the official end of the signing, and many of us will simply sign until we run out of people or time. There are a few (rumour says) who will leave at the end of their hour no matter what; if they want to give a bad impression to a large number of readers, this is their choice. Be stoical about it, bear in mind that there may be another event that day, and it may have been a very long week already. A good publicist should have budgeted the time correctly, but we're all prey to unexpected six-mile tailbacks on the motorway.

Care and feeding of authors

Since many signings take place over the lunch hour, a snack is appreciated before or after the signing. A sandwich is fine, although the author may well have been living on sarnies for weeks and would be pathetically grateful for a jacket spud or something exotic. Haughty demands for smoked salmon and champagne – well, that's up to you. I can't help you there, but you will probably be prosecuted if you hit anyone with a fire extinguisher.

Authors have their likes and dislikes and these get magnified as shops pass on the information. According to rumour I demand sushi, Australian Chardonnay, kumquats, chocolate-coated coffee beans, those little blue things in Liquorice Allsorts, and gin and tonic. No, it's all a mystery to me, too. Some shops go out of their way to put on a good spread (so's the staff can fall on it when the author has gone) and this is good PR, but in truth an author tends to eat lightly on tour because their stomach is knotted into a figure eight.

Stock signings

These are 'signings-lite'; the author and publicist drop in while they're in town to sign some stock. Do not underestimate them. A bit of friendliness and a sense that this is a welcome occasion will pay off. Treat it like a proper signing, but without people. The author will remember. Trust me on this. I've done stock signings at shops that left me feeling guilty that they weren't given a 'proper' event, and insisted that we do them 'properly' next time we're in town.

Please make sure that whoever arranged this event is either there or at least has made it known to the rest of the staff. There's going to be some icy looks if the author is greeted with 'You're here to do what?' and there will also be a feeling that if a shop cannot manage a stock signing that doesn't leave the author feeling like a scribbling intruder they may not get behind a full signing either.

Fond farewells . . .

Do make sure there's someone around to say 'goodbye'. Perhaps you'd be surprised at the number of shops who seem to think an author is an automated signing engine. My publicist and I have wandered mystified out of empty shops at the end of a long signing because the staff have all bogged off somewhere to count the money.

Authors are impressionable, especially on tour. Some shops have impressed me so much that they are the shop I will sign at in that particular town. Organizing a good successful signing is part of that, of course, and that does not have to mean a huge queue, just a sense that the shop made an effort. What authors recall is 'That was the shop where they did that really good coffee/cracking window display/ were nice people', and you get a reputation as a good shop to sign at (which spreads among authors, believe me).

Sometimes shops shyly give little presents, like a bottle of wine. This is nice, but really, really is not required or expected by real authors (and may even be an embarrassment if the author is travelling light). If generosity sweeps you up, then suggesting that they select a book is a good idea all round. But a simple 'Many thanks' works wonders.

No Worries

SFX, June 1998

*That wonderful, prestigious, and above all influential UK
magazine* SFX *asked me for a signing-tour report on Australia.
Actually, it's composed from several 'real' reports, just like it says.*

*Oh, and the current PR lady in Australia is not fearsome at
all, really.*

Australia had the best *de facto* national anthem in the world.
Even people living in swamps in Brazil knew that if you
heard the strains of 'Waltzing Matilda' you'd soon be
swamped by young men and women with orange com-
plexions and the heaviest knapsacks in the world. So, when
Australians actually got the chance to vote in a replacement
for 'God Save The Queen', what did they vote for? 'Advance
Australia Fair', that's what. Now, true, it's more hygienic
than most anthems, singing the praises of sunshine and fresh

air rather than, say, bashing other countries, but it does sound so . . . worthy. Why didn't 'Waltzing Matilda' get chosen? Because it wouldn't have been respectable. Australians care a lot about what other people think.

I had this conversation with an Aussie on the edge of a swimming pool at Ayers Rock:

Aussie: 'So what do the poms think about us wanting to kick out Queenie, then?' (The 'republic v. monarchy' debate was big at the time.)
Me: 'Doesn't worry us. We've been thinking along the same lines.'
Aussie: 'You don't mind?'
Me: 'Nope. It's fine by us.'
Aussie: 'So . . . you poms don't mind, then . . .'
Me: 'Nope.'
Aussie: 'Oh. Right.'

I saw him once or twice again that day, and he was clearly uneasy. He wanted us to mind, so he could say that it was none of our bloody business.

Because . . . well, Australia is still very English, down at bone level. You can see it everywhere, especially in the letters columns of its newspapers. There's the same hair-trigger fear that someone somewhere might be getting more than their fair share; the same low-grade resentments, the same tone of voice . . . it's just like being back home. I love the place, and must have been back at least a dozen times.

I did my first Australian tour in 1990. It was a bit of an

eye-opener. They talk about UK and Commonwealth rights in the contracts, and the author says 'yeah, yeah' and signs – and then you go out there, and there's all these real people. Let's see, what were the highlights on that tour . . . oh, yes, going into a bookshop in some tiny place called Toowoomba and finding a huge crowd of people, and on the signing table was a Vegemite sandwich and a cup of Milo, cornerstones of the Australian Experience. One of the others is 'a chunder', which I didn't have. Incidentally, an early Australian rival to Marmite was tentatively called Pawill, although the proposed slogan, 'If Marmite, Pawill', was never used as far as I know, possibly because of police intervention. I was also pissed on by a koala, because that's what they do. A taxi driver ran after me in the street to give me my change, a thing that's never ever happened anywhere else in the world. And we shifted a lot of books, in this huge continent hitherto known to me as a word in the small print on page 28.

Since then I've done a tour most years, sometimes linked up with SF cons either in Australia or in New Zealand. And after every tour I do The Report, of things we did, things that went wrong (and right), and all the other stuff that might be useful in the future.

It'd be sort of suicidal to print one. So I looked at all the reports, and tinkered with them . . .

In *The Last Continent* I tried to make it clear that the Discworld continent of Fourecks is not, of course, Australia. It's just a bit . . . Australian. So this is a report of a tour that never was in some place that doesn't exist. But it all happened, somewhere. I've just moved things around a bit to protect the innocent, which in this case means me.

Day 1

Off on BA009, 10.25 p.m. from Heathrow. Watched *Mars Attacks*; shame Mars didn't attack earlier, like before this waste of space went into production. Rowan Atkinson and Mel Smith were also in the cabin, so there was understandably a genteel air of silent gloom which meant I could get some sleep.

Day 3

(Day 2 is confiscated by Customs when you arrive but they give it back to you when you go.)

Arrived feeling fragile but okay, checked into hotel, slept for six hours, woke up feeling as though every sensory organ in my body had been wrongly wired. A vital piece of equipment on tour is a small torch and a notebook. Every night you're in a new room. It's not just that you don't know where the bathroom is, you don't even remember where the light switch is. Before the jetlag wears off, you don't even know if you're the right person. This is where the notebook comes in handy.

Up and shower and do some local media and then it's time for a talk and signing.

This was something originally dreamed up by some fans as a little chat, got bigger at the insistence of the fearsome PR lady who likes my time to be filled edge to edge, and ended up in this big hall with 400 people. Nice bunch.

Someone congratulates me on my deadpan delivery. Haven't the heart to say that this is because bits of my body think it's 5.00 a.m.

Day 4

Morning doing more media, many of whom I'd met before. One keen guy conducts entire interview with the mike of his recorder plugged into the auxiliary power socket. I didn't like to point this out, because it would be impolite, so when he found out by himself we did the interview again.

Noon: Small Mainstream Bookshop signing.

A very small shop – 250 square feet or so, I'd guess, but with a very mixed and friendly queue that took up more or less the whole ninety minutes allocated. This is one of those shops where the owners seem to know half the customers by name, and probably ring them up to find out how they are if they don't see them for a month. Couldn't fault it. Banana daiquiri supplied, entirely unasked.

Straight on to: University of Bananabendin, Worralorrasurfa.

A good crowd that took two hours to get through. Pet wallaby brought along to see me, and a fan presents me with a bag of dried bush tomatoes, of which I'm known to be rather fond. Oh, and here's a banana daiquiri. And someone's holding a baby kangaroo.

Then a phone interview with a journalist doing a preview piece for the signing a few cities down the line. She's never read a Discworld book, but nervously admits to sharing a home with someone who's read them all. And reads out bits to her.

On to Small Family Bookshop, for a talk outside in the rather nice back garden. Nibbles and, hey, a banananana dakry. Overhead, possums swoop from tree to tree, unless I mean wombats. Hard to get away from this shop because the owner is one of those lovely people who tries to give you his entire stock to take away, but I make it in the end.

Day 5

Damn – the cooling fan in the laptop has stopped working. Ring up local office of Wasabi Computers, who might be able to fix it tomorrow, except that tomorrow we're somewhere else . . . It might be a software problem, says the engineer, and there's a fix on their bulletin board, but time is pressing . . . 10.00 a.m.: Bookshop in a Mall, Outinasuburba.

Nice big queue and I eye the early arrivals carefully, espying a fan I'd met before. Explain problem. He nips off. An hour later he's back, and slips me a disk with the freshly downloaded fix. I sign all his books. No worries.

1.00 p.m.: Small Bookshop, Worralorrasurfa.

Still enough fans around to take the queue to about seventy-five minutes. As a charity wheeze, they can have their picture taken with me. One lady has made me an entire box of origami turtles. No worries.

Day 6

8.10 a.m.: flight to Arthur.

11.00 a.m.: Interview with Big Radio Journo (said to be first-division media). I was prepared to dislike the man but in fact we got on pretty well; he avoided the usual dumb questions and we had a decent twenty minutes. Sometimes it's a bit embarrassing to be interviewed by a journalist who's a fan because fan-type questions don't work well on air (they say things like 'So . . . is Rincewind coming back, then?' and you can hear a hundred thousand people looking at their radios and saying 'What the — is he on about?').

On to Small Yet Seriously Worthy Bookshop, Innasuburb.

This shop is seriously behind all aspects of Discworld. They sell the Clarecraft models and had even imported the videos. Don't know how many people there were, because everyone was keen and wanted to chat and a bunch of actors in costume from an upcoming production of *Wyrd Sisters* also turned up. A fun event; every tour should contain at least one. I was allowed to kiss Granny Weatherwax. Few people can say the same. Not without having a very croaky voice, at any rate.

On to Big Specialist Bookshop.

Big Forbidden Planet type of queue, heavy with carrier bags. One nice lady had brought a banana daiquiri in an esky. Another one opens the violin case she's carrying and it turns out to contain a polished scythe blade on a black velvet lining.

Will I sign it so's she can have the name etched on? What would you do, boys and girls?

Signing overruns, so the tail end of the queue follows me down the road to Big Mainstream Bookshop and tags on to the end of the one already there. Among the people waiting is Ruby, who describes herself as my biggest fan and may well be, and a lady with some books to be signed to her psychiatrist. I sign them, advising her to change her psychiatrist.

Nip back to the Specialist shop to sign orders, and we spot a young lady fan surreptitiously walking out with the empty lager can that I'd been drinking from earlier. We shall never know why and dare not ask.

Check into very posh small hotel. There's a letter from the manager, assuring me of his attention at all times.

Go out with publishers to a fish and chip supper. Ah, but this is Doyles Fish Restaurant, where they serve barramundi and chips, and a barramundi is what a cod becomes if it's been a good cod in this life.

Back to the hotel, where there's a letter in the room from the deputy manager, assuring me of his attention at all times. I wake up at 2.00 a.m. at the sound of an envelope being pushed under the door. It's from the night manager, assuring me of his attention at all times. I think if you stay in this hotel for more than a fortnight you have to marry one of the staff.

Day 7

On to Large Mainstream Shop, Nothersuburb.

Eighty or ninety people, I guess. One guy turned up as Death and was rewarded with a big poster. At least, I assume it was someone dressed up as Death, but who knows?

On to New Specialist Bookshop, Yettanothasuburb. Big queue. Lady surreptitiously attempts to bribe me to put her son in a future book. Trouble is, he's called John (or Sam, or Tony . . . can't quite remember). Explain that if she changes his name to Sweevil or Chalcedony she might be in with a chance.

Off to airport for flight to Vulcana . . .

Signing-tour hotels are like a box of chocolates – you never know whether you're going to get the nasty hard one that someone else has already sucked. Sometimes you get one lit by forty-watt lightbulbs, sometimes you get a suite where you have to phone reception in the end to find out where the bed is. I'm in luck tonight – this one's got a bath so big you can lie down in it, completely flat.

Day 8

Media in the morning, then on to University for big talk in their lecture theatre, organized by the librarian, who is a fan. Make ape-like gestures behind his back while he's doing the introduction, then give him a 'Librarians Rule Ook' badge. Sign for queue afterwards, and get hit by a drive-by manuscript dumper. That is, when it's over there's this unexpected brown envelope on the desk, with a note asking me to read it and send my comments to the author. Sigh.

4.00 p.m.: Small Yet Lovely Specialist Bookshop. The owner knows her stuff, so it's always a pleasure to sign here. Long friendly queue, and there's a bowl of black jellybeans on the signing table; it is impossible to eat only one black jellybean. One lady had travelled more than fourteen hours on a train to get to this signing. Sent her a poster when I got home.

Rush off to airport for flight to Bugarup. Dinner on the plane is Chicken Congealé. No worries. Well, perhaps one or two.

Day 9

Breakfast with a journo, who's really a fan in disguise who has come up with a good way of not having to wait in a queue, some down-the-line interviews, and on to:

Book signing, Bigmallsomewherea.

They've really tried, but somewhere someone came up with the idea that fantasy = horror = coffins, and obtained an actual coffin, on wheels, for use as a signing table. This raises a few problems. One of them, of course, is of good taste, but more practical is the fact that coffins are made for lying in or kneeling by, not sitting at, and since this one is on castors it gently slides away as I sign until it's at arm's length. In the end we settle for a dull but practical table and they save the coffin for Anne Rice, who knows how to do this stuff.

On to:

Another Big Specialist Bookshop, Citycenta.

Nice place, this. Been there on every tour. Despite this, loads of people with lots of backlist. And a banana dakry. Oh, and a Goth. Fourecks seems to have a thriving Goth culture, if 'thriving' is the right word. I think Goths are fun. It's not a proper signing queue unless you get at least one Goth. In Worralorrasurfa they've got surf Goths.

Back to the hotel where, hooray, I have a suite with extensive views of the curvature of the earth.

Day 10
So's I don't get bored on my day off, there's a set of proofs been sent here from the UK. Read them and make three pages of corrections. Plan is that, since hotel has got a Business Centre, I can use one of their printers and then fax the pages back . . .

. . . except that today the person who knows how their setup works is away. Spend an engrossing hour until I find out that their printer switch box is wired back to front. Oh, and the default printer on the network is not, in fact, the one next to this machine. I find this out when someone rings down and says, 'There's some rather odd stuff coming out of the Laserjet in the manager's office. Who is Captain Vimes, mate?'

Day 11
Fly to Purdeigh Island.

Noon: Busy signing at general bookshop; foreign authors don't often come here, so everyone's got everything.

And down the length of the island to:

Evening talk/signing organized by local bookshop in the Country Comfort Hotel. What a lovely name for a hotel.

And then a real early night because:

Day 12
Up at 4.30 a.m. for flight to Crowtown. Aargh! There'd been a much more sensibly timed flight, which got cancelled. This isn't life in the fast lane, it's life in the oncoming traffic.

Crash out for an hour or so at hotel. Today we're going to

try four signing sessions with bits of media in between, just so no shop feels hard done by. This means starting signing at a couple of shops a few doors from one another, splitting about two hours of queue between them. Then down to some mall for sushi fast food, which Eckians have really taken to. That's something you don't see in England – ladies who look like your great-grandmother scarfing California roll and sashimi off a fork.

Then round the corner to a Small Specialist Bookstore, which is another one that makes an effort. They got someone to ride his Harley into the shop on the *Soul Music* tour, and for the *Feet of Clay* one they built a 180kg golem in the shop. This guy knows his stuff – he's provided a bucket of ice cubes to combat wrist-ache, too.

6.00 p.m.: Off to a talk organized by one of the morning's shops, which has managed to browbeat enough people to fit a large hall. And more signing. A few MS dumpers, but one guy has brought in a flask of Wow-wow Sauce, made to the recipe in *The Discworld Companion*.

And then off with the shop manager to a meat-pie floater wagon to sample this most famous local delicacy. Forgoing, for reasons of economy, the Gourmet Pie Floater (containing named meat) at $3.60, I opted for the basic variety at $3.30.

It was piquant. No worries.

Day 13

Long flight to Sand City. Got a suite in the hotel, wow. But it's sort of odd. There's this huge room but the furniture is arranged as if it's a small room, so there's the sofa and chairs and table and stuff and then an acre of carpet all around.

Off to a signing in a mall. People say, hey, you must see a lot of the world on your travels, but what you mainly see is malls. This is a good mall.

The shop reported a huge crowd when we were on the way, although it was easily dealt with in under forty-five minutes, which just goes to show.

Back to the hotel for an interview. Journo and I take a taxi across the carpet to the distant sofa.

6.30 p.m.: Talk/signing.

One of the most enjoyable events of this tour. A full house – about 250 people – and I was fairly relaxed so it felt as if it was going well, and it seemed that everyone had a book/ books to be signed.

On the way home, the captain of the 747 came over the speaker and said, 'Good evening, I am your captain, Roger Rogers,' and in a cabin full of sweaty business types getting pie-eyed on free booze I was the only one who noticed . . .

Conventional Wisdom

Introduction to the Third Australian Discworld Convention programme book, April 2011

The 2011 Australian Discworld Convention was perfectly wonderful. It wasn't a large convention, but it was crowded, somehow, with so many things going on. It set the benchmark for every subsequent Discworld convention.

However, I still remember fondly the first Discworld Convention, held in a (badly) converted department store in Manchester back in 1996. I watched the fans shuffle in, looking at each other in amazement and realizing they were not alone. They're a loveable lot who drink like the rugby club and fight like the chess club.

Ladies and gentlemen,

Welcome to the Third Australian Discworld Convention! It may well be that this is the first ever convention for some of you; I know that in the UK about one half of attendees are first-timers. When the first ever Discworld Convention took place in Manchester, England, back in 1996 nearly a thousand people turned up, each one expecting to be the only one there. Nevertheless, this fledgling convention boasted several panels, drinking, an extremely good maskerade, drinking, a gala dinner (which included quite possibly the last ever appearance of the genuine pre-immigration English Curry made from swede, sultanas and urine) and, of course, drinking. At the end of the three-day event people were quite genuinely in tears at having to leave and certainly there were many friendships made that still endure; something that's unusual in the general world of fandom.

Discworld conventions (there are five worldwide this year) are now limited to the size of the biggest hall that can be realistically hired; in the UK and US that means an attendance of around a thousand people. I attended my first Antipodean convention in New Zealand only a couple of years after my first ever signing tour down under in August 1990 and made certain that I came again at frequent intervals. The publishers were so pleased that I actually *liked* spending twenty-four hours in an aeroplane that until not long ago I was turning up probably every other year. Quite often my wife joined me and that meant that at one stage, when I was alternately coming down for a big signing tour and going back for a holiday later in the same year, I ordered some trousers in Perth which had to be altered and so I simply collected them when I next went past three months later. Yes, I actually do like the journey, especially since I have been upgrading myself to First Class!

Frankly, I'm looking forward to enjoying myself at this convention and hope that you are too. I am sufficiently keen on talking to people that I often have to get dragged away to do the more formal events, but I always welcome a keen fan who knows the magic words 'What would you like to drink?'

A small embarrassing detail: I am over sixty and, as above, people *will* be buying me drinks and drinks have this terrible problem of being temporary. And so if you see me heading purposefully in the general direction of the dunny do not try to engage me in conversation if you want to live. Yes, it's actually true; once I was communing with nature and somebody actually pushed a book under the door for me to sign.

And on the subject of signings, please read and take note of the formal instructions; signings take an awful lot out of the hand and decades of signings have made my hand rather weak. However, it's still strong enough to pick up a glass.

I really am looking forward to the convention and that's no lie.

Best wishes,
Terry Pratchett
Wiltshire, UK – February 2011

Straight from the Heart, Via the Groin

Speech given at Noreascon 2004, WorldCon

I had a whole speech prepared on my computer, but in the event it wouldn't open, so this is what I was able to recall from memory. The main thing in speeches is to get that first laugh in, and once you've got it, you have the audience in the hollow of your hand.

My name is Terry Pratchett. If this comes as a surprise to you, you have a little bit of time left in which to leave.

Some six months ago I wrote a worthy and learned treatise to deliver to you today. However, some events eventuated in the meantime. So, having got you all here, I'm going to tell you about my operation. It turned out that I had very high blood pressure, so for three months I had high blood pressure and pills that weren't doing any good, which made my blood pressure go up higher. Then for three months I had low blood pressure and pills that did work, but they were the maximum-strength Beta Blockers which are, brothers and sisters, the Devil's face flannel. It was like having a hot towel on my brain.

And then they got it all sorted out, and they found that since I had no history of heart disease in my family, a low cholesterol level, didn't smoke, didn't drink strong drink – much – wasn't overweight, and exercised regularly, of course I had heart disease. I complained about this and they said, 'Tough luck, even plastic people get struck by lightning.' They weighed my wallet and found it was far too heavy for a man of my age and off I went for an angiogram, where they look at your heart via your groin. Now, the heart and groin are sometimes linked in other ways, but it did seem to me they were taking the long route. They give you a little some-thing which makes you a wee bit sleepy and hey, you are allowed to watch the operation on television.

They said, 'Is there any particular music you would like to listen to?' And I said, 'Well, I hadn't thought about it, really. Er . . . you got some Jim Steinman?' And they said 'Sure', put on 'Bat Out Of Hell' and got on with the job. I was watching what they were doing and there was my heart on the screen, and I realized I was nodding off and I thought, 'But this is so cool! The last thing I'm seeing is my heart, still beating!'

Then I had to have the stents put in. You know, these things that collapse. You've probably been following the various legal cases if you have any heart problems, as I have, but mine apparently are okay. And that's rather a more serious operation. Beforehand, you go and talk to the surgeon and he explains, 'There's nothing to worry about, it's quite simple, you will be out next day, oh by the way will you sign this document?'

'Oh yes, what's this document for?'

'That enables us to take you away and give you full-on open heart surgery if necessary. By the way, my son really likes your books.'

I said, 'If you would like your son to continue to be happy, may I advise some caution tomorrow?'

And again I was wheeled into the surgery and gently slid into a happy state. Woke up in my room, God knows how many hours later, with a nurse pressing hard on my groin. What can a man say? 'Where were you when I was eighteen?' In fact I settled for: 'What happened? Did it all work? Did the stents go in?'

'Yes, they've gone in fine, no problems,' she said, 'but we had to stop you bleeding from the artery.'

And the thing about bleeding from the artery, well . . . bleeding from the vein, you get drops of blood. Bleeding from an artery, the ceiling goes red. Then in comes the surgeon and said, 'It's fine, it's fine, everything is fine.' But there was just a hint of not-quite-fine in his voice, so I said, 'So, it all went well, did it?' in a meaningful sort of way, to which he replied, 'Well, there were some fun and games.'

I said, 'How long was I on the slab?' And he said, 'Oh, about an hour and a half, and please stop calling it a slab.' I said, 'Fun and games, I take it, is a medical term meaning "You nearly died"?'

He said, 'Well you reacted rather badly to the dye which is used to illuminate the heart, but we hit you up with —— [something I can't remember, but it sounded like nitro-glycerine] and everything was . . . fine.' Apparently some part of my brain shuts my arteries down when I'm stressed. How my bloodline managed to survive five million years of evolution with this amazing trait, we shall never know, but they changed the medication as a result and I feel, well, fine.

Then the surgeon said: 'What we don't understand is why you kept on shouting about sandwiches. You kept trying to sit up on the operating table, which is not the slab, saying, "There he is – with sandwiches!"'

And I said, 'Yes, I remember that, there was a man – and he had sandwiches! He had a sort of tray and he was standing in the corner!' And the doctor said, 'What kind were they?' And I said, 'I don't know! You wouldn't let me get near! And sometimes there was this big nose looming in front of me and something like the voice of God saying THERE ARE NOOOOOO SANDWICHES . . .'

He said, 'Yes, that was probably me.'

So that's it, brothers and sisters. I'd have loved to find out if they were going to be cucumber with the crusts cut off. That means you're going to go to hell. In England, if they are Branston Pickle and cheese that means you are on the way to heaven. But alas, it was only a near sandwich experience and I survived. But it is nice to know that wherever you are going to go, you are going to get something to eat on the way.

However, when this happens to a man, he starts to think, and asks the questions that have been bugging him for some time, like 'What's it all about then, when you get right down to it?' and 'Is it really too late to get a Porsche?'

But mostly, 'What's it all about then really when you get down to it?' And you know, I just don't know. But I'm pretty sure that you should not head towards the sandwiches.

Two weeks ago we had a Discworld convention in the UK. A major one is held every two years. Lots of Americans came to it this time. You can tell the Americans, they were the ones that spent a lot of time in the bar singing songs like 'Roll Me Over In The Clover'. They had been let out of California, where you are not even allowed to think songs like that.

And it was great and it was very international and they capped the numbers at 750 which is big for a con in the UK. On Sunday night, I looked down at this hall and people were having fun and there were lots of people in costume and they were kind of continuously creating Discworld . . . and I looked upon it and saw that it was pretty good.

As a kind of experiment, a guild system had been set up, and guilds had to vie with one another to get points for their guild. And as I was telling the kids earlier, you're sitting there and a sweet little munchkin who is now working for the Assassins' Guild comes up and goes 'Stabbity, stabbity, stab. That will be two dollars.'

'No,' I say, 'that's not how assassination works. You do not charge the corpse.' So she thinks about it and says, 'My friend

Keith,' (another small munchkin salutes) 'he's from the Guild of Alchemists and will bring you alive again for three dollars.' So with rigor mortis setting in, I stuck my hand in my pocket and gave them some of the fake convention money and then she smiled sweetly and said, 'And for five dollars, I won't kill you again.'

It was amazing to see how this Ankh-Morpork system evolved during the con. Within a few hours of it starting, the head of the Merchants' Guild embezzled his guild's money to purchase the assassination of the head of the Assassins' Guild so he could take it over, and on the second day, the forged money started to appear. It was magnificent! It was Ankh-Morpork come to life. And I looked down at the hall at the people having fun and enjoying themselves and occasionally charging one another to kill them and I thought, 'My Work Here is Done . . .'

My next book out is *Going Postal*. It's about a fraud, a criminal, a conman, who to some extent becomes redeemed through the book, and learns that in addition to fooling everybody else that he's a nice guy, he can even fool himself. And a friend of mine who read a draft copy said, 'There is a little bit of autobiography in all books, isn't there?' Only friends will tell you that.

And, indeed, I think I am a fraud. I am a Guest of Honour at this convention. When I was a kid, Guests of Honour, as I said the other night, were giants made of gold and half a mile high. They had names like James Blish, Brian Aldiss, Arthur C. Clarke . . . I'm five foot seven and I'm never going to get any taller.

I wish I could say I had any purpose in mind when I started the Discworld series. I just thought it was going to be fun. There was an awful lot of bad fantasy around in the early 1980s. There was plenty of good fantasy around, I have to add, but there were just too many dark lords, or differently pigmented lords as we call them now. I thought it was time to have fun with this. *The Colour of Magic* and *The Light Fantastic* were the result. Then I found that they were selling. This came as a huge surprise to me. So I wrote *Equal Rites*. I wrote a third of *Equal Rites* in one weekend. In fact, after one of the nuclear power stations I was a press officer for exploded. Well, it didn't really explode. Well, not much. I mean, it more sort of leaked a bit. But not much. You could hardly see it. And no one died. Trust me on this.

The nervousness here comes from eight years as a nuclear press officer. I never really had to deal with a genuine nuclear accident, but some of the things I did have to deal with were slightly worse, from my personal point of view.

There was, for example, the man who came to a nuclear power station on a public Open Day and turned out to be too radioactive to be allowed into the power station. He set off the machine that shouldn't go bing, which is only supposed to go bing, or rather, not to go bing, when you are leaving the place. That presented a problem: when a man goes through the machine that shouldn't go bing and it goes bing, you just know that the Health and Safety Executive is going to ask questions if he still goes bing when he leaves, and you'll have to prove that he brought the bing in with him.

It turned out that he had been dismantling a Second

World War aircraft altimeter on his kitchen table – that's the kind of thing we Brits do for fun – the night before, and had got pure radium all over his hands. So we scrubbed him up and the power station sent some men in nice clean white suits to take his kitchen table away and put it in the low-level-waste depository. Not many kitchen tables end up like that, or go bing.

Oh, while I think about it, I'll mention there's something about spending a lot of time with engineers that makes you burst out laughing when you hear the term 'three completely independent fail-safe systems'. I learned all about the 'Fred Factor'.

It works like this. Someone decides we'll have a nuclear power station and they call in leading technical architects, and they design it. Subsystems are designed by competent engineers and sub-subsystems are designed by equally competent engineers and so it goes down and down and then you get to Fred. Fred is not a bad person, or even a bad workman. He is just an innocent victim of other people's assumptions.

Fred has been given a job sheet and some tools and told he's got an hour to do the task. Fred has got to wire up three, as it might be, completely independent fail-safe systems and he wires them up and they are indeed completely independent except for one crucial wire from each system which must go through the wall and into the control room. And Fred sits there thinking, 'Why should I drill three holes when one will clearly do?' So he takes out his drill and he drills one hole through the wall and he runs all the wires through it and he positions them just under the Acme Sharp-Edged Shelving System, in a bay where a very small truck is shunting goods around and backing up an awful lot and good heavens, one day all three systems fail at once. That's a terrible surprise, even to Fred.

We had various Fred-type emergencies when I was working for the industry. For example, it should be impossible, completely impossible, to pour nuclear waste down a lavatory. But no one told Fred. So when, after a job of work, he was cleaning the top of the reactor, he tipped a bucket of, well to him, dirty water down the lavatory; and it just so happened that the health physicists, checking the sump outside shortly afterwards, heard the Geiger counter suddenly go 'bing!'. And there, lodged in the sump, was a bit of iron like a piece of grit.

Unfortunately, just before they had done this, a big tanker had already taken a lot of the sewage sludge away from the station to a big holding tank at a local sewage works. That was good. It was going nowhere, at least. But how do you find a few tiny lumps of welding spatter, smaller than a pea and, frankly, not highly radioactive, in eighty thousand gallons of crap? Just feeling around is not an option.

There was a meeting between the sewage workers and the nuclear workers, and it was interesting to see the relative concepts of danger and risk. The nuclear workers were saying, 'Hey, we know about nuclear material, we can handle it, it's detectable, it's no problem, we can deal with this; but that? That's sewage!' And the sewage workers were saying, 'This is sewage. We're used to sewage, we eat and drink sewage, we know about sewage, but that? That's nuclear!'

And finally they came up with a masterstroke: all the stuff was pumped out into tankers and taken up to a coal-fired power station in the Midlands and burned to ash. The ash was put on a conveyor belt and run under a Geiger counter. It detected three little pieces of welding spatter that were slightly radioactive and that was that. I was impressed. A lot of effort had gone into finding these specks, which were rather less dangerous than our friend's altimeter, and it seemed to me to be a matter of honour as much as safety. Contrary to popular belief, nuclear engineers are quite keen to keep the ticking stuff on the inside.

I remember speaking to the guy who had actually hauled the stuff in his tanker. And I said, 'Were you worried?' And he said, 'Well, not really. The last load I had to haul was prawns three months beyond their sell-by date. That did worry me a bit.'

All those involved in the enterprise – including me, because I'd handled the media – got a little informal certificate commemorating our efforts. And since engineers are sophisticated humorists, it was printed on dark brown paper.

And then one day . . . well, I can't remember what happened at which power station at this particular point, I think Fred had done something. I spent all day answering the phones and I was so hyper when I got home late on Friday night that I opened up the computer and started to work. On Sunday morning, my wife came up quietly, saved the work in progress, and tucked me up in bed. And that was the last third of *Equal Rites*.

I decided I had to get out of the industry as quickly as I possibly could. There was such a never-ending level of media interest it was messing with my head. Besides, the early Discworld books were selling well enough to make turning pro a possibility. I gave them a month's notice. It was a fairly pleasant farewell, and they gave me a lovely statuette made of a kind of nice dull grey metal which I really treasure and I keep it by my bed because it saves having to switch the light on while I read.

I finished *Equal Rites* and then I wrote more – and possibly began a work rate which has led to the fact that I am now on blood-pressure pills. I lived in dread of not having work in progress. And I developed the habit of starting a book on the same day as I'd finished the last one. There was one period where I had a schedule of four hundred finished words a day. If I could finish the book in three hundred words, I wrote a hundred words of the next book. No excuses. Granddad died, go to funeral, four hundred words. Christmas time, nip out after dinner, four hundred words. And I did that for years and years and years, because I was fixated on the idea that if you have not got work in progress, you are in fact not a writer at all, you are a bum. And somehow I thought that if I stopped writing, the magic would go away. And I was getting some successes. The books were selling very well. *Mort* got to no. 2 in the bestseller lists. *Sourcery* got to no. 1 and stayed in the list for three months. And that started a trend which has continued to this day. I've lost count of how many books I've sold. I've heard fifty million, I'm sure of forty-five million. It's hard to keep track. There are so many books and translations and all the back lists and things . . .

America turned out to be a problem. Some of you may have been privy to me begging on my knees for a Hugo last night. For a wannabe stand-up comedian like me, you'll do anything for a laugh. Would I like a Hugo? I gather it's unusual to be a WorldCon GoH without several. Well, I know that for most of my writing career I have been ineligible because my publishing history in the US in the early days was marked by sliding publication dates, publishing out of sequence, publishing uncorrected, publishing with my name printed wrong. There were so many things . . . oh and publishing and not telling anyone that you had done it, which is not uncommon. By 1998 I was so depressed about it all that I was quite prepared to officially hand over the US publication rights to a UK publisher because some of you people, in fact many of you people, I suspect, were part of the new underground railroad by which tens of thousands of British hardcovers were being imported into the United States by the fans who didn't like/didn't want to wait for the US versions. My publishers at the time didn't seem to get their heads around this. You'd see me at a US WorldCon signing UK hardcover after UK hardcover for a long, long queue; is there not something wrong with this picture? My editor tried to help, but without back-up it all seemed an uphill struggle.

Then my American agent said, 'No, wait a bit. I think things are going to change.' And what happened was that there was a big shake-up at HarperCollins and at last I had a publisher who thought 'This guy is selling gazillions, but not here! Let's do something about it!' And they gave me a publicist who actually knew my name, which is generally a good start. In 2000 they even asked me to tour.

Back in 1996 I did a signing tour which was miserable and horrible and I spent all my time flying backwards from hub to hub and living on lard balls and salt licks which is what you live on at airports. And it was a terrible tour and I didn't want to do another one so when they asked me to this time I sent them a big list of demands, like:

I'm not going to do any radio station called Good Morning City-I've-never-been-to-before-and-will-be-leaving-in-two-hours . . .

I'm not going to take any flight that gets me into a hotel later than about seven o'clock in the evening . . .

Oh, yes . . . arriving at a hotel at midnight is not good. I think it was Rocky Frisco who saved me in Madison, Wisconsin, because the hotel did no food but he had some cold pizza. That's life in the fast lane, folks. You get in at midnight, you get cold pizza. And you're up at 6.30 to do Good Morning, City-where-the-pizza-is-so-cooold . . .

They agreed to everything. I was astonished. And on the 2000 tour the smallest signing I did was bigger than the biggest signing I did in 1996. I did a tour a couple of years ago, same size crowds, a bit bigger maybe than an English tour. Suddenly, it seems, I'm selling in the US. And who knows, with a bit of effort all round, within a few years, I might get up to where we could have been in about 1996.

And yet, I still feel like a fraud. It's all been done in fun, folks. I had no big plans. I wrote the first few books for fun. I wrote the next books for fun. I did it because I really wanted to do it. I did it because I got something out of it.

I was a fan, a real convention-going fan, for only maybe three years. Went to a couple of them in the early 60s. Went to a WorldCon. Got a job. Started courting girls. And suddenly I was whirled away into what may loosely be called 'Real Life'. While I have to say, when you work on a newspaper, life doesn't appear to be all that real.

In 1973 there was a convention in my area, and I thought, I ought to go back. You know, it's been, what, eight years since I last went to a con. And I walked in, and there was no one I recognized, and I just couldn't get a handle on it. Sometimes I wonder what would have happened if I had gone in and gone back into fandom right there and then. Mind you, I do recall that Salman Rushdie actually came second in a science fiction writing competition organized by Gollancz in the late 1970s. Just imagine if he'd won – Ayatollahs from Mars! – he would have had none of that trouble over *The Satanic Verses,* 'cos it would have been SF and therefore unimportant. He'd have been coming along to cons. He'd be standing here now! Ah, but the little turns and twists of history . . .

Where do the ideas come from? I do not know. But one of the things I did learn from my science fiction reading was that there were other things you could read besides science fiction. I developed a love of history, which school had singularly failed to inculcate into me. I am now in correspondence with my old history master and we get on very well. But his lessons hadn't told me the things that were really interesting: that, for example, during a large part of the eighteenth century, you could actually get pubs to pay you to take urine away and the tanners would actually pay you to have urine delivered to them. That's an interesting fact. It must be even more fun to know it when you are fourteen years old.

I have to admit that I am currently in a position of having more bookshelf space than I have books [Cries of 'Oh!']. However, this is, of course, not counting all those books in the attic, the books under the bed in the spare room, the books wrapped up in protective paper in the garage. Those are the books you kind of, well, just have, they're like Stonehenge. No one is ever going to do anything with them now, but obviously you keep them. Yep, I actually have empty shelves. I have got at least eight feet of blank shelves in my new library. I am sorry. But we went off to an antiquarian bookseller's the other week, and I spent several hundred quid and now I've got probably only about four feet of shelving to fill.

I've made a lot of money out of the writing. A considerable amount. But I am horizontally wealthy, which is the way to go. I advise you all to consider horizontal wealth. If you are vertically wealthy, you think 'I am rich. So I had better do what rich people do.' What do rich people do? Well, they find out where the hell Gstaad is, and then they go skiing there. They buy a yacht. They may go to beaches a long way away. Well, first of all, never buy a yacht. Yachts are like tearing up hundred-pound notes while standing under a cold shower. A nail, a perfectly ordinary nail, costs five times as much if it is a nautical nail. My PA is on at me to buy a light aircraft because he could fly it, but he was training to be a fighter pilot and maybe it wouldn't be a good idea.

But horizontal wealth means not letting your increased income dictate your tastes. You like books and now you have money? Buy more books! Change those catenary bookshelves for good hardwood ones! In my case, build a library extension to your office. And, of course, you buy what will be useful for that most wonderful of pursuits, blind research, which is research without direction for the sheer joy of it.

Let me tell you, for example, the story of tarlatane, uncovered in newspaper accounts from the mid 1850s. Tarlatane was a kind of false silk, made in, I think, lower Saxony. A mineral was ground up, and mixed with paste, and rubbed into cloth, and polished in such a way that you got something that looks a bit like silk. It was a lovely brilliant green, and this young lady attended a ball for troops going to the Crimea, in London, one sultry summer's night, and she had a dress made of tarlatane and shoes made with tarlatane and a bag made of tarlatane. Thus dressed, she danced the night away in this closed, rather humid ballroom, and no doubt little flecks of green spiralled off her dress as she whirled and danced from partner to partner, and then she went home and she felt a bit ill. And then she felt very ill – and after a couple of days of horrible torment, she died of acute arsenic poisoning. How do you make tarlatane? You make it out of copper arsenate. And this is terrible. And this is tragic. But as an author, you look up and you see the glow, the whirling dancers, the beautiful girl, the deadly green glitter in the air. And this is so cool! Sorry . . . but you know what I mean.

I was reading an old book on alchemy and it talked about an alchemist in Austria, who got – I can't remember which emperor it was – to pardon him. He was brought before the emperor on charges of falsely claiming to be able to make gold. He could see the man was unwell, recognized the symptoms of arsenical poisoning, and made a bargain that if he could cure the emperor of Austria he would be allowed to go free.

He tested everything. He tested bread, he tested meat, he tested the water. The emperor got worse and worse. Then he got hold of one of the big candles used in the royal bedroom and weighed it. He went down to the market and bought another candle the same size and weighed that, and found that the royal candle was a pound heavier than the other, because the wick was almost solid arsenic. Lovely stuff, arsenic. I have several different ores of it, it's quite my favourite poison. And every night, when the candles were lit, the emperor was slowly poisoned – and that became part of the plot of *Feet of Clay*. Where do you get your fantastic ideas from? You steal them. You steal them from reality. It outstrips fantasy most of the time.

And I wish I could tell you how many other incidents like this there are. In *The Wee Free Men*, the village has a tradition of burying a shepherd with a piece of wool on his shroud, so that the recording angel will excuse him all those times during lambing when he failed to attend church – because a good shepherd should know that the sheep come first. I didn't make that up. They used to do that in a village two miles from where I live. What I particularly liked about it was the implicit loyalist arrangement with God. Americans, I think, sometimes get puzzled by people in Ireland who call themselves loyalists yet would apparently up arms against the forces of the crown. But a loyalist arrangement is a dynamic accord. It doesn't mean we will be blindly loyal to you. It means we will be loyal to you if you are loyal to us. If you act the way we think a king should act, you can be our king. And it seemed to me that these humble people of the village, putting their little piece of wool on the shroud, were saying, 'If you are the God we think you are, you will understand. And if you are not the God we think you are, to Hell with you.' So much of Discworld has come from odd serendipitous discoveries like that.

I read and read and read throughout my teens. I was a child born just before the TV generation so it never really caught me. I haunted all the bookshops. I read every book I could find. I picked up stuff like a Hoover, and remembered it out of the sheer joy of finding out that the universe is stuffed with interest. Knowledge kind of drifted down out of the atmosphere.

The first book I ever bought for myself was *Brewer's Dictionary of Phrase and Fable*. There are some milestones in my career, and one I am possibly most proud of is that I was asked to write an introduction for the book's Millennium edition. I've got just about all possible editions of it. A great, great help to a fantasy writer. When I needed to find out exactly how you build a clock of flowers in order to tell the time by the opening and closing of the blooms, I turned first to *Brewer's Dictionary of Phrase and Fable* and there it was. So that's where I get my ideas from. I look them up in books. How do you write the stories? You make it up as you go along. This is a terrible thing to have to tell people. But I've spoken to other authors and when there is no one else near by, that's what we agree that we do. We just have different definitions of 'make up', 'go' and 'along'. And possibly of 'it', too.

Currently, I'm writing the next adult Discworld book. What I have is a title. I know that in this story there is a children's book, and the children's book is called *Where's My Cow?* and Commander Vimes is reading it to young Sam Vimes, who is just over a year old. And young Sam Vimes must be read to at six o'clock every night. No matter what the Commander of Police is doing, no matter how serious the political murder he's investigating, he will go home to read to his little boy out of *Where's My Cow?*. It is important to both of them.

Where's My Cow? has a very small vocabulary. It has been chewed all around the edges. And the narrative runs: 'Where's my cow? Is that my cow? It goes baa! It is a sheep. That's not my cow!' . . . and so on, through various barnyard creatures; parents here will know what I mean. Vimes reads this every night and thinks, 'This kid lives in a city. A big, big city. The only sound that animals make in the city is sizzle.' And he looks around and the nursery has got sheep on the wallpaper, and bunny rabbits and foxes and giraffes with waistcoats. Why? And he thinks, 'What would the urban children's story book be like, with all the seamstresses and the beggars and things like that? What kind of noise does a beggar make? "Blaugh! For some money I won't follow you home!'"

And I know, I know, that in this book, which is barely under construction, there's going to be a moment where Vimes is reading through it for the umpteenth time – and this book is soggy, his son goes to sleep chewing this book – and he is going to look at it, and in the back of his mind is this terribly complex crime, and somehow that little book is going to become pivotal to the solution. I don't even know what the crime is yet!*

I spoke to Neil Gaiman about this the other day, and he said exactly the same thing. You have this little oasis of exactly the right piece of plot, and you know it's going to work, and you have no idea yet what the connective tissue is. The book's called *Thud!* because it is based on a game called Thud which is actually available in the UK. It's a game between trolls and dwarfs. It's specifically designed to be played by trolls and dwarfs. Maybe that's why we're not selling many to humans! But also, in a kind of nod towards Dashiell Hammett, it's a good way of starting a murder mystery. 'Thud! That's the sound he made when he hit the ground.' From there, you can go anywhere.

Unfortunately for me, at the same time as this I am also writing the next book in the *Wee Free Men* series.

Writing two books at the same time – which is incredibly bad for your health, I'm on six pills a day already, which has given me the water-retaining capabilities of a drainpipe – is actually quite nifty because you can take a rest from writing

---

* [later] And thus it happened – but not in the way I'd expected.

one, to write the other. Now you know how I got where I am today. And again, I'm writing scenes which are good, and I don't know where they are going to fit in the book.

But it's what I call 'The Valley Filled With Clouds' technique. You're at the edge of the valley, and there is a church steeple, and there is a tree, and there is a rocky out-crop, but the rest of it is mist. But you know that because they exist, there must be ways of getting from one to the other that you cannot see. And so you start the journey. And when I write, I write a draft entirely for myself, just to walk the valley and find out what the book is going to be all about.

I'm sure true writers do not work like this. I know for a fact that Larry Niven uses lots of little postcards, and writes the outline of each scene on one. I know this, because once upon a time we discussed doing a beanstalk story together. Both of us wanted to do it, and after some discussion, we agreed two things. One was that any of the ideas we came up with in that discussion, either of us could use, because they were only ideas after all. And the other was that there was no way on God's good earth that the two of us could ever collaborate on anything, because the styles of working simply would not interlock.

Nobody ever taught me to write. No one ever told me what I was doing wrong. My first novel was published by the first publisher I sent it to. And so I've been learning as I go, and I find it now rather embarrassing that people beginning the Discworld series start with *The Colour of Magic* and *The Light Fantastic*, which I don't think are some of the best books to start with. This is the author saying this, folks. Do not start at the beginning with Discworld.

The books I'm really most proud of having written are the children's books. It was brought home to me today when I was talking to the kids, why this is. They started asking about the turtles. Then they continued asking about the turtles. And I said, 'Okay, no more turtle questions.'

They said: 'Okay, well, about the elephants then . . .'

The thing is that when you write for kids you have to be more precise. You have to answer the questions. You can't leave people hanging around. You can't rely on them filling in too many gaps for themselves. But kids are also remarkably astute about narrative these days. They've got plot savvy. I remember my daughter watching a movie many years ago, she was about eight or nine perhaps, and it was an action-adventure and she said, 'That black guy is going to survive.'

And this is about a third of the way through, and we knew it was that kind of movie where lots and lots of people are going to get killed. And I said, 'How do you know it's going to be him?'

'That guy's going to survive, and that woman's going to survive, and the black guy is going to survive because the other black guy got killed earlier.' Actually she was wrong, but her reasoning was spot on. Already she had been working out how plots work, and lots of bright kids are doing that. So it really stretches me to write the children's books. You have to stay ahead of them.

I think I have probably done great harm to the world of fantasy. Fortuitously, although I'm not very cerebral about what I write, lots and lots of people are doing theses and doctorates on me. So, apparently, I'm a post-modern fantasy writer. I think this is because I've got a condom factory in Ankh-Morpork. Admittedly, the troll that does all the packing wonders what the women are laughing about when he is packing the 'Big Boys'. But you cannot imagine a condom machine in Middle-earth. Well, actually, I can, regrettably. But you certainly can't imagine one in Narnia, and nor should you. But the curious thing is Ankh-Morpork can survive this. Ankh-Morpork does survive most things.

I was told one day, by a fan in the business, that I could get a coat of arms.

I said, 'Could it have hippos on either side of it like the Ankh-Morpork one?' 'No, you can't do that; you have to be either the Queen or a city.' I said, 'Well, I'm personally not a city so I can't, but I could do it anyway, couldn't I? I mean, what happens if I do it?' 'We won't like it.' So I thought, 'This is 2004, I could live with that.' But he really wasn't impressed with the city motto of Ankh-Morpork: 'Quanti canicula ille in fenestra' which does translate very nicely as 'How much is that doggie in the window?'

Anyway, once the shuttle is flying again there are secret plans afoot to get the mission patch from *The Last Hero* on board it somewhere. I suspect that the Latin motto, when translated, reads 'We who are about to die, don't want to'. My contact tells me the astronauts would have no problem with that.

It has been tremendous fun. It's made me a lot of money. I wish I was a real author. I truly do. I haven't thought a great deal about what I've done. I've gone ahead and done it. It comes as a huge shock to read these theses, that sneak in at a rate of one every month or two, and find out about my wonderful use of language and the cleverness with which I do these things. I think 'Nah!' I just do it because that's what it's like . . . That bit goes there because it's impossible to imagine it going in any other place. And then they go and make me a Guest of Honour. There are far, far better authors out there, folks. But I thank you very much for reading this one. It has been tremendous fun. Discworld is twenty-one years old next month, which kind of means something in England, even now. Once upon a time, it was when you were allowed to drink. But now you are officially allowed to drink at the age of about eight years old, although here in the US you have to be thirty. But, somehow, it means you have come of age.

I am pleased to tell you that my heart is holding out very well, but I now intend to write only one book a year. The trouble is that would give me spare time. My wife pointed out recently that the last time we went on holiday I wrote a quarter of a book in two weeks. Well, it was in Australia. It was great. You'd get up early, the birds were singing, there was a fridge full of cold beer, it was 6 a.m., the sun was out, so I sat and wrote, it was great fun. The place we go to in Australia is a little lodge up in the rainforest, but close to the sea. There are no kids and no dogs. Why not? Because the sharks eat them. If the sharks don't get you, the saltwater crocodiles will have a go. And if the saltwater crocodiles don't find you, the box jellyfish will. Come on in, the water's heaving! We like the place. What we particularly like about it is the tennis court and golf course, because it doesn't have them.

And I remember our first walk in the rainforest there. You go around the corner and there is a spider the size of the palm of your hand, bouncing in its web going 'woingggg'. And what do you do? Well, you creep round, a long way round, like half a mile round if necessary. And we were climbing up this cliff, holding on to a rope, and it was starting to rain, and I was looking where I put my feet . . . and there was this big snake strangling a goanna. So I called down to the guide and said, 'There's a snake!' And he said, 'What sort?' And I cried out, 'I'm halfway up a cliff, it's raining hard, I'm holding on to a rope, I'm beginning to slip, and I'm not going to play "What's My Snake!" but I think it's a kind of python.' 'Why do you think it's a kind of python?' 'Because the iguana's eyes are going out like this . . . mwaa.' And so he came up and said, 'That's all right, yeah, no worries, kick it into the bushes.' So we prodded it gently into the bushes. And that was my first walk in the Australian rainforest. And from that, *The Last Continent* came.

I remember the first time I went to Australia, flying over the Pacific in the middle of the night. The Pacific has these ultra-cumulus clouds that grope for the sky – by moonlight they look like Marge Simpson's hairstyle. I watched them for a while, sipping a brandy (this wasn't the coach cabin, you understand) and all was quiet. Then I trotted along to clean my teeth before settling down and I caught sight of myself in the mirror and said: 'What happened? Why should you be here? Thank goodness there's no justice in the world!'

I feel like that right now.

Thank you very much, ladies and gentlemen.

Discworld Turns 21

**Discworld Convention programme, 2004, titled
'A Word from Terry on being 21'**

*It rumbles along, the whole business. Once a book is finished it
isn't mine any more; I stop thinking about it. But sometimes I
look back.*

*Ten years have passed since I wrote this, and Granny is still
going. Moist von Lipwig, who made his first appearance in*
Going Postal, *has now been found in various places, and I
think I shall shortly need someone who is not him. I really like
Moist – he grew, just like Commander Vimes grew, although
that was because Vimes had a child. Once there are children, you
have different people. And so now, again, I'm looking at the old
characters and wondering which new ones are going to strut on
to the stage. Discworld changes, but it changes in its own way.*

So . . . here we are then. Twenty-one years. It's been a good ride, no small children were hurt, and there wasn't much screaming.

I'm not sure *why* twenty-one. We could have made a big fuss about the twenty-fifth book, *The Truth*, which had the advantage of being a bigger number, or maybe everyone could have waited another handful of years for the 50,000,000th sale, or ten years or so in case I manage the big golden Fiftieth Discworld book.

That's a chilling thought. Already there are hulking great fans who got started by reading their parents' Discworld collection. A couple of years ago I did a talk at a school where the *headmaster* recalled, as a student, queuing at a Discworld signing. That was unnerving. There are *families* of Discworld readers. Stay alive long enough, and the years just fall over.

But we're stuck with this magic twenty-one, a legacy of the days when you had to wear short trousers until you had been shaving for five years. Twenty-one, then, and the best part of three million words.

The trouble is, I can't remember a lot of it. I'm told I had fun. What I *can* remember is looking around the posh cabin of a 747 high over the Pacific, in the summer of 1990. People were sleeping. Outside there were huge towering clouds in the moonlight. Some hours ahead was my first Australasian tour. There was an orchid in a vase in the toilet. I looked at myself in the mirror and thought: this isn't real, is it. Not really . . .

That general state of amazement has never left me. It's followed me into Buckingham Palace, the halls of various universities, behind the scenes of the Library of Congress and into innumerable bookshops: oh yes. At least a year and a half of those twenty-one years was spent sitting in bookshops. It followed me to Alice Springs and upriver in a rainforest in Borneo, where I did a small impromptu signing at a camp that rehabilitates orphaned orangutans back to the wild. (None of them joined in, but I signed three books for the British kids who'd just arrived there to work on various 'green' projects; the baby orangs had better things to do, like pillage the carelessly fastened knapsacks in the dormitories for anything edible, such as, e.g., toothpaste and vitamin pills.) My name's been given to an extinct species of turtle, and various characters are commemorated in the Latin names of small plants and, I think, insects.

And all the time there's been this slight feeling that it was happening to someone else.

I never took writing seriously. In fact, that's not entirely true. I took writing very seriously, which was probably the right thing to do at the time. I read books that explained how hard it was to make *any* money from writing, and, seriously, journalism looked a much better bet. I wrote as a hobby and made some early sales, but the thought of trying to make a living from it never crossed my mind. (I was probably sensible. Then, as now, writing for most authors was buttressed by a *real* job, that could be relied upon to pay the bills.)

When I found I *could* make a living – oh, that wonderful Saturday morning when I looked at the figures and realized that if I played my cards right I might never have to do an honest day's work ever again – I never thought I'd get *rich*.

See? Life is what happens while you're making other plans.

Maybe it's time to make some plans now. Two books a year as a reliable thing? That is stopping, not gradually, but as from now. There isn't the *time* any more. The US market has opened up. Everyone wants me to tour and, bluntly, two books a year get in one another's way. They don't get the review coverage because, well, Pratchett books are always *there*, a kind of biographical constant, and twice a year there's a month of high stress when three books are happening all at once. One's being started, one's being proofed and edited (in two countries at once, now) and one's due to be toured. It's a juggling act. If anything goes wrong, it's a train wreck. It's dawned on me that I don't need to do it, not every year. Within a few days of a book the readers, God bless 'em, ask: 'What's next in the pipeline?' There is no pipeline. It's just me.

The children's books will continue. They take as much time as the adult books, but they work, and a change is nearly as good as a rest. Nearly. Two more 'Tiffany Aching' books are planned.

As for Discworld, it *will* carry on. One reason I started the children's Discworld series was to give me a different area to play in, because 'adult' Discworld is filling up. Granny Weatherwax may have a crotchety but lengthy life expectancy (magic seems to extend life and there's no evidence that her own grandmother is dead) but Vimes is feeling the cold mornings these days. How much of a major overhaul would readers tolerate? Blow *them*, how much could I tolerate? Someone else running Ankh-Morpork? Or the Watch? Or Unseen University? I suspect there's a few ghosts that won't go away.

Fortunately, Discworld time moves slower than ours. But *Going Postal* will contain all-new major characters, because that's what the plot requires. Next year's book, which just has a working title right now (and that is not being divulged to *anyone* lest Amazon begin taking orders for it next week) is Watch-based and looking rather good. After that, I'm pleased to say, the future is a mysterious fog that might contain anything at all.

And then there's been the fans, who write me letters and invite me to their weddings and without whose constant interest and advice I wouldn't have a clue where I was going wrong. They know when to take the joke seriously and let it become more than a joke.

But what is a typical fan? Can you spot them? Some can. Those of you who standeth upon the face of the Earth in queues, watch carefully next time as the local newspaper photographer enters the bookshop. Yes, he's looking for the legendary Typical Terry Pratchett Fan! Watch him pace up and down, past the people in suits, the people who look like someone's mum or dad, the people who look like they have a job and are on their lunch hour. What's this? Three hundred people in the queue and not one of them with the decency to wear a pointy hat?

Or, as one puzzled security man said, after watching a

queue that had amiably refrained from doing the expected but curiously weird things for three hours, 'They're all so . . . so normal!'

To which I replied, 'Oh, no, they're not that bad . . . '

It's been fun. It is fun. Long may it be fun.

Thank you.

Kevins

The Author, Winter 1993

Back in the golden days when I was first writing, my wife Lyn used to bring me elevenses. And with the elevenses came a lot of manuscripts and a lot of letters . . .

My wife christened them Kevins. It's quite unfair. It was just that . . . well . . . one day the post included three letters all from boys called Kevin, and she wrote 'Kevins' on the small folder and somehow the name stuck.

So now, once a week or whenever I'm feeling guilty, I write replies to the Kevins. Many of them are female. Some of them are grandmothers. I've never really counted them. All I know is that I write almost 200,000 words, about two novels' worth, of letters every year. Most of them are letters to Kevins.

They never tell you about this in those How to Write

books. Make some time to write every day . . . *yes*. Use one side of the paper only . . . *yes*. But do they tell you how to deal with almost thirty identical letters from Form 5A? No. Do they tell you how to reply to the man who accuses you of stealing his ideas by laser beam before he had time to write them down? Unaccountably not. Nor do they tell you that you might have to buy a guide to New Zealand to help identify badly written return addresses (you can make a reasonable stab at UK names like Newsquiggle-upon-Tyne, but almost anywhere in New Zealand that isn't called Auckland or Wellington is called Rangiwangi . . . or at least looks as if it is).

I suppose all this comes under the heading of fan mail. As a genre author, I am probably perceived by my readers as 'belonging' to them in a rather more direct way than, say, Martin Amis belongs to *his* readers – I effect, according to one reviewer, 'a snug mindfit of opinion between reader and writer' (he meant it nastily – he was a *Sunday Times* man, after all).

So they don't hesitate to ask for new titles featuring favourite characters. ('Dear Sir Arthur, Why not bring Sherlock Holmes back to track down Jack the Ripper . . . ?') Or for autographs. Or signed photographs. (This beats me. I mean who cares what an author looks like? You finish a book, perhaps the gripping narrative has left white-hot images snugly mindfitting into the brain – and then you turn to the back flap and there's this short bald guy with a pipe . . .)

Why do people write to authors? Field evidence here

suggests that some are aspiring authors themselves and want the map reference of the Holy Grail. People really do ask us: how do you get published?, with a strong implication that there must be more to it than, well, writing a decent book and sending it to publishers until one of them gives in. They want the Secret. I wish I knew what it was.

People really do ask: where do you get your ideas from? And I've never come up with a satisfactory answer. 'From a warehouse in Croydon' is only funny once. After that you have to *think*.

Sometimes they want to encourage us, as did the librarian who wrote: 'I think it's *marvellous* that young readers enjoy your work, because that means we can get them into libraries and introduce them to *real* books.'

Or occasionally to chastise us. A teacher complained about the bad grammar of an eighty-year-old rural witch who'd never been to school ('Dear Mr Dickens, You really must do something about the way Sam Weller talks . . .'). On the other hand, I had a most interesting correspondence with a French academic on the correct modern usage of the word 'careen', which went on for some time.

And the younger ones doing GCSE don't hesitate to write on the lines of (to be read in one breath): 'Dear Mr Pratchett I have read all your books You are my favourite author I am doing a project on you Could you please answer these 400 questions by Friday because I have to hand it in on Monday . . .'

I get around these by selecting the twenty most interesting questions and getting the computer to print out a Q&A

sheet in really tiny print, which is updated every month or so. I suspect that many a narrow pass mark has been achieved by a bit of careful copying . . .

It's easy to tell a letter from a teenage reader. They tend to have numbered sentences, as in 'Dear Mr Pratchett, I would like to be a writer when I leave school. Can you tell me 1) Are you on Flexitime? 2) What are your wages?' Every year, as regular as the arrival of the cuckoo, at least one of them writes asking if I could give them a week's Work Experience, which I always think of in Hardyesque terms ('It were in 1993 that Master Pratchett took oi on as a prentice boy at one farthing a week . . .').

Further down the age range, pencil and crayon creep in. These letters are quite short. They tend to get answered first. They are often accompanied by pictures. Anyone who has written anything for children knows what I mean. Sometimes they contain the toughest questions. And a list of all the household pets by name. At the other end of the scale the Kevins often begin, 'I bet you don't get many letters from 75-year-old grandmothers . . .'

Actually, I do. Lots of adults who read me don't always let on. It's like those surveys you see in the literary papers at the end of the year – the celebs are asked what books they've enjoyed this year, and everyone knows they've been reading Joanna Trollope and Jilly Cooper and Tom Clancy, but they all go waxy-faced and gabble the first five 'serious' titles they can remember.

A statistically significant number of correspondents write to say they met someone else reading one of my books on a remote Greek island. It may of course always be the same person.

Many of them have this in common, though: they express doubts that the author will read the letter, let alone answer it. The letter is an act of faith. It's as though they've put a message in a bottle and tossed it into the sea. But . . .

. . . well, when I was young, I wrote a letter to J. R. R. Tolkien, just as he was becoming extravagantly famous. I think the book that impressed me was *Smith of Wootton Major*. Mine must have been among hundreds or thousands of letters he received every week. I got a reply. It might have been dictated. For all I know, it might have been typed to a format. But it was *signed*.

He must have had a sackful of letters from every commune and university in the world, written by people whose children are now grown up and trying to make a normal life while being named Galadriel or Moonchild. It wasn't as if I'd said a lot. There were no numbered questions. I just said I'd enjoyed the book very much. And he said thank you.

For a moment, it achieved the most basic and treasured of human communications: you are real, and therefore so am I.

After thinking about that, I've tried to persuade myself that the mail isn't a distraction from writing but some kind of necessary echo of it. It's part of the whole process. A kind of after-sales service. There is, admittedly, the terminally weird letter, although these are rare. And sometimes the handwriting defeats us. And readers who want to continue a lengthy correspondence sometimes have to be gently let down, because of God's lack of foresight in putting only twenty-four hours in one day. But apart from those rarities, they all get answered sooner or later . . . I hope. It's part of the whole thing, if ever I manage to work out what the whole thing is.

Wyrd Ideas

The Author, Autumn 1999

. . . these days, of course, there are as many emails as letters.

'Hey U R 1 kewl dood, can U give Me some Tips about Writing?' You may be familiar with emails like this, if you're known to be an author with an internet address. On the internet, no one cares how you spell. Dyslexia is imitated, not as an affliction, but as a badge of coolth. Some of the younger users regard as suspicious any suggestion that vaguely competent English has a part to play. I suggested to one correspondent that, if he wished to be a writer, he should allow grammar, spelling and punctuation to enter his life; he bridled, on the basis that 'publishers have people to do that'!

Ahem . . .

My email address is public, and easily tracked down. I am

a popular author. I no longer count the emails I get every day. I answer as many as I can.

Fairly early on, I learned that a filter on my mailbox was essential to electronic survival; that decision was made, in fact, in the days when I still used a 2,400 baud modem and someone decided to email me their illustrated manuscript – all three megabytes of it (the ethos of the internet was evolved by people who did not have to pay their own phone bills). Besides, a filter also helps cut out all that spam addressed to 'friend'. No stranger who is up to any good calls you 'friend'.

That was just irksome. Now I've hit what I think is a real problem.

One of the traditions of the fantasy and science fiction genre is communication; fans like to be in touch with lots of other fans and they embraced the internet with amazing speed as an alternative to the mimeograph machine or computer printer. And another tradition has been 'fan fiction'.

Plenty of other genres have their fans, but 'fanfic' is unique to F&SF, as far as I know. People, out of the love of doing it, write further stories set in some professional author's universe and using established characters and background, and publish them on an amateur basis for the pleasure of their friends.

Traditionally, since in many cases they themselves were once fans (it's hard to imagine becoming a science fiction writer without having a liking for science fiction) the genre authors have turned a benign or blind eye to this legally dubious activity. Be happy that you have fans, has been the consensus, and if you have fans they will be . . . fannish. It's not a bad training ground for writers. It's just part of the whole thing.

Authors who write a popular series find that readers are not passive receivers: they take the view that the author writes the script but the movie is played out in the reader's own head, and therefore the enterprise is in some ways a collaborative or interactive one in which the reader has rights, if only the right to an opinion. This sort of thing has gone on for years in a private kind of way ('Dear Miss Austen, I think it would be really cool if one of your heroines were to fall in love with Napoleon . . .'). It's probably healthy. The trouble is that the net is not private and it magnifies everything, good and bad.

I used to read the two newsgroups devoted to me and my work. It is fun to see one's books publicly deconstructed by an Oxford don on the same newsgroup as they are deconstructed by someone who thinks *Star Wars* is a really old movie. But I recently stopped reading them, after seven years.

I started to get nervous when people began posting, on the public newsgroups, plot suggestions for future books and speculation about how characters would develop. The net is still new, and it is big and it is public, and has brought with it new perceptions and problems. (One minor one is that people are out driving their language on a worldwide highway without passing a test. Take the word 'plagiarize'. I know what it means. You know what it means. Lawyers certainly know what it means. But I have seen it repeatedly used as a synonym for 'research', 'parody', and 'reference', as in '*Wyrd Sisters* was plagiarized from Shakespeare'. That was a book of mine and, yes, well, it certainly does add to the enjoyment if you've heard of a certain Scottish play and . . . er . . . where do I start?)

Now add to this the growth of strange ideas about copyright. At one end of the spectrum I get nervous letters asking 'Will it be all right if I name my cat after one of your characters?' At the other are the emails like: 'I enjoyed the story so much that I've scanned it in and put it on my web page . . . hope you don't mind.' Copyright is either thought to exist in every single word, or not at all.

In short, I began to worry, in this overheated atmosphere, about what would happen if I used a storyline that a fan had already posted on the net or on some fan-fiction web page.

I've already had a few emails on the lines of 'I see you have used that idea of mine, then', when the idea in question was 'Why doesn't Terry Pratchett write a book about Australia/ pirates/football?' (I once had one – and I'm sure I've not been the first – which quite frankly said, 'I've got a great idea that will make us both a lot of money if you write the book, but obviously I can't tell you about it until we've signed a contract . . . ')

We all soon become aware that to many otherwise intelligent people 'the Idea' is the heart, soul and centre of a novel, and all that stuff about plot, point, character, dialogue and 100,000 written words is a clerical detail. Get the Idea, and all you need then is someone to 'write it down'.

I may be worrying too much, but there *is* something to worry about. It isn't the law that worries me. Come to that, it isn't 99.99 per cent of fans on the net. It's simply that in every crowd there's a twerp. All any twerp needs to do is protest loud and long, and he or she will get attention from other twerps who'll go along for the ride – after all, if such people didn't exist, the *Ricki Lake Show* wouldn't have an audience. And then you just need a journalist who thinks it'd make a good story on the lines of 'Famous Author Stole My Idea, Says Disappointed Fan', and if you don't think a journalist would run something like this, you haven't been reading the papers. Even the participation of a journalist isn't necessary. The net itself is, as a publicity device, available to all.

Unfortunately, very little imagination is needed for this scenario. There have already been hints of it in the US where, as we know, people sue as automatically as they breathe and there's soon to be a class action against God for making an imperfect world. It has certainly been enough, rumour says, to cause other authors to shun 'their' newsgroups.

It's a shame, but I think I've very publicly got to log off, too. I've got lots of ideas. Now, if only people would let me have some Time.

Notes from a Successful Fantasy Author: Keep It Real

Writers' & Artists' Yearbook 2007

I'm always labelled as a fantasy author, but I've been heard to say that I'm mainstream, because the books that people read are surely the mainstream. The books in shops are mainstream. And now that includes fantasy. 'Real' writers have been stealthy. They've taken the tropes of fantasy or science fiction and twisted them – but those books don't get called science fiction or fantasy, because the people writing them don't think of them like that.

Since a lot of fiction is in some way fantasy, can we narrow it down to 'fiction that transcends the rules of the known world'? And it might help to add 'and includes elements commonly classed as magical'. There are said to be about five sub-genres, from contemporary to mythic, but they mix and merge and if the result is good, who cares?

If you want to write it, you've probably read a lot of it – in which case, stop (see below). If you haven't read any, go and read lots. Genres are harsh on those who don't know the history, don't know the rules. Once you know them, you'll know where they can be broken.

Genres are also – fantasy perhaps most of all – a big bulging pantry of plots, conceits, races, character types, myths, devices and directions, most of them hallowed by history. You're allowed to borrow, as many will have done before you; if this were not the case there would only ever have been one book about a time machine. To stay with the cookery metaphor, they're all just ingredients. What matters is how you bake the cake; every decent author should have their own recipe, and the best find new things to add to the mix.

World building is an integral part of a lot of fantasy, and this applies even in a world that is superficially our own – apart from the fact that Nelson's fleet at Trafalgar consisted of hydrogen-filled airships. It is said that, during the fantasy boom in the late eighties, publishers would maybe get a box containing two or three runic alphabets, four maps of the major areas covered by the sweep of the narrative, a pronunciation guide to the names of the main characters and, at the bottom of the box, the manuscript. Please . . . there is no need to go that far.

There is a term that readers have been known to apply to fantasy that is sometimes an unquestioning echo of better work gone before, with a static society, conveniently ugly 'bad' races, magic that works like electricity and horses that work like cars. It's EFP, or Extruded Fantasy Product. It can be recognized by the fact that you can't tell it apart from all the other EFP.

Do not write it, and try not to read it. Read widely outside the genre. Read about the Old West (a fantasy in itself) or Georgian London or how Nelson's navy was victualled or the history of alchemy or clock-making or the mail coach system. Read with the mindset of a carpenter looking at trees.

Apply logic in places where it wasn't intended to exist. If assured that the Queen of the Fairies has a necklace made of broken promises, ask yourself what it looks like. If there is magic, where does it come from? Why isn't everyone using it? What rules will you have to give it to allow some tension in your story? How does society operate? Where does the food come from? You need to know how your world works.

I can't stress that last point enough. Fantasy works best when you take it seriously (it can also become a lot funnier, but that's another story). Taking it seriously means that there must be rules. If anything can happen, then there is no real suspense. You are allowed to make pigs fly, but you must take into account the depredations on the local bird life and the need for people in heavily over-flown areas to carry stout umbrellas at all times. Joking aside, that sort of thinking is the motor that has kept the Discworld series moving for twenty-two years.

Somehow, we're trained in childhood not to ask questions of fantasy, like: how come only one foot in an entire kingdom fits the glass slipper? But look at the world with a questioning eye and inspiration will come. A vampire is repulsed by a crucifix? Then surely it can't dare open its eyes, because everywhere it looks, in a world full of chairs, window frames, railings and fences, it will see something holy. If werewolves as Hollywood presents them were real, how would they make certain that when they turned back into human shape they had a pair of pants to wear? And in *Elidor*, Alan Garner, a master at running a fantasy world alongside and entwined with our own, memorably asked the right questions and reminded us that a unicorn, whatever else it may be, is also a big and very dangerous horse. From simple questions, innocently asked, new characters arise and new twists are put on an old tale.

G. K. Chesterton summed up fantasy as the art of taking that which is humdrum and everyday (and therefore unseen) and picking it up and showing it to us from an unfamiliar direction, so that we see it anew, with fresh eyes. The eyes could be the eyes of a tiny race of humans, to whom a flight of stairs is the Himalayas, or creatures so slow that they don't see fast-moving humanity at all. The eyes could even be the nose of our werewolf, building up an inner picture of a room by an acute sense of smell, seeing not just who is there now but who was there yesterday.

What else? Oh yes. Steer clear of 'thee' and 'thou' and 'waxing wroth' unless you are a genius, and use adjectives as if they cost you a toenail. For some reason adjectives cluster around some works of fantasy. Be ruthless.

And finally: the fact that it is a fantasy does not absolve

you from all the basic responsibilities. It doesn't mean that characters needn't be rounded, the dialogue believable, the background properly established, the plots properly tuned. The genre offers all the palettes of the other genres, and new colours besides. They should be used with care. It only takes a tweak to make the whole world new.

Whose Fantasy Are You?

Bookcase (W. H. Smith), 17 September 1991

They wanted about 400–500 words 'on fantasy'. Imagine the start of this being uttered in the same tone of voice Dr Elizabeth Allaway uses to the recalcitrant grants committee in the movie Contact.
Besides, it's true.

You want fantasy? Here's one . . . There's this species that lives on a planet a few miles above molten rock and a few miles below a vacuum that'd suck the air right out of them. They live in a brief geological period between ice ages, when giant asteroids have temporarily stopped smacking into the surface. As far as they can tell, there's nowhere else in the universe where they could stay alive for ten seconds.

And what do they call their fragile little slice of space and time? They call it real life. In a universe where it's known that whole galaxies can explode, they think there's things like 'natural justice' and 'destiny'. Some of them even believe in democracy . . .

I'm a fantasy writer, and even I find it all a bit hard to believe.

Me? I write about people who live on the Discworld, a world that's flat and goes through space on the back of a giant turtle. Readers think the books are funny – I can prove it, I get letters – because in this weird world, people live normal lives. They worry about the sort of things we worry about, like death, taxes, and not falling off. The Discworld is funny because everyone on it believes that they're in real life. (They might be – the last I heard, physicists have discovered all these extra dimensions around the place which we can't see because they're rolled up small; and you don't believe in giant world-carrying turtles?) There are no magic swords or mighty quests. There are just people like us, give or take the odd pointy hat, trying to make sense of it all. Just like us.

We like to build these little worlds where everything gets sorted out and makes sense and, if possible, the good guys win. No one would call Agatha Christie a fantasy writer, but look at the books she's most typically associated with – they're about tiny isolated little worlds, usually a country house, or an island, or a train, where a very careful plot is worked out. No mad axeman for Agatha, no unsolved crimes. Hercule Poirot always finds the clues.

And look at Westerns. The famous Code of the West largely consisted of finding somewhere where you could safely shoot the other guy in the back, but we don't really want to know that. We'd rather believe in Clint Eastwood.

I would, anyway. Almost all writers are fantasy writers, but some of us are more honest about it than others.

And everyone reads fantasy . . . one way . . . or another . . .

Why Gandalf Never Married

Speech given at Novacon, 1985

This was written while Equal Rites *and its female wizard heroine, Esk, were taking shape. Shortly after that, similar ideas about women seemed to turn up in the zeitgeist. I still enjoy writing for the witches: Granny Weatherwax and Nanny Ogg, Tiffany and all the others. Even the pig witch, Petulia – I really liked writing her.*

I want to talk about magic, how magic is portrayed in fantasy, how fantasy literature has in fact contributed to a very distinct image of magic, and perhaps most importantly how the Western world in general has come to accept a very precise and extremely suspect image of magic users.

I'd better say at the start that I don't actually believe in magic any more than I believe in astrology, because I'm a Taurean and we don't go in for all that weirdo occult stuff.

But a couple of years ago I wrote a book called *The Colour of Magic*. It had some boffo laughs. It was an attempt to do for the classical fantasy universe what *Blazing Saddles* did for Westerns. It was also my tribute to twenty-five years of fantasy reading, which started when I was thirteen and read *The Lord of the Rings* in twenty-five hours. That damn book was a half-brick in the path of the bicycle of my life. I started reading fantasy books at the kind of speed you can only manage in your early teens. I panted for the stuff.

I had a deprived childhood, you see. I had lots of other kids to play with and my parents bought me outdoor toys and refused to ill-treat me, so it never occurred to me to seek solitary consolation with a good book.

Then Tolkien changed all that. I went mad for fantasy. Comics, boring Norse sagas, even more boring Victorian fantasy . . . I'd better explain to younger listeners that in those days fantasy was not available in every toyshop and bookstall, it was really a bit like sex: you didn't know where to get the really dirty books, so all you could do was paw hopefully through *Amateur Photography* magazines looking for artistic nudes.

When I couldn't get it – heroic fantasy, I mean, not sex – I hung around the children's section in the public libraries, trying to lure books about dragons and elves to come home with me. I even bought and read all the Narnia books in one go, which was a bit like a surfeit of Communion wafers. I didn't care any more.

Eventually the authorities caught up with me and kept me in a dark room with small doses of science fiction until I broke the habit and now I can walk past a book with a dragon on the cover and my hands hardly sweat at all.

But a part of my mind remained plugged into what I might call the consensus fantasy universe. It does exist, and you all know it. It has been formed by folklore and Victorian romantics and Walt Disney, and E. R. Eddison and Jack Vance and Ursula Le Guin and Fritz Leiber – hasn't it? In fact those writers and a handful of others have very closely defined it. There are now, to the delight of parasitical writers like me, what I might almost call 'public domain' plot items. There are dragons, and magic users, and far horizons, and quests, and items of power, and weird cities. There's the kind of scenery that we would have had on Earth if only God had had the money.

To see the consensus fantasy universe in detail you need only look at the classical Dungeons and Dragons role-playing games. They are mosaics of every fantasy story you've ever read.

Of course, the consensus fantasy universe is full of clichés, almost by definition. Elves are tall and fair and use bows, dwarfs are small and dark and vote Labour. And magic works. That's the difference between magic in the fantasy universe and magic here. In the fantasy universe a wizard points his fingers and all these sort of blue glittery lights come out and there's a sort of explosion and some poor soul is turned into something horrible.

Anyway, if you are in the market for easy laughs you learn that two well-tried ways are either to trip up a cliché or take things absolutely literally. So in the sequel to *The Colour of*

Magic, which is being rushed into print with all the speed of continental drift, you'll learn what happens, for example, if someone like me gets hold of the idea that megalithic stone circles are really complex computers. What you get is, you get druids walking around talking a sort of computer jargon and referring to Stonehenge as the miracle of the silicon chunk.

While I was plundering the fantasy world for the next cliché to pull a few laughs from, I found one which is so deeply ingrained that you hardly notice it is there at all. In fact it struck me so vividly that I actually began to look at it seriously.

That's the generally very clear division between magic done by women and magic done by men.

Let's talk about wizards and witches. There is a tendency to talk of them in one breath, as though they were simply different sexual labels for the same job. It isn't true. In the fantasy world there is no such thing as a male witch. Warlocks, I hear you cry, but it's true. Oh, I'll accept you can postulate them for a particular story, but I'm talking here about the general tendency. There certainly isn't such a thing as a female wizard.

Sorceress? Just a better class of witch. Enchantress? Just a witch with good legs. The fantasy world, in fact, is overdue for a visit from the Equal Opportunities people because, in the fantasy world, magic done by women is usually of poor quality, third-rate, negative stuff, while the wizards are usually cerebral, clever, powerful and wise.

Strangely enough, that's also the case in this world. You don't have to believe in magic to notice that.

Wizards get to do a better class of magic, while witches give you warts.

The archetypal wizard is of course Merlin, adviser of kings, maker of the Round Table, and the only man who knew how to work the electromagnet that released the Sword from the Stone. He is not in fact a folklore hero, because much of what we know about him is based firmly on Geoffrey de Monmouth's *Life of Merlin*, written in the twelfth century. Old Geoffrey was one of the world's great writers of fantasy, nearly as good as Fritz Leiber but without that thing about cats.

Had a lot of trouble with women, did Merlin. Morgan Le Fay – a witch – was his main enemy but he was finally trapped in his crystal cave or his enchanted forest, pick your own variation, by a female pupil. The message is clear, boys: that's what happens to you if you let the real powerful magic get into the hands of women.

In fact Merlin is almost being replaced as the number one wizard by Gandalf, whose magic is more suggested than apparent. I'd also like to bring in at this point a third wizard, of whom most of you must have heard – Ged, the wizard of Earthsea. I do this because Ursula Le Guin's books give us a very well thought out, and typical, magic world. I'd suggest that they worked because they plugged so neatly into our group image of how magic is ordered. They serve to point up some of the similarities in our wizards.

They're all bachelors, and sexually continent. In this fantasy is in agreement with some of the standard works on magic, which make it clear that a good wizard doesn't get his end away. (Funny, because there's no such prohibition on witches; they can be at it like knives the whole time and it doesn't affect their magic at all.) Wizards tend to exist in Orders, or hierarchies, and certainly the Island of Roke reminds me of nothing so much as a medieval European university, or maybe a monastery. There don't seem to be many women around the university, although I suppose someone cleans the lavatories. There are indeed some female practitioners of magic around Earthsea, but if they are not actually evil then they are either misguided or treated by Ged in the same way that a Harley Street obstetrician treats a local midwife.

Can you imagine a girl trying to get a place at the University of Roke?* Or I can put it another way – can you imagine a female Gandalf?

Of course I hardly need mention the true fairytale witches, as malevolent a bunch of crones as you could imagine. It was probably living in those gingerbread cottages. No wonder witches were always portrayed as toothless – it was living in a 90,000-calorie house that did it. You'd hear a noise in the night and it'd be the local kids, eating the doorknob. According to my eight-year-old daughter's book on wizards, a nicely illustrated little paperback available at any good bookshop, 'wizards undid the harm caused by evil witches'. There it is again, the recurrent message: female magic is cheap and nasty.

* Of course, if you've read the later Earthsea novels you can. But in 1985 that was still to come.

But why is all this? Is there anything in the real world that is reflected in fantasy?

The curious thing is that the Western world at least has no very great magical tradition. You can look in vain for any genuine wizards, or for witches for that matter. I know a large number of people who think of themselves as witches, pagans or magicians, and the more realistic of them will admit that while they like to think that they are following a tradition laid down in the well-known Dawn of Time they really picked it all up from books and, yes, fantasy stories. I have come to believe that fantasy fiction in all its forms has no basis in anything in the real world. I believe that witches and wizards get their ideas from their reading matter or, before that, from folklore. Fiction invents reality.

In Western Europe, certainly, wizards are few and far between. I have been able to turn up a dozen or so, who with the 20-20 hindsight of history look like either conmen or conjurors. Druids almost fit the bill, but Druids were a few lines by Julius Caesar until they were reinvented a couple of hundred years ago. All this business with the white robes and the sickles and the oneness with nature is wishful thinking. It's significant, though. Caesar portrayed them as vicious priests of a religion based on human sacrifice, and gory to the elbows. But the PR of history has nevertheless turned them into mystical shamans, unless I mean shamen; men of peace, brewers of magic potions.

Despite the claim that nine million people were executed for witchcraft in Europe in the three centuries from 1400 – this turns up a lot in books of popular occultism and I can only say it is probably as reliable as everything else they contain – it is hard to find genuine evidence of a widespread witchcraft cult. I know a number of people who call themselves witches. No, they are witches – why should I disbelieve them? Their religion strikes me as woolly but well-meaning and at the very least harmless. Modern witchcraft is the Friends of the Earth at prayer. If it has any roots at all they lie in the works of a former colonial civil servant and pioneer naturist called Gerald Gardiner, but I suggest that it is really based in a mishmash of herbalism, sixties undirected occultism, and *The Lord of the Rings*.

But I must accept that people called witches have existed. In a sense they have been created by folklore, by what I call the Flying Saucer process – you know, someone sees something they can't or won't explain in the sky, is aware that there is a popular history of sightings of flying saucers, so decides that what he has seen is a flying saucer, and pretty soon that 'sighting' adds another few flakes to the great snowball of saucerology. In the same way, the peasant knows that witches are ugly old women who live by themselves because the folklore says so, so the local crone must be a witch. Soon everyone locally KNOWS that there is a witch in the next valley, various tricks of fate are laid at her door, and so the great myth chugs on.

One may look in vain for similar widespread evidence of wizards. In addition to the double handful of doubtful practitioners mentioned above, half of whom are more readily identifiable as alchemists or windbags, all I could come up with was some vaguely masonic cults, like the Horseman's

Word in East Anglia. Not much for Gandalf in there.

Now you can take the view that of course this is the case, because if there is a dirty end of the stick then women will get it. Anything done by women is automatically down-graded. This is the view widely held – well, widely held by my wife ever since she started going to consciousness-raising group meetings, who tells me it's ridiculous to speculate on the topic because the answer is so obvious. Magic, according to this theory, is something that only men can be really good at, and therefore any attempt by women to trespass on the sacred turf must be rigorously stamped out. Women are regarded by men as the second sex, and their magic is there-fore automatically inferior. There's also a lot of stuff about man's natural fear of a woman with power; witches were poor women seeking one of the few routes to power open to them, and men fought back with torture, fire and ridicule.

I'd like to know that this is all it really is. But the fact is that the consensus fantasy universe has picked up the idea and maintains it. I incline to a different view, if only to keep the argument going that the whole thing is a lot more metaphorical than that. The sex of the magic practitioner doesn't really enter into it. The classical wizard, I suggest, represents the ideal of magic – everything that we hope we would be, if we had the power. The classical witch, on the other hand, with her often malevolent interest in the small beer of human affairs, is everything we fear only too well that we would in fact become.

Oh well, it won't win me a PhD. I suspect that via the insidious medium of picture books for children the wizards will continue to practise their high magic and the witches will perform their evil, bad-tempered spells. It's going to be a long time before there's room for equal rites.

Roots of Fantasy

'The Roots of Fantasy: Myth, Folklore & Archetype', *The Book of the World Fantasy Convention*, ed. Shelley Dutton Berry, 1989

I've adjusted this slightly and filled in some detail. The stuff about the nuclear pixie is stone-cold true.

There's another story about that power station that's just waiting to happen.

You see, power stations take a long time to build. Large items of construction plant spend their entire working life on the site, until they break down beyond hope of repair. What can you do with a clapped-out bulldozer? Well, you've got lots of spoil and junk anyway, and you need to landscape the place, so you bury it in a huge mound, maybe along with a couple of mechanical diggers to serve it in the Next World.

People visiting the site now see this and think it's the Pixie

Mound. It isn't. That is on the other side of the road, and quite unimpressive by comparison.

But, you know, I'd like to think that on some dark and stormy night lightning will strike both mounds at the same time. It will be that slow, blue, crackling lightning that you only get in movies, of course.

And then there will be a moment of deep silence, that is broken by the muffled yet distinctive cough of a big diesel engine starting up . . .

Now, there's a Press Release you wouldn't want to miss . . .

Last year an American writer told me, 'I'm afraid your books won't sell well over here, because in your books you can't hear the elves sing.'

Well, it looks as though time is proving him wrong, but not hearing the elves sing is fine by me. I think they probably do far more interesting things. Besides, if the job of elves is to sing, then the elf I'm interested in is the one who's tone deaf. Half of the fun of writing funny fantasy is the search for clichés to bend. But enough of this . . .

The roots of fantasy go far deeper than mere dragons and elves, and it's a shame that writers now spend so much time in the consensus high fantasy universe . . . you know the one.

Somewhere down towards bedrock level is the desire to make worlds which, however apparently complex, bizarre, and downright dangerous they may be, have graspable rules and probably also a moral basis. We know the third brother who gives food to the poor old woman is going to win through, we know the last desperate million-to-one chance that might just work *will* work, we know that any item presented to the main character in mysterious circumstances will be a major plot token. We know the humble swineherd is really the royal heir in disguise because in our hearts we know that we are, too, but in this little secondary world there are understandable imperatives and prohibitions which he, unlike us, can thread through to achieve the . . . well, the end of the book.

There is a dark side. Take *The Lord of the Rings*, which for many of my generation was the first fantasy book they read. My adult mind says that the really interesting bit of *LOTR* must have been what happened afterwards – the troubles of a war-ravaged continent, the Marshall Aid scheme for Mordor, the shift in political power, the democratization of Minas Tirith. Well, that could be a funny fantasy. Or a satire. But not a straight fantasy, because it's too close to our reality. What we want is heroes and solutions, and, yes, singing elves.

We also know in our hearts that the universe isn't really like that. We always have, ever since the first little circle of firelight when the shaman told us about Zog, who could kill mammoths. The world isn't really like that but it ought to be, and if we believe it enough we might get through another night.

Fantasy imposes order on the universe. Or, at least, it superimposes order on the universe. And it is a human order. Reality tells us that we exist for a brief, beleaguered span in a cold infinity; fantasy tells us that the figures in the foreground are important. Fantasy peoples the alien Outside, and it doesn't matter a whole lot whether it peoples it with good guys or bad guys. Putting 'Hy Brasil' on the map is a step in the right direction, but if you can't manage that, then 'Here be Dragons' is better than nothing. Better dragons than the void.

Right at the bottom, at the tip of the root, is the fear of the dark and the cold, but once you've given darkness a name you have a measure of control. Or at least you think you have, which is nearly as important.

The desire to build structures is as strong as ever even now, among brilliant, intelligent us, who know all about Teflon and central heating. For example: reality tells me that, when I'm bored on a long journey, I stop off at a gas station and buy a cassette tape from the rack, and, since these racks are invariably stocked by someone with the musical taste and discernment of a duck egg, I generally play safe and buy a compilation album by a middle-of-the-road group I won't actually throw up listening to. So odd corners of the car fill up with cheap compilation albums. That's reality's story, anyway. But I'd found myself developing the superstition that any tape cassette, if left in a car for about a fortnight, turns into a 'Best of Queen' album. Friends say this is ridiculous. They say their cassettes turn into Bruce Springsteen compilations.

Okay, it's a gag. I hardly believe it at all. I've found the rational explanation. Like the whispering in our old house; I traced that to starlings roosting under the eaves. If you want a definition of the word 'susurration', it's the noise starlings make at night. And the great beast that stood behind me, breathing heavily, while I was reading one day; someone down the street was mowing their lawn with one of those old-fashioned push mowers, and the noise was bouncing around, hitting the corner of the room behind me, and sounded, with the clatter of the cutting stroke and the free-wheeling of the chain, like – well, like some horrible beast. The twenty seconds it took for me to analyse the sound without moving my head seemed to last a whole lot longer.

Let me tell you about the nuclear power plant built on – well, nearly on – an Iron Age burial mound. The Pixie Mound, the locals called it. And during the course of its construction the station workers got into the habit of blaming everything from a lost hammer to a major project delay on the malign influence of the Pixie (apparently someone had accidentally driven a lorry over his mound, which is the sort of thing pixies really hate). Of course, they didn't believe it. And as a joke, when the station was finished, the contractors presented the first station manager with a model garden gnome – the Pixie. And it was put in the station's trophy cabinet. And a story sprang up that if it was ever moved, something would go wrong on the site. And one day it was put in a cupboard. Three weeks later a freak storm swept up the estuary and flooded the pump house to a depth of six feet, knocking four reactors and hundreds of megawatts of generating capacity off-line.

TV crews came out the next day to film the clean-up and, yes, one of the work crew mentioned the Pixie, who was duly exhumed from his cupboard for his moment of celebrity.

Ho ho ho, the pixie curse shut the station. Ho ho ho.

In those days you could still be funny about nuclear power. It made a good story on the TV news, and headed up quite a decent piece about the speed with which the station had been brought back on line.

The story went round the world. Somewhere early in its travels the vitally important 'ho ho ho' element got removed. And we got letters from everywhere. What was then West Germany led the field, I seem to remember. 'Please tell us more about the creature that shut down a nuclear power station,' they said.

I was told to draft a suitable form of reply, and I have to say it was a pretty good one.

It talked about the concept of gremlins, and how lots of trades created little superstitions and mythologies. But as a PR man for the place, I became aware that not everyone on the site was one hundred per cent behind my cheery statements saying that, of course, we didn't actually believe it. They were engineers. They knew about Murphy. They weren't about to upset no pixie.

In fact, I had a conversation with one senior engineer, in the shiny, bright and modern power station, that went like this:

'You can't say that no one here believes it.'

'Do you want me to say that people here do believe it, then?'

'No. Say it's just . . . a story.'

And later one of them said, 'I wonder what legends will accumulate around this place in a thousand years' time, when

it's just a mound. The villagers will probably say that at midnight you can see a team of physicists walk their rounds.'
And we agreed that, if people didn't think very carefully
about warning signs, a dead and buried nuclear reactor would
make the classic cursed tomb: not long after breaking into it,
people would die mysteriously.

That impressed me. I didn't know engineers could think
like that. Already, the hard edges of the machinery were
being filmed with the grease of fantasy – or whimsy, you
might say, which is only fantasy with its shirt undone. I realized then that if ever there is a moonbase, or a Mars base, or
an L5 colony, then our interior decorator minds will furnish
the new landscape with reconditioned fantasies: shadowy
figures that live in the girderwork and steal electricity, maybe,
or dwarfs that come out of the computer panelling and clean
your helmet at night, if you leave them a bowl of nutrient
soup.

We spray our fantasies on the landscape like a dog sprays
urine. It turns it into ours. Once we've invented our gods and
demons, we can propitiate or exorcize them.

Once we've put fairies in the sinister solitary thorn tree,
we can decide where we stand in relation to it; we can hang
ribbons on it, see visions under it – or bulldoze it up and call
ourselves free of superstition.

Elves Were Bastards

Hillcon Programme Book, November 1992

I re-read this twelve years later and thought: wow, I must have been having a really bad day, do I still believe this?

And the answer is yes, for a given value of 'yes'.

In 1992, the boom in fantasy that had begun in the mid-eighties had just reached the crest of the wave. You couldn't move for the stuff, local and imported. A lot of it was good, but much of it was bad – not necessarily badly written, but bad in that it brought nothing to the party. I recall an issue of Locus *magazine that discussed or advertised three different titles that included a Dark Lord as the enemy (no, none of them was* LOTR*). Oh, dear. Dark Lords should be rationed.*

Convention bookstalls were crowded with the stuff. The covers had a certain sameness. There were good books in there, but how could you tell? So many unicorns, dragons, quests, elves . . . heroic fantasy was feeding on itself.

Bad for fantasy, good for me; it was a target-rich environment.

Anyway, that was then . . . I feel a lot calmer now. Probably it would be a good idea if I kept away from Disneyworld for a while.

I'm called a writer of fantasy, but I'm coming to hate the term. Why? Because what could be so good is often so bad. Because there's so much trash out there, so much round-eyed worship of mind-numbing myths, so much mindless recycling of ancient cycles, so much unthinking escapism.

I'm not against recycling. The seasons do it. So do panto-mimes, so do fairy stories. The retelling of oft-told tales is an honourable art – but there should be some attempt at texture and flair. *Star Wars* was the quintessential heroic fantasy story, with just enough twist and spin to give it an extra edge. *Robocop* retold an ancient tale in a new voice and was marvellous; *Robocop II* was superexpensive trash because people didn't understand what they'd got.

Unfortunately, there's still a market for rubbish. I picked up a recently written fantasy book at the weekend, and one character said of another: 'He will grow wroth.' Oh, my God. And the phrase was in a page of similar jaw-breaking, mock-archaic narrative. Belike, i'faith . . . this is the language we use to turn high fantasy into third-rate romantic literature. 'Yonder lies the palace of my fodder, the king.' That's not fantasy – that's just Tolkien reheated until the magic boils away.

I get depressed with these fluffy dragons and noble elves.

Elves were never noble. They were cruel bastards. And I dislike heroes. You can't trust the buggers. They always let you down. I don't believe in the natural nobility of kings, because a large percentage of them in our history have turned out to be power-crazed idiots. And I certainly don't believe in the wisdom of wizards. I've worked with their modern equivalents, and I know what I am talking about.

Fantasy should present the familiar in a new light – I try to do that on Discworld. It's a way of looking at the here and now, not the there and then. Fantasy is the Ur-literature, from which everything else sprang – which is why my knuckles go white when toe-sucking literary critics dismiss it as 'genre trash'. And, at its best, it is truly escapist.

But the point about escaping is that you should escape to, as well as from. You should go somewhere worthwhile, and come back the better for the experience. Too much alleged 'fantasy' is just empty sugar, life with the crusts cut off.

I'm writing this in Florida, home of fantasy – either the sort that you watch, or the sort that you stick up your nose. They've got some weird stuff here; for one thing, they've got Disney/MGM and Universal Studios.

And this is what's weird about them. They aren't really studios. Oh, they shoot some film here, but that's kind of secondary. They weren't built as studios. They were built as . . . well, as theme parks. Those false frontages, those artful backlots, those false-perspective streets, they were built for no other purpose than to look like something which in turn was built to look like something. Built to look like something that isn't real.

Whoever would have thought it?

Here in America – and in England, to a lesser extent – you can read newspaper articles and buy alleged books which treat the characters played by TV stars as if they were real people. The world has gone strange. You can't tell the reality from the fantasy any more. Think I'm kidding? On the racks at the supermarket are 'newspapers' like the *Sun*, the *Midnight Globe*, the *Weekly World News*. Typical lead story: Elvis has been found alive in a UFO dredged from the Bermuda Triangle. People read this stuff. It's not even good SF. They have a vote, same as you.

This is all 'escape from' stuff – the Disney rides, the elves, the stupid stories. It goes nowhere. The best stuff does take you somewhere. It takes you to a new place from which to see the world. An interest in fantasy when I was a child gave me an interest in books in general, and I found in books on astronomy and palaeontology a deep sense of wonder that not even Middle-earth could beat.

Let's not just leave here. Let's go somewhere else. And if we can trample over some elves to do it, so much the better.

Let There Be Dragons

The Bookseller, 11 June 1993

A speech in defence of fantasy given when guest of honour at the Booksellers Association Conference annual dinner in Torquay in 1993.

I have still got the first book I ever read. It was *The Wind in the Willows*. Well, it was probably not the first book I ever read – that was no doubt called something like *Nursery Fun* or *Janet and John* Book 1. But it was the first book I opened without chewing the covers or wishing I was somewhere else. It was the first book which, at the age of ten, I read because I was genuinely interested.

I know now, of course, that it is totally the wrong kind of book for children. There is only one female character and she's a washerwoman. No attempt is made to explain the social conditioning and lack of proper housing that makes stoats and weasels act the way they do. Mr Badger's house is an insult to all those children not fortunate enough to live in a Wild Wood. The Mole and the Rat's domestic arrangements are probably acceptable, but only if they come right out and talk frankly about them.

But it was pressed into my hand, and because it wasn't parents or teachers who were recommending the book I read it from end to end, all in one go. And then I started again from the beginning, because I had not realized that there were stories like this.

There's a feeling that I think is only possible to get when you are a child and discover books: it's a kind of fizz – you want to read everything that's in print before it evaporates before your eyes.

I had to draw my own map through this uncharted territory. The message from the management was that, yes, books were a good idea, but I don't recall anyone advising me in any way. I was left to my own devices.

I am now becoming perceived as a young people's writer. Teachers and librarians say, 'You know, your books are really popular among children who don't read.' I think this is a compliment; I just wish they would put it another way. In fact, genre authors get to know their reader profile quite intimately, and I know I have a large number of readers who are old enough to drive a car and possibly claim a pension. But the myth persists that all my readers are aged fourteen and called Kevin, and so I have taken an interest in the dark underworld called children's literature.

Not many people do, it seems to me, apart from those

brave souls who work with children and are interested in what they read. They're unsung resistance heroes in a war that is just possibly being won by Sonic Hedgehogs and bionic plumbers. They don't have many allies, even where you would expect them. Despite the huge number of titles that pour out to shape the minds of the adults, my Sunday paper reviews a mismatched handful of children's books at infrequent intervals and, to show its readers that this is some kind of literary play street, generally puts a picture of a teddy bear on the page.

Perhaps the literary editor's decision is right. In my experience children don't read reviews of children's books. They live in a different kind of world.

The aforementioned school librarians tell me that what the children read for fun, what they will actually spend their money on, are fantasy, science fiction, and horror and, while they offer up a prayer of thanks that the kids are reading anything in this electronic age, this worries them. It shouldn't.

I now know that almost all fiction is, at some level, fantasy. What Agatha Christie wrote was fantasy. What Tom Clancy writes is fantasy. What Jilly Cooper writes is fantasy – at least, I hope for her sake it is. But what people generally have in mind when they hear the word fantasy is swords, talking animals, vampires, rockets (science fiction is fantasy with bolts on), and around the edges it can indeed be pretty silly. Yet fantasy also speculates about the future, rewrites the past, and reconsiders the present. It plays games with the universe.

Fantasy makes many adults uneasy. Children who like the stuff tend to call it 'brill' and 'megagood'. This always disturbs people. (It worries them so much that when someone like P. D. James uses the mechanisms of science fiction, helpful people redefine the field, thus avoiding bestowing on her the mark of Cain; the book isn't science fiction 'because it's not all about robots and other planets'. P. D. James writing science fiction? Impossible. But *Children of Men* is a science fiction book, as is *Time's Arrow*, and *Fatherland*, as was Kurt Vonnegut's *Slaughterhouse 5*, and Philip K. Dick's *Man in the High Castle*. Science fiction, the stuff that is seldom reviewed, is often good; it doesn't need robots, and Earth is room enough.)

Of course science fiction and fantasy are sometimes badly written. Many things are. But literary merit is an artificial thing and exists in the eye of the beholder. In a world where Ballard's *Empire of the Sun* cannot win the Booker, I'm not too in awe of judgements based on literary merit.

Not long ago I talked to a teacher who, having invited me to talk at her school, was having a bit of trouble with the head teacher, who thought that fantasy was morally suspect and irrelevant to the world of the nineties.

Morally suspect? Shorn of its trappings, most fantasy would find approval in a Victorian household. The morality of fantasy and horror is, by and large, the strict morality of the fairy tale. The vampire is slain, the alien is blown out of the airlock, the Dark Lord is vanquished, and, perhaps at some loss, the good triumph – not because they are better armed but because Providence is on their side.

143

Why does the third of the three brothers, who shares his food with the old woman in the wood, go on to become king of the country? Why does James Bond manage to disarm the nuclear bomb a few seconds before it goes off rather than, as it were, a few seconds afterwards? Because a universe where that did not happen would be a dark and hostile place. Let there be goblin hordes, let there be terrible environmental threats, let there be giant mutated slugs if you really must, but let there also be hope. It may be a grim, thin hope, an Arthurian sword at sunset, but let us know that we do not live in vain.

To stay sane, if I may gently paraphrase what Edward Pearce recently wrote in the *Guardian*, it is frequently necessary for someone to take short views, to look for comfort, to keep a piece of the world still genially ordered, if only for the duration of theatrical time or the length of a book. And this is harmless enough. Classical, written fantasy might introduce children to the occult, but in a healthier way than might otherwise be the case in our strange society. If you're told about vampires, it's a good thing to be told about stakes at the same time.

And fantasy's readers might also learn, in the words of Stephen Sondheim, that witches can be right and giants can be good. They learn that where people stand is perhaps not as important as which way they face. This is part of the dangerous process of growing up.

As for escapism, I'm quite happy about the word. There is nothing wrong with escapism. The key points of consideration, though, are what you are escaping from, and where you are escaping to.

As a suddenly thirsting reader I escaped first of all to what was then called Outer Space. I read a lot of science fiction, which as I have said is only a twentieth-century subset of fantasy. And a lot of it was, in strict literary terms, rubbish. But this was good rubbish. It was like an exercise bicycle for the mind – it doesn't take you anywhere, but it certainly tones up the muscles.

Irrelevant? I first came across any mention of ancient Greek civilization in a fantasy book – by Mary Renault. But in the fifties most schools taught history like this: there were the Romans who had a lot of baths and built some roads and left. Then there was a lot of undignified pushing and shoving until the Normans arrived, and history officially began.

We did science, too, in a way. Yuri Gagarin was spinning around above our heads, but I don't recall anyone at school ever mentioning the fact. I don't even remember anyone telling us that science was not about messing around with chemicals and magnets, but rather a way of looking at the universe.

Science fiction looked at the universe all the time. I make no apology for having enjoyed it. We live in a science fiction world: two miles down there you'd fry and two miles up there you'd gasp for breath, and there is a small but significant chance that in the next thousand years a large comet or asteroid will smack into the planet. Finding this out when you're thirteen or so is a bit of an eye-opener. It puts acne in its place, for a start.

Then other worlds out there in space got me interested in this one down here. It is a small mental step from time travel to palaeontology, from swords 'n' sorcery fantasy to mythology and ancient history. Truth is stranger than fiction; nothing in fantasy enthralled me as much as reading of the evolution of mankind from protoblob to newt, tree shrew, Oxbridge arts graduate, and eventually to tool-using mammal.

I first came across words like ecologist and overpopulation in science fiction books in the late fifties and early sixties, long before they had become fashionable. Yes, probably Malthus had said it first – but you don't read Malthus when you're eleven, though you might read someone like John Brunner or Harry Harrison because their books have got an exciting spaceship on the cover.

I also came across the word neoteny, which means 'remaining young'. It's something which we as humans have developed into a survival trait. Other animals, when they are young, have a curiosity about the world, a flexibility of response, and an ability to play which they lose as they grow up. As a species we have retained it. As a species, we are forever sticking our fingers into the electric socket of the universe to see what will happen next. It is a trait that will either save us or kill us, but it is what makes us human beings. I would rather be in the company of people who look at Mars than people who contemplate humanity's navel – other worlds are better than fluff.

And I came across a lot of trash. But the human mind has a healthy natural tendency to winnow out the good stuff from the rubbish. It's like gold-mining: you have to shift a ton of dirt to get the gold; if you don't shift the dirt, you won't find the nugget. As far as I am concerned, escapist literature let me escape to the real world.

So let's not get frightened when the children read fantasy. It is the compost for a healthy mind. It stimulates the inquisitive nodes. It may not appear as 'relevant' as books set more firmly in the child's environment, or whatever hell the writer believes to be the child's environment, but there is some evidence that a rich internal fantasy life is as good and necessary for a child as healthy soil is for a plant, for much the same reasons.

Of course, some may read no other kind of fiction all their lives (although in my experience science fiction fans tend to be widely read outside the field). Adult SF fans may look a bit scary when they come into bookshops – some of them have been known to wear plastic pointy ears – but people like that are an unrepresentative minority and are certainly no weirder than people who, say, play golf. At the very least they are helping to keep the industry alive, and providing one of the best routes to reading that there can be.

Here's to fantasy as the proper diet for the growing soul. All human life is there: a moral code, a sense of order, and, sometimes, great big green things with teeth. There are other books to read, and I hope children who start with fantasy go on to read them. I did. But everyone has to start somewhere.

Please call it fantasy, by the way. Don't call it 'magical realism', that's just fantasy wearing a collar and tie, mark-of-Cain words, words used to mean 'fantasy written by someone

I was at university with'. Like the fairy tales that were its forebears, fantasy needs no excuses.

One of the great popular novelists of the early part of this century was G. K. Chesterton. Writing at a time when fairy stories were under attack, for pretty much the same reason as books can now be covertly banned in some schools because they have the word witch in the title, he said: 'The objection to fairy stories is that they tell children there are dragons. But children have always known there are dragons. Fairy stories tell children that dragons can be killed.'

Magic Kingdoms

Sunday Times, 4 July 1999

When the third Harry Potter book came out, the Sunday Times
*asked me to address the subject of why the British seem to be so
keen to write fantasy. I think the full brief was: 'We need it by
Thursday'. When it was printed, as 'Fantasy Kingdom', it
turned out that some editor had kindly assumed that 'numinous'
was a mistyping of 'luminous' and had changed it. Sigh.*

I remember a back garden I used to see from the train. It was
a very small garden for a very small house, and it was sand-
wiched between the thundering railway line, a billboard, and
a near-derelict factory.

I don't know what a Frenchman or an Italian would have
made of it. A terrace, probably, with a few potted plants and
some trellis to conceal the worst of post-industrial squalor.
But this was an Englishman's garden, so he'd set out to grow,

if not Jerusalem, then at least Jerusalem artichokes. There was a rockery, made of carefully placed concrete lumps (the concrete lump rockery is a great British contribution to horticulture, and I hope one is preserved in some outdoor museum somewhere). There was a pond; the fish probably had to get out to turn around. There were roses. There was a tiny greenhouse made of old window frames nailed together (another great British invention). Never was an area so thoroughly gardened, in fact, as that patch of cat-infested soil.

No attempt had been made to screen off the dark satanic mills, unless the runner beans counted. To the gardener, in the garden, they did not exist. They were in another world.

The British have a talent for creating imaginary worlds, and there's no doubt that we are major exporters. Joanne Rowling is currently leading the drive. She couldn't be selling more books if her young wizard Harry Potter was Hannibal Lecter's godson. Why are we so at home with fantasy?

Well, it's in the air . . . almost literally. The early Christian Church helped things along by deliberately refraining from stamping on the pagan religions of the time. Instead, some of their festivals and customs were given a Christian veneer. No doubt this saved a lot of trouble at the time. It also preserved them, which wasn't the intention. Since then we have been great accumulators of invaders' gods, creating a magpie mythology that grabbed hold of anything that shone nicely. Some of the pieces came together to form the Matter of Britain, the Arthurian legend spun out of other legends to become the great British story. It's built into the landscape, from one end of the country to the other. Every hill is Arthur's Throne, every cavern is Merlin's Cave.

Stories beget stories. I've always suspected that Robin Hood was just another robber, but he did have the advantage of a very powerful weapon. It was not the longbow. It was the voice of Alan a Dale, the minstrel. Weaponry will only keep you alive, but a good ballad can make you immortal.

Then this rich rural tradition was locked up in the mills of the early Industrial Revolution, which pressure-cooked it.

Of course there had always been fantasy. It's the Ur-literature from which all the others sprang, and it developed in the cave right alongside religion. They grew from the same root: if we draw the right pictures and find the right words, we can steer the world, ensure the success of the hunt, keep ourselves safe from the thunder, negotiate with Death. A phrase sometimes linked with fantasy is 'tales of gods and heroes', and the two go together. The first heroes were the ones who defied or tricked or robbed the gods, for the good of the tribe, and came back to tell the story.

But it was in the last century that fantasy took on an additional role as a means of escape, a way out of the perceived grimness of the industrializing world. Out of the same pot, I've always felt, came the English obsession with gardens, with the making of little private plots that could become, for an hour or so, the whole world.

Some vitriol was printed a couple of years ago when *The Lord of the Rings* was voted the best book of the century in a poll of Waterstone's readers. Certain critics felt that the public were being jolly ungrateful after all they had done for them, the beasts. It didn't matter. The book is beyond their control. They might as well have been throwing bricks at a mountain; it doesn't cause any damage and it makes the mountain slightly higher. The book is now a classic, and real classics aren't created by diktat.

J. R. R. Tolkien has become a sort of mountain, appearing in all subsequent fantasy in the way that Mt Fuji appears so often in Japanese prints. Sometimes it's big and up close. Sometimes it's a shape on the horizon. Sometimes it's not there at all, which means that the artist either has made a deliberate decision against the mountain, which is interesting in itself, or is in fact standing on Mt Fuji.

Fantasy worlds have a huge attraction. There are rules built in. The appeal is simple and beguiling in the complex world of the twentieth century. Evil has a map reference and a remedy – the finding of a sword, the returning of a Grail, the destruction of a ring. The way will be tough but at least it has a signpost. If the Good exhibit enough goodness, moral fibre and bravery they will win through, although at some cost. And for a span they'll live happily ever after . . . until they have to do it again.

And yet . . . *The Lord of the Rings*, while English to the bone, was not a typical British fantasy book. It was not part of the mainstream, even though it is now a river in its own right and has spawned numerous tributaries and has come to define 'fantasy' for many people.

It was unusual because it started and finished in a world which is like ours but which isn't ours, a world with different rules and created with meticulous attention to detail and, above all, a world that you cannot get to from here. There is no magic door to Middle-earth apart from the covers of the book. There is no entry by magic carpet, wardrobe, dream, or swan-drawn chariot. It is a separate creation.

Since and because of Tolkien there have been more fantasy universes than you can shake a curiously engraved sword at, but the British have traditionally desired their fantasy worlds to be a lot closer to home. We like them to be about as close as the other side of a door or the back of a mirror or even to be in here with us, numinous, unseen until you learn the gift. And this has been accompanied by an urge towards a sort of domesticity, an attempt to make gardens in the goblin-haunted wilderness, to make fantasy do something . . . to, in fact, bring it down to Earth.

In the *Poetics*, Aristotle said that poetical metaphor and language involve the careful admixture of the ordinary and the strange. G. K. Chesterton said that far more grotesque and wonderful than any wild fantastical thing was anything that was everyday and unregarded, if seen unexpectedly from a new direction. That is our tradition, and it has largely been kept alive by people writing for children.

Tolkien's great achievement was to reclaim fantasy as a genre that could be published for and read by adults. Traditionally, we had left the journey to the kids, who rather enjoyed it and found it easy. Adults got involved only to the extent that some teachers carefully picked up any 'escapist rubbish' the child was currently reading and dropped it in the bin. There are still, even now, some of those around – I believe a special circle of Hell is reserved for them. Of course fantasy is escapist. Most stories are. So what? Teachers are not meant to be jailers.

Escapism isn't good or bad of itself. What is important is what you are escaping from and where you are escaping to. I write from experience, since in my case I escaped to the idea that books could be really enjoyable, an aspect of reading that teachers had not hitherto suggested. The fantasy books led me on to mythology, the mythology led painlessly to ancient history . . . and I quietly got an education, courtesy of the public library.

For me, E. Nesbit's young heroes flew magic carpets, travelled in time and talked to magical creatures, but they were still Edwardian children. C. S. Lewis's children certainly lived Here but went through a magical door to get There. Magic doors are a huge part of the tradition. An enduring image, that symbolizes real fantasy far more than any amount of dragons and witches, is an early scene in Terry Gilliam's movie *Time Bandits*, where a mounted knight in full armour gallops out of the wardrobe in the ordinary room of an ordinary boy.

John Masefield's Kay Harker, in *The Midnight Folk* and *The Box of Delights*, did not even need a door, just the vision to see the magical world intersecting with this one and the characters that lived with one foot in each. Writers like Diana Wynne Jones and Alan Garner let their characters wander in and out of a similar magical world – this world, seen from Chesterton's different viewpoint.

The best fantasy writers don't write fantasy in the fluffy, hocus-pocus sense, they change the rules by which the world works and then write very carefully and logically by those rules. And it's no longer enough that there should be wizards and goblins and magic. We know about that stuff. Now we want to know how the wizards are dealing with the challenge of genetically modified dragons, and what the dwarfs are doing to stamp out racial harassment of gnomes. We're back to Chesterton again. Maybe a good way of understanding this world is to view it from another one.

Joanne Rowling's Harry Potter is firmly in this tradition. In truth, the stories do not contain a lot of elements new to anyone keeping up with modern fantasy writing for children. Young wizards and witches have been to school before. But that really does not matter. Genres work like that; if they didn't, there would only ever be one book with a Time Machine in it. Most crime novels are full of policemen, crimes, and criminals, and most cakes contain pretty much the same sort of ingredients. It's the cookery that counts. Cook it right, with imagination and flair and a good pinch of luck, and you have that rare and valuable thing – a genre book that's risen above the genre. And Harry Potter is beautifully cooked.

Cult Classic

From *Meditations on Middle-earth*, ed. Karen Haber, 2001

Hmm. When this was first published, US critics said I was being too populist in complaining about the critics' (other critics, that is) attitude to The Lord of the Rings.

Well, they were wrong. Tolkien had many fans in academia, it's true, but in the UK at least it was, up until a couple of years ago, quite normal for the London media-rocracy to be dismissive of Tolkien and the 'sad people' who read him. Then the movies happened, were very popular, and the carping got very muted indeed.

This was written pre-movie.

The Lord of the Rings is a cult classic. I know that's true, because I read it in the newspapers, saw it on TV, heard it on the radio.

We know what cult means. It's a put-down word. It means 'inexplicably popular but unworthy'. It's a word used by the guardians of the one true flame to dismiss anything that is liked by the wrong kind of people. It also means 'small, hermetic, impenetrable to outsiders'. It has associations with cool drinks in Jonestown.

The Lord of the Rings has well over one hundred million readers. How big will it have to be to emerge from cult status? Or, once having been a cult – that is to say, once having borne the mark of Cain – is it actually possible that anything can ever be allowed to become a full-fledged Classic?

But democracy has been in action over the past few years. A British bookshop chain held a vote to find the country's favourite book. It was *The Lord of the Rings*. Another one not long afterwards, held this time to find the favourite author, came up with J. R. R. Tolkien.

The critics carped, which was expected but nevertheless strange. After all, the bookshops were merely using the word 'favourite'. That's a very personal word. No one ever said it was a synonym for 'best'. But a critics' chorus hailed the results as a terrible indictment of the taste of the British public, who'd been given the precious gift of democracy and were wasting it on quite unsuitable choices. There were hints of a conspiracy amongst the furry-footed fans. But there was another message, too. It ran: 'Look, we've been trying to tell you for years which books are good! And you just don't listen! You're not listening now! You're just going out there and buying this damn book! And the worst part is that we can't stop you! We can tell you it's rubbish, it's not relevant, it's the

157

worst kind of escapism, it was written by an author who never came to our parties and didn't care what we thought, but unfortunately the law allows you to go on not listening! You are stupid, stupid, stupid!'

And, once again, no one listened. Instead, a couple of years later, a national newspaper's Millennium Masterworks poll produced five works of what could loosely be called 'narrative fiction' among the top fifty 'masterworks' of the last thousand years, and, yes, there was *The Lord of the Rings* again.

The *Mona Lisa* was also in the top fifty masterworks. And I admit to suspecting that she was included by many of the voters out of a sheer cultural knee-jerk reaction, mildly dishonest but well meant. Quick, quick, name of the greatest works of art of the last thousand years! Er . . . er . . . well, the *Mona Lisa*, obviously. Fine, fine, and have you seen the *Mona Lisa*? Did you stand in front of her? Did the smile entrance you, did the eyes follow you around the room and back to your hotel? Er . . . no, not as such . . . but, uh, well, it's the *Mona Lisa*, okay? You've got to include the *Mona Lisa*. And that guy with the fig leaf, yeah. And that woman with no arms.

That's honesty, of a sort. It's a vote for the good taste of your fellow citizens and your ancestors as well. Joe Average knows that a vote for a picture of dogs playing poker is probably not, when considered against the background of one thousand years, a very sensible thing to cast.

But *The Lord of the Rings*, I suspect, got included when people stopped voting on behalf of their culture and quietly voted for what they liked. We can't all stand in front of one picture and feel it open up new pathways in our brain, but we can – most of us – read a mass-market book.

I can't remember where I was when JFK was shot, but I can remember exactly where and when I was when I first read J. R. R. Tolkien. It was New Year's Eve, 1961. I was babysitting for friends of my parents while they all went out to a party. I didn't mind. I'd got this three-volume yacht-anchor of a book from the library that day. Boys at school had told me about it. It had maps in it, they said. This struck me at the time as a pretty good indicator of quality.

I'd waited quite a long time for this moment. I was that kind of kid, even then.

What can I remember? I can remember the vision of beech woods in the Shire; I was a country boy, and the hobbits were walking through a landscape which, give or take the odd housing development, was pretty much the one I'd grown up in. I remember it like a movie. There I was, sitting on this rather chilly sixties-style couch in this rather bare room; but at the edges of the carpet, the forest began. I remember the light as green, coming through trees. I have never since then so truly had the experience of being inside the story.

I can remember the click of the central heating going off and the room growing colder, but these things were happening on the horizon of my senses and weren't relevant. I can't remember going home with my parents, but I do remember sitting up in bed until 3 a.m., still reading. I don't recall going to sleep. I do remember waking up with the book open on my chest, and finding my place, and going on reading. It took me, oh, about twenty-three hours to get to the end.

Then I picked up the first book and started again. I spent a long time looking at the runes.

Already, as I admit this, I can feel the circle of new, anxious but friendly faces around me: 'My name is Terry and I used to draw dwarf runes in my school notebooks. It started with, you know, the straight ones, everyone can do them, but then I got in deeper and before I knew it I was doing the curly elf ones with the dots. Wait . . . there's worse. Before I'd even heard the word "fandom" I was writing weird fan fiction. I wrote a crossover story setting Jane Austen's *Pride and Prejudice* in Middle-earth; the rest of the kids loved it, because a class of thirteen-year-old boys with volcanic acne and groinal longings is not best placed to appreciate Miss Austen's fine prose. It was a really good bit when the orcs attacked the rectory . . . ' But around about then, I suspect, the support group would have thrown me out.

Enthralled I was. To the library I went back, and spake thusly: 'Have you got any more books like these? Maybe with maps in? And runes?'

The librarian gave me a mildly disapproving look, but I ended up with *Beowulf* and a volume of Norse sagas. He meant well, but it wasn't the same. It took someone several stanzas just to say who they were.

But that drew me to the Mythology shelves. The Mythology shelves were next to the Ancient History shelves. What the hell . . . it was all guys with helmets, wasn't it? On, on . . . maybe there's a magical ring! Or runes!

The desperate search for the Tolkien effect opened up a new world for me, and it was this one.

History as it was then taught in British schools was big on kings and acts of Parliament, and was full of dead people. It had a certain strange, mechanistic structure to it. What happened in 1066? The Battle of Hastings. Full marks. And what else happened in 1066? What do you mean, what else happened? The Battle of Hastings was what 1066 was for. We'd 'done' the Romans (they came, they saw, they had some baths, they built some roads and left) but my private reading coloured in the picture. We hadn't 'done' the Greeks. As for the empires of Africa and Asia, did anyone 'do' them at all? But hey, look here in this book; these guys don't use runes, it's all pictures of birds and snakes; but, look, they know how to pull a dead king's brains out through his nose . . .

And on I went, getting the best kind of education possible, which is the one that happens while you think you're having fun. Would it have happened anyway? Possibly. We never know where the triggers are. But *The Lord of the Rings* was a step-change in my reading. I was already enjoying it, but *The Lord of the Rings* opened me up to the rest of the library.

I used to read it once a year, in the spring.

I've realized that I don't any more, and I wonder why. It's not the dense and sometimes ponderous language. It's not because the scenery has more character than the characters, or the lack of parts for women, or the other perceived or real offences against the current social codes.

It's simply because I have the movie in my head, and it's been there for forty years. I can still remember the luminous green of the beech woods, the freezing air of the mountains, the terrifying darkness of the dwarf mines, the greenery on the slopes of Ithilien, west of Mordor, still holding out against the encroaching shadow. The protagonists don't figure much in the movie, because they were never more to me than figures in a landscape that was, itself, the hero. I remember it at least as clearly as – no, come to think of it, more clearly than – I do many of the places I've visited in what we like to call the real world. In fact, it is strange to write this and realize that I can remember stretches of the Middle-earth landscape as real places. The characters are faceless, mere points in space from which their dialogue originated. But Middle-earth is a place I went to.

I suppose the journey was a form of escapism. That was a terrible crime at my school. It's a terrible crime in a prison; at least, it's a terrible crime to a jailer. In the early sixties, the word had no positive meanings. But you can escape to as well as from. In my case, the escape was a truly Tolkien experience, as recorded in his *Tree and Leaf*. I started with a book, and that led me to a library, and that led me everywhere.

Do I still think, as I did then, that Tolkien was the greatest writer in the world? In the strict sense, no. You can think that at thirteen. If you still think it at fifty-three, something has gone wrong with your life. But sometimes things all come together at the right time in the right place – book, author, style, subject, and reader. The moment was magic.

And I went on reading; and, since if you read enough books you overflow, I eventually became a writer.

One day I was doing a signing in a London bookshop and next in the queue was a lady in what, back in the eighties, was called a 'power suit' despite its laughable lack of titanium armour and proton guns. She handed over a book for signature. I asked her what her name was. She mumbled something. I asked again . . . after all, it was a noisy bookshop. There was another mumble, which I could not quite decipher. As I opened my mouth for the third attempt, she said, 'It's Galadriel, okay?'

I said: 'Were you by any chance born in a cannabis plantation in Wales?' She smiled, grimly. 'It was a camper van in Cornwall,' she said, 'but you've got the right idea.'

It wasn't Tolkien's fault, but let us remember in fellowship and sympathy all the Bilbos out there.

Neil Gaiman: Amazing
Master Conjuror

Boskone 39 Programme Book, February 2002

*When I first met Neil, he called himself a ligger. Say there's a
new book being launched, and there might be drink and there
might be food. That's where the ligger is, looking for something
for his magazine, eating nondescript canapés and drinking
warm wine.*

*We were both writing fit to burst back then, and he would
ring me up in the middle of the night and chat about what we
were doing, mostly in darkness. We came to understand one
another – it's good to have someone like that to talk to, when
you're a writer.*

From him I learned the most precious words 'tax deductible'.

What can I say about Neil Gaiman that has not already

been said in *The Morbid Imagination: Five Case Studies*?

Well, he's no genius. He's better than that.

He's not a wizard, in other words, but a conjuror.

Wizards don't have to work. They wave their hands, and the magic happens. But conjurors, now . . . conjurors work very hard. They spend a lot of time in their youth watching, very carefully, the best conjurors of their day. They seek out old books of trickery and, being natural conjurors, read everything else as well, because history itself is just a magic show. They observe the way people think, and the many ways in which they don't. They learn the subtle use of springs, and how to open mighty temple doors at a touch, and how to make the trumpets sound.

And they take centre stage and amaze you with flags of all nations and smoke and mirrors, and you cry: 'Amazing! How does he do it? What happened to the elephant? Where's the rabbit? Did he really smash my watch?'

And in the back row we, the other conjurors, say quietly: 'Well done. Isn't that a variant of the Prague Levitating Sock? Wasn't that Pasqual's Spirit Mirror, where the girl isn't really there? But where the hell did that flaming sword come from?'

And we wonder if there may be such a thing as wizardry, after all . . .

I met Neil in 1985, when *The Colour of Magic* had just come out. It was my first ever interview as an author. Neil was making a living as a freelance journalist and had the pale features of someone who had sat through the review showings of altogether too many bad movies in order to live off the freebie cold chicken legs they served at the receptions afterwards (and to build up his contacts book, which is now the size of the Bible and contains rather more interesting people). He was doing journalism in order to eat, which is a very good way of learning journalism. Probably the only real way, come to think of it.

He also had a very bad hat. It was a grey homburg. He was not a hat person. There was no natural unity between hat and man. That was the first and last time I saw the hat. As if subconsciously aware of the bad hatitude, he used to forget it and leave it behind in restaurants. One day, he never went back for it. I put this in for the serious fans out there: if you search really, really hard, you may find a small restaurant somewhere in London with a dusty grey homburg at the back of a shelf. Who knows what will happen if you try it on?

Anyway, we got on fine. Hard to say why, but at bottom was a shared delight and amazement at the sheer strangeness of the universe, in stories, in obscure details, in strange old books in unregarded bookshops. We stayed in contact.

[SFX: pages being ripped off a calendar. You know, you just don't get that in movies any more . . .]

And one thing led to another, and he became big in graphic novels, and Discworld took off, and one day he sent me about six pages of a short story and said he didn't know how it continued, and I didn't either, and about a year later I took it out of the drawer and did see what happened next, even if I couldn't see how it all ended yet, and we wrote it together and that was *Good Omens*. It was done by two guys who didn't have anything to lose by having fun. We didn't do it for the money. But, as it turned out, we got a lot of money.

... hey, let me tell you about the weirdness, like when he was staying with us for the editing and we heard a noise and went into his room and two of our white doves had got in and couldn't get out; they were panicking around the room and Neil was waking up in a storm of snowy white feathers saying, 'Wstfgl?' which is his normal ante-meridian vocabulary. Or the time when we were in a bar and he met the Spider Women. Or the time on tour when we checked into our hotel and in the morning it turned out that his TV had been showing him strange late-night semi-naked bondage bi-sexual chat shows, and mine had picked up nothing but reruns of *Mr Ed*. And the moment, live on air, when we realized that an under-informed New York radio interviewer with ten minutes of chat still to go thought *Good Omens* was not a work of fiction ...

[Cut to a train, pounding along the tracks. That's another scene they never show in movies these days ...]

And there we were, ten years on, travelling across Sweden and talking about the plot of *American Gods* (him) and *The Amazing Maurice* (me). Probably both of us at the same time. It was just like the old days. One of us says, 'I don't know how to deal with this tricky bit of plot'; the other one listens and says, 'The solution, Grasshopper, is in the way you state the problem. Fancy a coffee?'

A lot had happened in those ten years. He'd left the comics world shaken, and it'll never be quite the same. The effect was akin to that of Tolkien on the fantasy novel – everything afterwards is in some way influenced. I remember on one US *Good Omens* tour walking round a comics shop. We'd been signing for a lot of comics fans, some of whom were clearly puzzled at the concept of 'dis story wid no pitchers in it', and I wandered around the shelves looking at the opposition. That's when I realized he was good. There's a delicacy of touch, a subtle scalpel, which is the hallmark of his work.

And when I heard the premiss of *American Gods* I wanted to write it so much I could taste it . . .

When I read *Coraline*, I saw it as an exquisitely drawn animation; if I close my eyes I can see how the house looks, or the special dolls' picnic. No wonder he writes scripts now; soon, I hope someone will be intelligent enough to let him direct. When I read the book I remembered that children's stories are, indeed, where true horror lives. My childhood nightmares would have been quite featureless without the imaginings of Walt Disney, and there's a few little details concerning black button eyes in that book that make a small part of the adult brain want to go and hide behind the sofa. But the purpose of the book is not the horror, it is horror's defeat.

It might come as a surprise to many to learn that Neil is either a very nice, approachable guy or an incredible actor.

He sometimes takes those shades off. The leather jacket I'm not sure about; I think I once saw him in a tux, or it may have been someone else.

He takes the view that mornings happen to other people. I think I once saw him at breakfast, although possibly it was just someone who looked a bit like him who was lying with their head in the plate of baked beans. He likes good sushi and quite likes people, too, although not raw; he is kind to fans who are not total jerks, and enjoys talking to people who know how to talk. He doesn't look as though he's forty; that may have happened to someone else, too. Or perhaps there's a special picture locked in his attic.

Have fun. You're in the hands of a master conjuror. Or, quite possibly, a wizard.

PS: He really, really likes it if you ask him to sign your battered, treasured copy of *Good Omens* that has been dropped in the tub at least once and is now held together with very old, yellowing transparent tape. You know the one.

2001 Carnegie Medal award speech

12 July 2002

This was the biggest medal there was, and I ate it. It was made of chocolate.

That is to say, the real medal wasn't chocolate, of course, but because I knew I was going to be awarded it in advance – they tell you that sort of thing – and I was a little skittish, my PA Rob and I looked around town for something the same size and shape as the medal. What we found was a perfect chocolate version. So after my speech I said, '. . . and what I really like is that I can eat it.' And I put it in my mouth. The librarian ladies didn't know what to do, and I thought to myself, 'Well, that's it, I'm bloody well not going to be given another one.'

I'm pretty sure that the publicists from this award would be quite happy if I said something controversial, but it seems to me that giving me the Carnegie Medal is controversial enough. This is *my* third attempt. Well, I say my third attempt, but in fact I just sat there in ignorance and someone else attempted it on my behalf, somewhat to my initial dismay.

The Amazing Maurice is a fantasy book. Of course, everyone knows that fantasy is 'all about' wizards, but by now, I hope, everyone with any intelligence knows that, er, whatever everyone knows . . . is wrong.

Fantasy is more than wizards. For instance, this book is about rats that are intelligent. But it is also about the even more fantastic idea that humans are capable of intelligence as well. Far more beguiling than the idea that evil can be destroyed by throwing a piece of expensive jewellery into a volcano is the possibility that evil can be defused by talking. The fantasy of justice is more interesting than the fantasy of fairies, and more truly fantastic. In the book the rats go to war, which is, I hope, gripping. But then they make peace, which is astonishing.

In any case, genre is just a flavouring. It's not the whole meal. Don't get confused by the scenery.

A novel set in Tombstone, Arizona, on October 26, 1881 is what – a Western? The scenery says so, the clothes say so, but the *story* does not automatically become a Western. Why let a few cactuses tell you what to think? It might be a counterfactual, or a historical novel, or a searing literary indictment of something or other, or a horror novel, or even, perhaps, a romance – although the young lovers would have to speak up a bit and possibly even hide under the table, because the gunfight at the OK Corral was going on at the time.

We categorize too much on the basis of unreliable assumption. A literary novel written by Brian Aldiss must be science fiction, because he is a known science fiction writer; a science fiction novel by Margaret Atwood is literature because she is a literary novelist. Recent Discworld books have spun on such concerns as the nature of belief, politics and even of journalistic freedom, but put in one lousy dragon and they call you a fantasy writer.

This is not, on the whole, a complaint. But as I have said, it seems to me that dragons are not really the pure quill of fantasy, when properly done. Real fantasy is that a man with a printing press might defy an entire government because of some half-formed belief that there may be such a thing as the truth. Anyway, fantasy needs no defence now. As a genre it has become quite respectable in recent years. At least, it can demonstrably make lots and lots and lots of money, which passes for respectable these days. When you can buy a plastic Gandalf with kung-fu grip and rocket launcher, you know fantasy has broken through.

But I'm a humorous writer too, and humour is a *real* problem.

It was interesting to see how *Maurice* was reviewed here and in the US. Over there, where I've only recently made much of an impression, the reviews tended to be quite serious and detailed with, as Maurice himself would have put it, 'long words, like "corrugated iron"'. Over here, while being

172

very nice, they tended towards the 'another wacky, zany book by comic author Terry Pratchett'. In fact, *Maurice* has no wack and very little zane. It's quite a serious book. Only the scenery is funny.

The problem is that we think the opposite of funny is serious. It is not. In fact, as G. K. Chesterton pointed out, the opposite of funny is not funny, and the opposite of serious is not serious. Benny Hill was funny and not serious; Rory Bremner is funny and serious; most politicians are serious but, unfortunately, not funny. Humour has its uses. Laughter can get through the keyhole while seriousness is still hammering on the door. New ideas can ride in on the back of a joke, old ideas can be given an added edge.

Which reminds me . . . Chesterton is not read much these days, and his style and approach belong to another time and, now, can irritate. You have to read in a slightly different language. And then, just when the 'ho, good landlord, a pint of your finest English ale!' style gets you down, you run across a gem, cogently expressed. He famously defended fairy stories against those who said they told children that there were monsters; children already know that there are monsters, he said, and fairy stories teach them that monsters can be killed. We now know that the monsters may not simply have scales and sleep under a mountain. They may be in our own heads.

In *Maurice*, the rats have to confront them all: real monsters, some of whom have many legs, some merely have two; but some, perhaps the worst, are the ones they invent. The rats are intelligent. They're the first rats in the world to be afraid of the dark, and they people the shadows with imaginary monsters. An act of extreme significance to them is the lighting of a flame.

People have already asked me if I had the current international situation in mind when I wrote the book. The answer is no. I wouldn't insult even rats by turning them into handy metaphors. It's just unfortunate that the current international situation is pretty much the same old dull, stupid international situation, in a world obsessed by the monsters it has made up, dragons that are hard to kill. We look around and see foreign policies that are little more than the taking of revenge for the revenge that was taken in revenge for the revenge last time. It's a path that leads only downwards, and still the world flocks along it. It makes you want to spit. The dinosaurs were thick as concrete, but they survived for 150 million years and it took a damn great asteroid to knock them out. I find myself wondering now if intelligence comes with its own built-in asteroid.

Of course, as the aforesaid writer of humorous fantasy I'm obsessed by wacky, zany ideas. One is that rats might talk. But sometimes I'm even capable of weirder, more ridiculous ideas, such as the possibility of a happy ending. Sometimes, when I'm really, really wacky and on a fresh dose of zany, I'm just capable of entertaining the fantastic idea that, in certain circumstances, *Homo sapiens* might actually be capable of thinking. It must be worth a go, since we've tried everything else.

Writing for children is harder than writing for adults, if you're doing it right. What I thought was going to be a funny story about a cat organizing a swindle based on the Pied Piper legend turned out to be a major project, in which I was aided and encouraged and given hope by Philippa Dickinson and Sue Coates at Doubleday or whatever they're calling themselves this week, and Anne Hoppe of HarperCollins in New York, who waylaid me in an alley in Manhattan and insisted on publishing the book and even promised to protect me from that most feared of creatures, the American copy editor.

And I must thank you, the judges, in the hope that your sanity and critical faculties may speedily be returned to you. And finally, my thanks to the rest of you, the loose agglomeration of editors and teachers and librarians that I usually refer to, mostly with a smile, as the dirndl mafia. You keep the flame alive.

Boston Globe–Horn Book Award speech for *Nation*

Speech read by Anne Hoppe, 2 October 2009

Nation *was one of those novels that came to me out of the blue. That's no lie – suddenly, there it was in my head, although my head of course was full of a lot of other things. And amazingly I didn't need to do much research – everything I wanted to know, somehow I got when it came to* Nation. *To cap it all, while I was writing it, Lyn and I went off to Australia, to a very nice place in far north Queensland, and I found myself walking down a path that all the maps will tell you is in Australia, but I knew was in Nation. And I looked out towards the sea and there it was, all of it – those great big trees that almost reach the sky. It was Nation. Somehow I was in the place I needed to be.*

I am sure that there are writers out there who are capable of telling the world, clearly and succinctly, why and how they wrote the books on which their names and likenesses now twinkle.

They would be real writers, who keep things in filing cabinets rather than in piles. They will have desks, quite probably glass-topped, which, unlike mine, are not infested with mice.

Yes, I know, this should not be possible, but it is an old Victorian desk with secret compartments in it; secret that is to me but not, alas, to the mice. Patch, the office cat, occasionally unleashes a pogrom, but what we have now is a stalemate at best. I cannot bring myself to poison them in situ, because of the thought of the little bodies mouldering in there somewhere among the mislaid Wills and long-lost maps to hidden treasure.

I have met real writers. They make lists. They plan out their books on file cards. They do proper research, with note-books, and unlike me, they don't get totally sidetracked by a wonderful book about the frozen-water trade on the US seaboard in the late eighteenth century.

It would be hard to describe my usual way of working, but I suspect it would look to a bystander, at least in the early stages of a novel, like the activity of a man who does not know what he is doing. That would be reasonable to surmise; generally I do not, and the purpose of writing the novel is to find out. Fortunately, this usually happens about halfway through the first draft. I tinker with ideas, invent characters, try out lines of dialogue, and generally play around with it until I have found a way to let myself know what I am thinking; often, one of the characters says something that tells me what the story is about.

Nation was not like that. It arrived like a tsunami; it took me over, more or less.

This happened about six months before the dreadful Asian tsunami of 2004, and when I saw the terrible news I told my editors that there was no way I could write the book at that time. It would simply be wrong.

But the story banged away at me nevertheless, to the point where I had to give in. It was that or go mad. And the first thing I did was to write the song.

It seems to me that I have always known that the tidal wave after Krakatoa sent a steamship a couple of miles into the rainforest. It is one of those things that you remember. And ever since I heard it, I have cherished the word 'calenture', a condition that affects becalmed sailors who begin to hallucinate green fields around their stricken ship. I wondered if the first man who looked over the side of the boat when it had been thrust into the jungle thought he had gone crazy. So I wrote the extra verse of 'For Those in Peril on the Sea' for poor Captain Roberts to sing as the *Sweet Judy* ploughed through the canopy, scattering birds and leaves. Here, indeed, was a sailor no longer in peril on the sea but suddenly – and urgently – in peril on the land.

And there it was, hanging in my mind like a vision, the white-sailed ship plunging out of the darkness, from the Old World to the New, with a near deranged captain tied to the wheel and making up, as his vessel disintegrates underneath him, a postscript to one of the finest Christian hymns. I sang it quite a lot while I wrote the book.

But all the time there was another vision squatting there, too. It is so clear in my mind that I can taste it even now. There was a boy, his back to me, holding a spear and screaming at the sea. I knew that he had lost something, and instantly realized that he had lost everything.

There had to be a girl. She would be a Victorian girl, with all the baggage that the word brings with it. She would have to be prim, and by the standards of the trouser-wearing peoples of the northern hemisphere, well brought up. But under those stiff Victorian clothes she would be as tough as nails. I took that as a given, because my creativity always appears to fail me if I try to write a soppy girl. I just can't. You could poke me with sticks, and it would have no effect. Oh, they sometimes start out soppy as anything, but as soon as they find that it doesn't work, they tend to become a reasonably close relative of Miss Piggy.

And so on. In short, I practically nearly drowned under the force of this book. In my mind, it is still totally visual, a sequence of images rather than words, as if I was getting a glimpse of the movie that was yet to be made (and probably never will be. See later).

Authors tend to have packrat minds as a matter of course, and I suspect that my mind packs more rats than most. *Nation* became a happy dumping ground for the hoarded junk of fifty years of joyfully undirected serendipitous reading. Hendrik Willem Van Loon's story of the Pacific gave me a good background. Various accounts of the Krakatoa explosion and its aftermath were dredged up. A whole three shelves of accumulated world folklore got distilled into the affairs of one island. Scientist friends dug out esoteric information on how you can measure the age of glass. And – this was a real coup – I found myself at a dinner sitting next to a man who not only knew that bullets can be slowed very, very rapidly by water and also that in some circumstances they might even ricochet off the surface, but who was able to set up some tests in his big tanks, just to check for certain. Blue Jupiter – viewing the giant planet in the daylight – is something I discovered for myself, one evening in early autumn, when I spotted Sirius just visible in the sky and realized that the highly sophisticated go-to function on my shiny new telescope would be able to use this data to locate Jupiter right at that moment.

And, five minutes later, there it was, blue and white like the daytime moon and with three of its own satellites visible.

They kept the universe turned on even during the daytime! I had always known that to be true, but it was a moment of epiphany; by whom, from what, and why I don't know, but any epiphany is worth having.

Even now, more than a year since the deed was done, I am still not sure what *Nation* is, because it seemed to me that I channelled half of it. I have a reputation, or possibly a crime sheet, as a comic writer, and indeed humour does break out sometimes in the book and a smile will force its way through. Yet it begins with a boy burying the corpses of almost everybody he has ever known. I admired Mau's dilemma as he single-handedly invented Humanism, railing at the gods for not existing, while at the same time needing them to exist to take the blame. I find it difficult to remember that I invented him: he seemed to create himself as the book progressed.

At this point, people say, in a kindly voice, the novel was clearly influenced by the fact that I was diagnosed with Alzheimer's disease during its completion.

That would be interesting if it were true, but it is even more interesting because it is not true. The first, and quite complex, draft had already been finished when I was diagnosed, and Posterior Cortical Atrophy, which is the official term for my variant of the disease, is quite hard even for an expert to discover. From what I have been told, the disease may have been quietly and unobtrusively taking over the territory for very many years before I had an inkling that anything was wrong.

All authors must occasionally wonder where the magic comes from, and sometimes I wonder where the strength of Daphne came from, and about the source of Mau's almost incoherent rage. Wherever their origins, I believe that *Nation* is the best book I have ever written or will write.

Finally, or perhaps I should say climactically, I must thank my editors on both sides of the Atlantic, who got the best out of me with *Nation* by pushing needles under my finger-nails, an ancient skill of the craft. I know it was for my own good, and I am grateful. Sincerely grateful, and this time I'm not kidding.

I would be astonished and gratified to be standing in front of you today, if indeed I was, in fact, standing in front of you today, because it would mark something very special – a second chance that worked.

Up until the mid-1990s I was barely known in the US, while already selling in great numbers almost everywhere else in the world. The publishing situation was woeful. I remember that one edition, in paperback, went out across America with my name spelt wrong on every other page. And yet, when I went to US science fiction conventions, I would be faced by a huge queue of fans, all burdened down with grey import UK editions – hardcover ones at that.

My agent did some calculations, and presented the publisher with figures to show how much their sloth was costing them. Things began to move. Not long afterwards my publisher either took over somebody else or got taken over themselves; in practice it's always a little difficult to be certain in these matters, because publishers tend to collide like galaxies, and you are never quite sure who ran into who, only that some stars have exploded and some constellations have gone freelance.

But, in short, I ended up with bright star editors who knew my work and cared about it, and even publicists who knew my name, which is always useful in a publicist.

Strange things began to happen. I began to get royalties, I began to get big crowds at events; at one signing a few years ago where the independent bookshop was stripped of all my titles within minutes of the beginning of an event, the crowd surged down to the nearest Barnes and Noble and did the same thing there. Who would have thought it?

Am I proud? Well, I am English, and a Knight and, of

course, properly modest and diffident. Hooray! Bingo! Ha ha ha ha ha ha!!!

I have always treasured having one of my novels named an Amelia Bloomer Book by the feminist task force of the ALA, because there is something heart-warming about a man with a beard receiving accolades for strong feminist writing. But this is the Boston Globe–Horn Book award. I am truly honoured to receive it, especially so, as it is given by people who, if they are not librarians themselves, are often in league with librarians.

Not long ago I was invited to a librarians' event by a lady who cheerfully told me, 'We like to think of ourselves as information providers.' I was appalled by this want of ambition; I made my excuses and didn't go. After all, if you have a choice, why not call yourselves Shining Acolytes of the Sacred Flame of Literacy in a Dark and Encroaching Universe? I admit this is hard to put on a button, so why not abbreviate it to: librarians?

As I am sure some of you know, I boast of the fact that for a couple of years I was a volunteer librarian, working weekends for no more reward than a cup of tea, a sweet biscuit, and a blind eye to the enormous number of books that I was taking home.

It seemed to me, even in those days, that librarians and their ilk were not mere 'providers'. Information sleets down on us like confetti; we are knee deep in the stuff.

But I saw my fellow librarians as subtle guides and givers of context, a view which must have taken root when, one day, one of them pushed across the counter three books bound together with string. He said, 'We think you might like this.' It was *The Lord of the Rings*. Now that's what I call real librarianship.

Postscript: *Nation* has done the rounds of Hollywood, but apparently is not of interest because it does not leave enough room for hilarious, wise-cracking animals. We must be grateful for small mercies.

Watching *Nation*

Daily Telegraph, 16 December 2009

Stage adaptations go wrong when someone thinks they know better than the author — it's as simple as that. Otherwise, it generally works. Last year, locally, a small company put on Going Postal. *They were amateurs, but bloody good and far more professional than the professionals. They got it exactly right, including the music. So I think I'll stick to amdram — I can beat them up if they get it wrong. But I don't need to because generally they get it right.*

Last Wednesday I went to the National Theatre to see the play *Nation*, based on my book, which by a happy coincidence was also called *Nation*. It is, I think, the best book that I have ever written or will write; it is certainly the one that took most effort.

(In short, *Nation* is set in an alternate nineteenth century, where a tsunami of Krakatoan proportions lays waste the oceans and leaves a native boy, Mau, alone on a devastated island with Daphne, a prim mid-Victorian girl marooned by the same wave. Their shy and difficult relationship becomes the centre of their drive to save the storm-washed refugees who reach the island, in the course of which they have to fight off attackers of all kinds to find the secret hidden in the island's traditions, that almost literally turns the world upside down.)

That is just an aside; what is important right now is that when the play opened to the press two weeks ago, it got rather more kicks than plaudits. There was praise for the staging, but the play on the whole got such epithets as 'racist', 'politically correct' and 'fascist', although to be fair, I think that whoever said that was probably confused.

All this for the play of a book which was universally well received last year and this year won the Printz Medal, given by the American Librarians Association and the highest US award for young adult literature that it is possible for a British author to win! I know some of those librarians. They are tough cookies. Racism, fascism and overt PC wouldn't stand a chance.

I was so depressed that fellow authors rallied round as a kind of small support group to say 'Don't take any notice of the critics' and to remind me that the author doesn't get blamed.

I hadn't seen the play in the previews. The people at the National said they didn't want me to see them until the play had been sufficiently tuned. They also made it abundantly clear that I had no say in the production.

The reason for this, apparently, is that 'writing a play is different from writing a book'. This is true: it's different, and is, I suggest, easier. The playwright has got sound, light, movement and music — and a lot of staff — as part of their palette; the book author has one lousy alphabet. And we don't get previews to help us tighten the work; we give it our best shot, press the send key, and pray.

Quite a large number of spies at the various incarnations fed me back dispatches from the front: it doesn't flow, difficult to follow, confusing even if you know the book, too much dance, 'a curate's egg', not enough explanation, not enough explanation, not enough explanation (I put that one in three times because it kept appearing), actors working hard, but it never had a chance to engage. No one was telling me they didn't like it; they were telling me that liking it took an effort. Mysteriously, they reported that nevertheless it was getting rapturous applause.

So last night I walked into the theatre like Wyatt Earp on a deceptively quiet street in Tombstone, my finger already on the trigger. And what I found is this: *Nation* is pretty good. You still have to pay attention, but according to the chief spy, attention has been made a lot easier. Cox, the chief villain, has an unnecessary back story, in my opinion; in the book he is a vicious psychopath, almost a force of nature. I wanted him to be not a two-dimensional but a one-dimensional character, evil incarnate. There were one or two places where the laws of narrative demand their due; if you're going to have a young Victorian girl sawing off somebody's leg during a musical number it's pretty important that the audience can understand why this is happening. And refugees arriving at a hospitable island after terrible suffering really should look close to death – which segues neatly into the amputation problem. And in my experience the ending needs approximately another twenty words of dialogue to make a complex and very delicate scene come into focus. All this being said at length, I couldn't help but love it. It isn't my book. The medium changes things. *Nation* the book whispers where *Nation* the play shouts; this is because the book has to reach your eyeballs, while the play has to reach the back of the theatre, and making things louder also makes them different. Plot exposition that can be gently wound out by the authorial voice and internal monologue of a character in the length of a page has to be delivered in a matter of seconds on the stage. In the book there is time to make certain that the reader, or even the reviewer, understands the difference between the grandfathers, the departed elders of the tribe, and the grandfather birds, vulture-like scavengers. In the play they collide, but not on the whole badly. In all fairness to Mark Ravenhill (the adaptor), to fully realize *Nation* on stage would probably require a performance of Wagnerian proportions, and much, sadly, had to go. As it is, it could be honed further to helpful effect, and I, who came prepared to be appalled, found myself charmed by it. The house was two thirds full, which would seem to me not too bad for a Wednesday. People sobbed, gasped, cheered and cried, and all moreover in the right places, as it dawned on me that what I was watching was, in a very strange way, a Victorian melodrama for the twenty-first century.

I spoke to a great many people after the show, because I signed a great many autographs, and heard nothing but good things. Even the older couple who vouchsafed to me that they thought there was a bit that they had not 'got', seemed quite happy that the idea had been there to be got, even if they personally hadn't got it.

And no theatre in the country would have been ashamed of the tsunami of applause. It is not my job to be a shill for the National. Remember the author doesn't get the blame. It could listen more, and earlier, and I must admit that we had an amicable conversation subsequently about further small tweaks to aid understanding and prevent confusion, so possibly I am not entirely useless. But the cast were great, and it is recognizably *Nation*, even if slightly out of breath. I will go back to see it again – probably more than once.

Doctor Who?

Honorary degree acceptance speech, University of Portsmouth, 2001

Nine times so far British universities have suffered short bouts of insanity during which they have awarded me honorary degrees as a Doctor of Letters.

It's now a tradition that I return the compliment and some suitable member of the faculty gets a degree from Unseen University (plus a badge and rather nifty UU scarf). It gets a laugh and a picture in the papers and everyone seems to enjoy it. I used to do the oration in Latin, or the Discworld equivalent, which coincidentally looks like very bad Latin, but it had to be very bad indeed before most people 'got it'; Jack Cohen at Warwick University got his for 'habeum tonsorius per Alberto Einstineum'.

This one, from the happy day in Portsmouth, was how the English ones go.

Vice-chancellor, venerable staff, guests, students, and graduates, I hope that no one will take it amiss when I say that what we are in fact doing today is celebrating ignorance. Ignorance is generally an unregarded talent among humans, but we are in fact the only animal that knows how to do it properly. We've got where we are today by starting out ignorant.

It wasn't always like this. A few thousand years ago, we knew everything – how the world began, what it was for, our place in it . . . everything. It was all there, in the stories the old men told around the fire or had written down in a big book. No more questions, everything sorted out.

But now we know that there's vast amounts of things that, well, we simply don't know. Universities have made great efforts in this area. Think about how it works: you arrive at university, the gleam still on your A-levels, and you've pretty well got it all sussed. Then the first thing they tell you – well, the second thing, obviously, because they have to tell you where the toilets are and so on – is that what you've learned so far is not so much the truth as a way of looking at things. And after three years or so you've learned there's a huge amount that you don't know yet, and that's when they give you a scroll and push you out. Ignorance is a wonderful thing – it's the state you have to be in before you can really learn anything.

Well done for surviving and thank you, Vice-chancellor, on behalf of the graduates, and also on behalf of myself.

I'm not quite sure why you've given me a Doctorate of Letters. Certainly the biggest service I have performed for literature is to deny on every suitable occasion that I write it but, nevertheless, I am honoured. I suspect the award has really been for persistence. I have been writing Discworld books for the better part of two decades. They have, I hope, brought pleasure to millions, and it almost seems unfair to say that at least they've brought fun and money to one. They've taken me around the world a dozen times, I've had a species of turtle (an extinct species, I'm afraid) named after me, and I think I've signed more than three hundred thousand books; I've even done a signing in the middle of a rainforest in Borneo and three people turned up – four if you include, as you should do, the orangutan.

But I've always wondered what life would have been like if a convenient journalistic job hadn't opened up on our local paper and I had gone on to university instead. I'm sure I would have enjoyed the cheap beer. On the other hand, that was in the late sixties, and as we know from our politicians the only thing you were sure of learning at university in the sixties was how not to inhale, so maybe I made the right choice. After all, now I have my degree, which I believe means I'm allowed to throw my hat into the air, something I've always wanted to do. Once again, many thanks to all of you from all of them and all of me. Thank you – and now for a small but important change in your advertised programme.

I said I did not go to university but I have since made up for it by owning one. Unseen University as the premier college for wizards came into being about eighteen years ago in the very first Discworld book and seems to be becoming more real every day. And since I have some influence there, I have prevailed upon the Archchancellor to allow me to perform a little reciprocal ceremony to celebrate the bond between our two great seats of learning. So . . . forward, please, Professor Michael Page.

Although he is far too thin to be a real wizard, Michael has nevertheless impressed me by having a sense of humour while nevertheless being an accountant, an achievement of such magnitude that it most certainly earns him an honorary degree in magic. In order to make him a member of Unseen University, of course, he must don . . . the official hat . . . the official scarf, with the University's crest . . . and the Octagonal badge worn by all alumni. There . . . you are now, professor, causas diabolici volentus, an honorary Bachelor of Fluencing. Due to a lack of foresight this does mean that you will have to have the letters BF after your name, but that is a small price, I am sure you will agree, to pay for greatness.

Thank you very much, Vice-chancellor, ladies, and gentlemen.

A Word About Hats

Sunday Telegraph Review, 8 July 2001

I like hats, particularly the black wide-brimmed Louisianas
which most people think are called fedoras. Coming as I do from
a family where the males go bald around twenty-five, I prefer to
have more than a thickness of bone between my brain and God.

The article says it all, and got commissioned merely because
of a remark I made to a journalist at a party. You'd think there
was something funny about hats.

I was obviously very upset when my hat was kidnapped. You
hear such stories. Was it going to be chained to a radiator?
Would I get a photo of it holding a newspaper? Or – terrible
thought – would it side with its captors and refuse to leave
them? I think that's called the Stockholm Syndrome,
although the Swedes aren't hugely famous for hats.

So I just paid up with a cheque for £75 to the student Rag

Day charity, which was the object of the whole exercise. The dreadful drama was over in ten minutes, and I didn't even get an opportunity to speak to the hat on the telephone.

I got the big black hat back and was, once again, myself.

I like hats. They give me something to do with my head.

In my family the men go bald in their twenties, to get it over with. It stops it coming as a nasty shock later in life. But it means that there's nothing there to absorb all those bumps and scratches that the hairy people never even notice. The modern remedy is a baseball cap. A baseball cap? I'd sooner eat worms.

I spotted the first big black hat in a shop called Billie Jean in Walcot Street, Bath, back in the late eighties. There it was, on a shelf. It was everything I wanted in a hat although, up until that point, I hadn't realized that I did, in fact, want a hat.

It was black, of course, and wide-brimmed, and quite tough, and flexible enough to hold a decent curve once I'd done a bit of work with a steaming kettle.

Sometimes you see something and you just have to go for it.

Since then I must have owned about ten of them, all identical to the inexpert eye. All right, I'll own up: when I was a kid I remember being impressed by John Steed of *The Avengers* opening a wardrobe door to reveal, disappearing into the distance, apparently endless lines of bowler hats and furled umbrellas. That taught me something. If you're going to be serious about hats you can't have just one.

Some, after a decent airing, have been donated to charity

auctions or used as competition prizes ('Win Terry Pratchett's Hat!'). One is the proud possession of my Czech translator. One just died. It was one of the best ones – thin felt that looked like velvet, a perfect fit, and as black as the Ace of Spades. It was like wearing a head glove. Never found another one like it. Took me a year to get it exactly as I wanted it, and two years to wear it out.

No two hats are alike. Every hat has its own character. All confirmed hat-wearers know this. I've got a heavy felt stunt hat, useful if I'm doing a school visit where half the class are probably going to end up trying it on, a quality hat for those select occasions, and some suitably rugged ones for signing tours. A black fedora or Louisiana wouldn't do for Australia, though, where I prefer an Akubra 'Territory', the largest hat they do short of a sombrero. If you look closely you can still see where the koala bear pissed on it.

When I became an officially famous author, the black hat became a kind of trademark. It wasn't on purpose, but photographers liked it. 'One with the hat on, please,' they'd say. And you always do what the photographer wants, don't you? And so the hat – sorry, the Hat – turned up in PR photos and I was stuck with it. It became me, according to all the photographs.

For that reason, people assume that I should be wearing it all the time. 'Where's your hat?' is the demand when I'm signing in a shop, as if people aren't sure who this little bearded bald guy is unless the Hat confers the official personality. Readers want to be photographed with me at bookshop events, and that's fine and part of the whole business, but I just know that as the camera is elevated they'll give that little gasp of realization and 'with the hat, of course'.

There have been a couple of foiled attempts at hat theft.

Then there was the hat-stretching. I bought a new hat for a tour last year. It turned out to be on the tight side, and I had foolishly not brought the spare hat. But a wonderful bookshop in the town of St Neots had once been a gentleman's outfitters and there, on a high shelf, was a Victorian hat-stretching engine. No bookstore should be without one. They kindly racked the hat in front of the crowd while I signed the books. I believe that some people thought it was a way of forcing me to sign.

People ask me if I feel naked without my hat. The answer is no. I feel naked without, say, my trousers, but if you walk down the street without wearing a hat the police take very little interest at all. But, yes . . . I've grown very attached to the hat, over the years.

Aha, people say, it's like some kind of prop, right? A magic mask? You think you become a real person when you put your hat on? You are the hat, right?

And that just goes to show why people shouldn't go around saying 'Aha' and getting their psychology from bad movies. No, I don't become a real person with the hat on. I become an unreal person with the hat on. There's this man who's sold 25 million books and goes on huge and gruelling signing tours and has seen the inside of too many hotel rooms. He's the one under the hat. It's tough under there, and sometimes the hat has to come off.

The hat's an anti-disguise, one that you remove in order to be unrecognized. It's amazing. It works beautifully. Without the hat I can join the huge fraternity of bald men with glasses, and amble around the place without people looking hard at me and saying, 'You're you, aren't you? Here, could you sign this for my wife? She won't believe me when I tell her.' It's not that I mind that stuff, but sometimes a man just wants to go out to buy a tube of glue and some spanners.

Without the hat I can leave home without a pen.

Without the hat, in fact, I can be myself.

A Twit and a Dreamer

On schooldays, scabby knees, first jobs, frankincense,
Christmas robots, beloved books and other off-duty thoughts

The Big Store

✩
✩ ✩
✩ ✩

Programme for Bob Eaton's stage adaptation of
Truckers, **March 2002**

*It's all true. Even so, I doubt that I could get across the real
magic of that first visit to a big store. This was a pre-TV age, at
least for anyone on a working man's wage. Nothing had
prepared me for all that colour and sound, those endless, endless
racks of toys, those lights. The visit etched its pictures in my head.*

Truckers started to be written when I was four or five years
old.

My mother took me up to London to do some Christmas
shopping. Picture the scene: I lived in a village of maybe
twenty houses. We had no electricity and shared a tap with
the house next door. And suddenly there I was in London,
before Christmas, in a large department store called Gamages.
I can remember it in colours so bright that I'm surprised that

the light doesn't shine out of my ears. If I close my eyes I can still hear the rattling sound the canvas clouds made as they were rather unsteadily rolled past the 'aeroplane' in the toy department. It was 'flying' us kids to see Father Christmas. I can't remember him, of course. It would be like trying to remember the face of God.

Later, drunk with sensory input, I got lost. My frantic mother found me going up and down on the escalators, looking at the coloured lights with my mouth open.

Nothing much happened for thirty-five years or so, and then I wrote *Truckers*: small people in a huge department store that they believe is the whole world. I think my hands on the keyboard were wired directly back to that five-year-old head. I remember the mystery of everything, and pretty much everything is a mystery at that age. Nothing made sense and everything was amazing.

That is what it was like for the nomes, trying to find the meaning of the universe in their indoor world without a map. What is 'Everything Must Go' telling you? And 'Dogs and Pushchairs must be Carried'? In order to understand what they mean, you have to, well, know what they mean. Of course, most of us are brought up by people who help us fill in the gaps, but the nomes have to work it out for themselves, and get it gloriously wrong. They achieve impossible things because no one has told them they can't be done.

Diggers and *Wings* followed shortly, and completed the trilogy, and by then I was in charge. But the first book was written entirely for the kid on the moving stairs.

(There are different kinds of fantasies, of course. Six years ago a Russian translator told me how hard it would be to translate the book. I said: surely Russian children don't find it too hard to believe in little people? She said: that's not the problem. The problem is making them believe in a store stuffed with merchandise.)

Roundhead Wood, Forty Green

Playground Memories, Childhood memories chosen by the famous in support of Elangeni Middle School and Chestnut Lane Lower School, Amersham, ed. Nick Gammage, 1996

Forty Green is near High Wycombe, in the Chilterns. I lived there when I was at primary school, and it was there that I learned how to spit, how to live with scabby knees and how to run away. My parents were wonderful – they were parents who wouldn't mind taking you out of school for the day to go to Lyme Regis in search of fossils. Once we went to a place called Church Cliff, and my dad brought a bucket – you could pick up winkles. We put lots of winkles in the back of the car – it didn't fall over, which was good – and when we got home, we gave some to all the neighbours. I got to enjoy being a boy, living in Forty Green.

My favourite play area was – it still *is* – called Roundhead

Wood, although it has fewer trees and more barbed wire now. And here four or five of us roared around like some screaming multi-legged animal, building camps, climbing trees, riding bikes around the little chalk pit in the middle and growing up a little bit more every day. It stood for every woodland, every jungle and, eventually, the surface of alien worlds. And you could hear your mum if she called.

One game involved climbing up a young beech tree, standing on a fork in the branches, and leaping across to another smooth-trunked tree about five feet away. The important thing was to hit the tree full on and instantly wrap your arms around it, otherwise you dropped into the holly bushes ten feet below. And then, having successfully adhered to the tree, you slid down, getting your trousers all green. There would be this solemn procession of kids . . . scramble LEAP splat slitherslither. Or LEAP grab panic ARGGGGHHH.

Of course, we had to make our own entertainment in those days.

A Star Pupil

**From *Celebrating 60 Years: Holtspur School
1951–2011*, 2011**

*I didn't enjoy primary school. I was the boy who came late. Not
one of the real dunces, but more goat than sheep. H. W. Tame,
the master, apparently believed he could divine in a six-year-old
which secondary school that boy or girl would go on to – and
since I was a goat, he had me down as one of the losers. My mum
wasn't going to have any of that, so she did what a lot of mums
do – found a teacher locally who could help me.*

*I remember the day of the eleven-plus results when H. W. Tame
went around the classroom to tell us where we were going. There was
silence as I got out of my chair to go and tell my parents, who were
waiting outside. I was the only goat that passed.*

There was a book about H. W. Tame called Selected At Six,
*but if my mother had been a teacher, she would have been head
of something.*

Of course I remember my first headmaster, H. W. Tame, a giant of a man, about 600 miles high as I recall. He was a pioneer of sex education for older primary school children, and I remember when I was about eleven going home from his talk, which we had all been looking forward to with considerable trepidation and excitement. I walked through the autumn leaves kicking them into the air and in my head weighing up the likelihoods and possibilities and deciding to my own satisfaction that he had definitely got it wrong.

In all truth, I cannot say that my memories of Holtspur School were of the warmest, but possibly that was entirely because I was an absolutely quintessential example of a twit and dreamer. Fortuitously I survived, and the talent of dreaming I subsequently found, when under control, to be remarkably rewarding. That which does not kill us makes us strong. Seriously, it was, well, school, decent enough in its way, and later, depending on your mood at the time, you decide which spectacles to wear when recalling your thoughts.

I also remember the pantomimes, which H. W. Tame wrote and occasionally appeared in, especially if a giant was wanted. Some time later on, as an adult, I met him at an event and was amazed at the miracle that meant he was now about the same size as me. It was school and if you managed to come out the other side in a reasonably amiable state of mind that must have been a plus.

On Granny Pratchett

False teeth and a smoking mermaid: Famous people reveal the strange and beautiful truth about themselves and their grandparents, Age Concern, 2004

Granny Pratchett was very small, very intelligent, badly educated and rolled her own cigarettes. She carefully dismantled the dog-ends and kept them in an old tobacco tin from which she rolled future fags, occasionally topping it up with fresh tobacco. As a child this fascinated me, because you didn't need to be a mathematician to see that this meant there must have been some shreds of tobacco she'd been smoking for decades, if not longer.

She spoke French, having gone off to be a ladies' maid in France before the First World War. She met Granddad Pratchett by chance, having taken part while she was there in a kind of pen-pal scheme for lonely Tommies at the Front. I suppose it was a happy marriage – when you're a kid, grand-parents just *are*. But I suspect it would have been a happier one for her if she'd married a man who enjoyed books, because they were her secret vice. She had one treasured shelf of them, all classics, but when I was around twelve I used to loan her my science fiction books, which she read avidly.

Or so she said. You could never be quite sure with Granny. She was one of the brightest people I've met. In another time, with a different background, she would have run companies.

Tales of Wonder and of Porn

Noreascon 4: WorldCon Programme Book, September 2004

The things we love when we're young stay with us – like astronomy, for me. The day I found out I had PCA, I'd just got a nice new piece for my telescope. And PCA has a lot to do with the eyes – you see, but sometimes you don't see because the brain is having difficulties processing the signal from the eyes. It's something I can deal with, but I can't read small type very easily. And as for the telescope . . . well, hanging around with a beer while Rob operates it is still good.

Still, I don't feel hard done by. I've read, oh lordy how I've read – I have books stashed everywhere. Those comic books that started everything for me were mostly rather cheapo, but some of them survive to the present day and can still be found somewhere in one of my libraries.

Well, well, well . . . My first WorldCon was in 1965. It was in London, of course. Only Americans and very rich people (the terms were considered interchangeable) flew the wide Atlantic in those days. Brian Aldiss was the GoH, and Arthur C. Clarke spoke at the banquet, illustrating his uplifting talk by flourishing a nail from the *Mayflower* and a piece of the heatshield of, I think, *Friendship 7*.

Over breakfast, James Blish complained to me about the lack of waffles. I was so proud! The author of the *Cities in Flight* trilogy had chosen *me* in whom to confide his displeasure at the narrow choice of British breakfast products!

There were giants in the world in those days or, at least, people who were very considerably taller than me.

But that was later.

I think it all started with a Superman comic that another kid gave to me when I was on holiday. I must have been nine. By the end of the holiday I was wearing my red towel tied round my neck *all the time*. For what it's worth, I always preferred Batman. Most local kids did. If you ate up your broccoli and drank your milk you could theoretically be Batman when you grew up, whereas in order to be Superman you had to be born on another planet. My friend Nibbsy, who was a Superman fan, reckoned you could be a *kind* of Superman if *this* planet blew up and your dad had the foresight to build a space rocket for you ahead of time. He thought I was in with a chance because my dad could weld. I feared his theory was unsound.

There were fights at school over the question of whether or not Batman could fly. Those of us who said he couldn't were in the minority and, therefore, got beaten up by the thick kids. But, hahaha, it wasn't us who broke limbs by jumping out of their bedroom windows. Shouting 'Batmaaagh!' on the way down didn't work, did it . . .

But the undercurrents were stirring. Gotham City had altogether too many carnival floats and too many dumb plots even for a nine-year-old. At about this time, Brooke Bond Tea started bringing out collectable cards in every packet of tea – more particularly, a series called *Out Into Space*.

I have them here, now, as I type. Never mind Proust and his biscuit, *my* ticket to the past is card nine, 'Planets and Their Moons'.

The colours are garish, the paintings are not great, but my family drank tea until their eyeballs floated just so I could get 'em all. Memorize the back of every card and you'd know more than most people today know about the night sky. Admittedly, some of what you'd know would be wrong: Mars was shown with canals. But they got me hooked on space, which is a great addiction because there's lots of it and it's obtainable free. And that was great, because they'd just decided to start the Space Age.

My parents, as they do, bought me a telescope. It was the kind of 'scope kind parents, as they were, buy without the benefit of reading a book on telescopes. Jupiter was a wobbly ball of rainbows but I learned my way around the moon.

I was going to be an astronomer, because when you were an astronomer you didn't have to be in bed by ten.

But it turned out not to matter if you were in bed by ten, because I'd found these stories about space . . .

I'm glad to say I did it right. I found a proper SF book-shop. Of course, a *proper* SF bookshop, one where the owner is a fan and whose customers are so well known to him that sometimes they help out behind the counter, is handily situated between a tattoo parlour and a porno bookstore.

My source of supply was *inside* the porn store. Its main line of business, conducted by a dear old lady who sat knitting in between dealing with customers, was porn.* Yet for some reason, possibly to add some weight to the claim to be a bookshop, half the floor space of the tiny place was occupied by cardboard boxes full of second-hand British and American SF magazines, quite often in mint condition.

Where did they come from? I never found out. All I know is, they filled up as fast as I emptied them. I never saw any other SF fans in there. There were occasionally some men in raincoats staring at the material on the upper shelves in a Zen-like trance when I came in, but they never took any notice of the kid scrabbling through the boxes below. The owner, who took quite a shine to me as possibly her one customer not yet interested in the upper shelves (and some-times made me a cup of tea), just said gnomically that 'people drop them in'.

Astounding, Analog, Fantasy and SF, Galaxy, New Worlds, Science Fantasy . . . untold riches, they sleeted down on me at sixpence each. They weren't the old lady's main stock in trade

---

* Soft core, as far as I can recall, although if customers approached the counter they could, after some sombre conversation, obtain mysterious brown envelopes. These may of course have been really rare SF magazines.

and she didn't know anything about SF, so about three times a week I came out with my school bag bulging. I still found time to do my homework.

Then, in one of the UK mags, there was a mention of the British Science Fiction Association.

Contact. And that led to the cons, and to that general encouragement to write that is part of the atmosphere. I wrote. I wrote rubbish, mostly, but some of it was okay, and I took notice of those guys on the panels who said: 'If you want to be a writer, get another job.' That was newspaper journalism and, for a trainee, a wonderful opportunity to work every god-given hour; the guys should have said: 'Get another job but not one which takes over your whole life.' And there were girls. The other job and, indeed, the girls took over.

The 1965 WorldCon was my last convention for twenty-one years. I'd been formally in fandom for a mere three years, not counting the apprenticeship in the little shop, and didn't find my way back until I'd written four novels. It's nice to be home.

Last time I went past, the shop had totally vanished under the concrete forecourt of a car dealership.

Either that or, the day I left for the last time, the little lady, her work done, pulled the lever under the desk and the whole place just folded up and slipped away . . .

Letter to *Vector*

Vector, 21 September 1963

When I was an adolescent, everything was happening – it was the sixties – but at school I still got into trouble for bringing in copies of Mad *magazine! I found the stuff we were being given was really rather stupid.*

TERRY PRATCHETT (Beaconsfield)

The article 'SF in Schools' in No. 20 [*Vector*] interested me mainly because

a) I'm a schoolboy, and

b) I'm very interested in SF.

First of all, I think Ron Bennett's pupils are dead lucky in having a Master who is interested in Science Fiction. All we get at my school are the same old dreary titles 'My Pets' or 'A Day at a Railway Station'. However charming they are the first time round, they begin to pall after five or six laps. (I exaggerate only slightly, I assure you.)

Of course, the cry goes up: 'Not everyone is interested in Science (ugh!) Fiction.' So what? 'A Day at a Railway Station' isn't everyone's cup of tea either. Besides, most of the blokes in my form copy the stories out of various magazines; it might interest them to crib out of *New Worlds*, etc. or *Science Fantasy*.

[Editor's reply: The two composition titles you mention are easily adaptable to SF themes, surely. 'My Pets' – a Little Fuzzy and a small thoat (I had a banth once but they banned it). 'A Day at a Railway Station' – digging among the ancient ruins in some future time when teleportation is universal. AM]

Writer's Choice

Waterstones' *Books Quarterly*, **12, 2004**

My granny had one bookshelf. I recall it contained a large book which was a great help to her in times of trouble and confusion, and it was the only one I ever saw her open: it was called *The Crossword Puzzle Solver's Dictionary*.

But the shelf also contained G. K. Chesterton's *The Napoleon of Notting Hill*, a book that distils the heart and soul of fantasy – which, I have to say, has little to do with wizards and everything to do with . . . well, everything. When you're a kid you fill your local landscape with perils and terrors (there was a barn a few miles from us where, I knew for a fact, giants lived). Chesterton knew why, and could achieve in a sentence what some philosophers can't manage in a book. He taught one lesson that I took to heart: there's nothing so strange as the 'normal'.

I came to reading late but hungry and so read adult and

children's books together, without distinguishing very much between them. *The Wind in the Willows* was the book that dragged me in; I've still got my original cheap copy somewhere, in a plastic folder because the spine evaporated years ago. Next time you read it, pay attention to what size the animals are. It changes throughout the book and yet it doesn't matter.

By sheer luck I also picked up *Mistress Masham's Repose*, by T. H. White, and loved it because it was a children's book that made absolutely no concessions to children. It was also a work of fiction in which another work of fiction (*Gulliver's Travels*) was real; that Chinese box of an idea is wonderful to discover when you're eleven. In fact I'd developed a taste for works that show us reality from a different perspective, and that led me to slink down towards the science fiction shelves.

Every literary novelist apparently knows that science fiction is 'all about' robots and spaceships and other planets. Oh, there's plenty of that stuff as top dressing, but at its best science fiction is about us and our Faustian bargain with our big brains, which dragged us out of the trees but may yet drag us into the volcano. The best science fiction book ever is only erratically in print, and it is *The Evolution Man* by the late Roy Lewis. Look in vain for robots. In fact, look in vain for *Homo sapiens*, probably, since the cast is a family of Pleistocene humanoids.

They've learned to walk upright and now they're ready for the big stuff – fire, cookery, music, arts and the remarkable discovery that you shouldn't mate with your sister. Because it's too easy, says Father, the visionary horde leader. In order to progress, humanity must create inhibitions, frustrations and complexes, and drive itself out of an animal Eden. To rise, we must screw ourselves up. Wonderful stuff, and my annual read. It's about time it had a mass-market publisher again.

Finally, you won't find this one in a modern bookshop but most good second-hand bookshops have it (unless I've been past, because I buy them up and press them on friends). It's *The Specialist*, by Charles Sale, and is only a few dozen pages long. Strictly speaking, it's the reminiscences of a privy builder, but it's really a gentle education in the nature of humour. That stuff needs deep soil; you can grow wit on a damp flannel.

Introduction to Roy Lewis's
The Evolution Man

Corgi, 1989

You hold in your hands one of the funniest books of the last 500,000 years.*

At its simplest, it is a comic account of the discovery and use, by a family of extremely Early Men, of some of the most powerful and fearful things the human race has ever laid a hand on – fire, the spear, marriage and so on. It's also a reminder that the problems of progress didn't start with the atomic age but with the need to cook without being cooked, and eat without being eaten.

* Well, sadly, you don't – at least not *The Evolution Man* – but if you can you should get your hands on it.

It's also a reminder that the *first* weapon to kill people but leave buildings standing was a club.

It hasn't been a best-seller yet (at least in the commonly accepted sense of the word), and perhaps that is because it is so difficult to categorize – nothing hurts a book more than people not knowing what shelf to put it on. Since it was first published in 1960, it has gone through a variety of printings and a variety of names (not just *The Evolution Man*, which is what Brian Aldiss wisely rechristened it that year when he chose it as one of the first novels to start the Penguin SF list, but also *Once Upon an Ice Age* and *What We Did to Father*).

Aldiss spotted what had not, until then, been noticed by anyone else, including the author – that it was, in fact, extremely good science fiction. The genuine article. Of course it didn't have rockets in it. So what? You don't need rockets. We all know this now. In 1960, that perception was less general.

I bought my copy then because it had 'SF' on the cover. I'd buy *anything* that had 'SF' on the cover in those dark days, in the same way that you'll drink anything marked 'liquid' if you're in a desert. And then I realized that I was reading something literate, novel, and very, very funny. After twenty-eight years that original copy has been loaned to friends so often that the print has nearly been worn off the pages by eyeball pressure.

If you've read this far, it's probably safe to tell you that this is a cult book. But don't worry about it. The term simply means that people have stumbled upon it not because of massive advertising but by happy accident, and then cherished the wonderful warm feeling that they're the only ones who know about it. In other words, it's a *good* cult book. By the time you've finished it, the cult will be bigger by one.

It will change your life in little ways. For example, the opening scenes of *2001* will never look the same again, because you'll be wondering which ape is Uncle Vanya. And you'll find yourself thanking, next time you see one of those helpful little books that identify edible and poisonous mushrooms, all those hundreds of research ape-men who sacrificed their lives to establish precisely which was which.

And you can savour the true story that the germ of the idea for all this came to Roy Lewis when, as *The Economist*'s Commonwealth Affairs reporter in the mid-fifties, he asked the renowned anthropologist Louis Leakey to explain the meaning of some prehistoric cave paintings. Leakey *danced* the meaning for him.

From this, and from observations of the dismantling of British colonial rule in Africa, and from reflections on the depths of history that lay under the political goings-on, Lewis crafted this book.

The famous French biochemist Jacques Monod subsequently wrote to point out one or two technical errors, but added that they didn't matter a damn because reading the book made him laugh so much he fell off a camel in the middle of the Sahara.

So sit on something solid.

April 1988 (somewhere in the Holocene)

The King and I

or How the Bottom Has Dropped Out of the Wise Man Business

Western Daily Press, 24 December 1970

Working at this paper was my second job – I had just started there, after leaving the Bucks Free Press, *when I wrote this piece. It was at the* Bucks Free Press, *my first job out of school, that I knew three real wise men: Mr Church was a solemn one. He took his position seriously and he made us newcomers take it seriously as well. Then there was Bugsy Burroughs, who would bawl you out when you did something wrong. They taught me a lot between them. On my first day I saw my first dead body – an* extremely *dead body. I was scribbling away with Mr Alan, the third wise man, showing me the ropes and I thought, 'I've learned more today than I think I ever did at school . . . At least, I've learned that a man can turn a lot of colours.'*

All I wanted was gold, frankincense and myrrh. Like a latter-day oriental king. That's all. There couldn't be a simpler Christmas shopping list. Easy, I thought. Basic.

I ended up in the middle of Broadmead, Bristol, in the rain, dressed like a refugee from *The Desert Song* and feeling like a very recently deposed Middle Eastern potentate.

I kept thinking: 'You're not cut out for this sort of thing. If they gave you a camel you wouldn't know what to do with it.'

I started out happily enough, I even took a carrier bag. That shows how innocent I was.

Gold. Well, that's common enough, you get it in rings and teeth. Frankincense turned out to be a bittersweet-smelling powder; myrrh a medicinal gum.

Medicinal: I headed for Boots.

'Frankincense? Who makes it?' asked the lady in the perfume department.

Oh well. There were other chemists, and I tried them.

Cool lot, Bristol chemists.

They can take a request for frankincense and snap back a 'Sorry sir, we don't stock it' without batting an eyelid. Actually one did say, 'Good God!'

I was advised to try the Association of the British Pharmaceutical Industry.

'What? Oh. Really? We'd better telephone you back,' they said.

They came back to say:

'You've had us all searching. Apparently myrrh used to be

used in a mouthwash. If you find the old type of chemist you might possibly still get it.'

Mouthwash didn't sound right, but I pressed on. I found Mr Pughe-Jones, a chemist in West Street, Bedminster.

'There isn't the call for that type of thing now,' he said. 'We used to sell myrrh before the war. There might be a bit left somewhere, but I doubt if I could find it.'

Then I began thinking: Perhaps it's you. What you want is a bit of style. Perhaps people aren't getting the message.

So off to Bristol Arts Centre to be kitted up at short notice as an oriental prince.

The robe was last worn by Herod. I said I wasn't snobbish.

'It's not too bad,' said the wardrobe mistress, surveying me critically, 'after all, they'd been on a long journey.'

Cool lot, Bristol shoppers. No one took a blind bit of notice of an oriental prince hopping along trying to keep his cloak out of puddles.

This is what happens to a Wise Man who wants to buy gold in Bristol . . .

If he goes to the Bank of England he gets handed a form by a sympathetic young man. He soon learns that it's no good asking for gold just because you want some.

He is told: 'I don't want to sound pessimistic, but that's just about the worst possible reason you can give.'

If he's a real wise guy he gives up then. That form is awfully ominous. A third of it is in capital letters, and full of phrases like FAILURE TO COMPLY WITH CONDITIONS.

If he's just persistent he visits a few jewellers. I did. I was shown a solid gold napkin ring which I very nearly bought till I snapped out of it.

It's no good. Gold, frankincense and myrrh don't get a look in.

Next year I'll just buy a hamper.

Three kings in Bristol would just find their camels towed away for parking offences.

But of course they didn't pass through Bristol – wise men.

Honey, these bees had a heart of gold

Bath and West Evening Chronicle, 24 April 1976

I was a subeditor at this paper, some years into my career as a journalist. They still had lead type, like the old days, and I was fascinated by that. When it's hot metal printing, it's real journalism.

Every newspaper needs to have someone who can write – not simply journalese, but other things, too. So I wormed my way into that and I had a little shed on the roof with birds I could feed. And I got paid for those pieces – countryside pieces, mostly.

It was a brief shopping list I took to London: gold. I got it. But that's hardly a beginning, is it?

Michael Ayrton, sculptor, novelist, artist and wide-ranging

genius, died not long ago. I met him twice. I can think of no other person whose death has affected me so much, even so.

He wrote a book called *The Maze Maker*, based on the life of the half-mythical craftsman Daedalus. He was the father of Icarus, and built the wings – in the book, the primitive hang-glider – on which his son failed so spectacularly to defy the sun.

I don't think it was ever a best-seller, but for many people it is still a book to return to again and again.

Well, anyway. One achievement Daedalus is credited with is the casting, in gold, of a honeycomb, and in the book Ayrton suggested how it might have been done.

To cast in metal you can make a wax model, envelop it in a sort of plaster cast, melt out the wax and fill the impression. And a honeycomb is its own wax mould. Was it really possible? So compelling was the description, I decided to have a go.

Daedalus decorated his honeycomb with bees cast in gold. You can treat the dead insect like wax, and burn out the ash of its creation in its mould.

It was November. I enrolled at a local silversmithing evening class, which enabled me to buy gold. Gold! They sell it in high-countered little shops in London, festooned with the stuff like a metal delicatessen. I bought enough – well, enough to see, if you looked closely – and rather more silver. Silver's okay, you can buy silver like sweets, it's gold that has the mystery.

It was winter, but the Bee Research Association came to my aid with a matchbox full of dead ones, a piece of wild honeycomb, and their most interested best wishes.

I made a pyramid of wax, and on it placed a bee – poised in flight. I ran tiny wax threads to antennae and wings, so that the molten metal would flow into every crevice, working with tweezers and a heated needle.

And in the workshop I mantled it in an okay cocoon, baked it to red heat, melted a fragment of 22-carat gold in a crucible, spun the whole lot in a centrifugal caster, and dropped the mould into a bucket of cold water. It exploded. And from the steaming water we took a gold bee, eye-faceted, wing-perfect, pollen bags still full – but full of gold. It took two days to free it from its golden web and remove the last trace of clay.

Then I melted it down. Well, why not? I needed the gold. Some fast talking got me some five locusts from London Zoo – a dozen flew out when I went into the little locust breeding rooms under the insect house, where they're bred for the zoo's insectivores. It's *Quatermass and the Pit* in there, I can tell you. But the ones that escaped didn't defoliate the country – they can't breed in Britain.

I cast locusts in silver. And the Natural History Museum donated four dead grasshoppers surplus to requirements. In gold you could have used their back legs as saws – and in fact they were once used, in bronze, for that purpose. I cast a honeycomb in silver, a few inches square. It took days to prepare and dripped with silver honey. And finally the gold was used in another bee, which stayed out of the crucible this time.

It worked, and I had become a minor expert in the ways

of transforming insects into gold. Trouble is, anything else would have been repetitive, so I stopped. But at least I knew it could be done.

Michael Ayrton did it too. When I met him later, I saw the golden honeycomb he had cast after a challenge by a rich reader of the book. On it were seven golden bees, the best of forty attempts. The whole thing was worth, I suppose, £1,000 at the time. When the new owner set it in the grass by his beehives, the bees visited it. I've always wondered whether they filled it with honey, and if the honey was unusually sweet.

That sounds fungi, it must be the dawn chorus

Bath and West Evening Chronicle, 2 October 1976

I think I was possibly one of the first people to find out about working from home. I looked at what work I was doing and where I needed to be for it, and I said to my boss, 'I could take a day off each week, for only a little less money.' So I would motorbike all the way back home to the Mendips, and it was a good time. I had just become a father and we had less money, but plenty of time together.

The song of the mushrooms woke me from my bed. And I groped my way into the laid-out clothes and crept downstairs, it being somehow wrong to put the lights on at five in the morning.

Past the cat, asleep on her chair, and the evening's last log crumbling into ash. Up the garden a cockerel starts to crow. Damn thing seen kitchen light flicker on at last; where hell paper bag? Ah—

And out past the sleeping houses, keeping to the grass because boots ring like bells on the road at this hour. I've probably been spotted, even so. (My father recalls trying to fit a new windscreen on his old Singer, on a driveway completely surrounded by bushes and, furthermore, up a grassy lane. It didn't fit. When he went to the pub that night, a man from the other side of the village gave him a grin and said, 'Dint fit, didit . . .')

Mist curls like a cliché over the fields, and there's half a mile of them to cross. Rabbits scatter. A larger mammal, possibly a hippo, trundles away through a spinney.

There's many a clump of ink-caps along the forestry track. They're fungi, and melt into an alarming black goo when ripe. But they're edible, and taste like mushrooms, and are shunned by the ignorant masses, thank goodness, which means I can pick them without competition and eat them by the plateful as mushrooms should be eaten.

But this morning picking them would be like shooting a hen. The quarry is more elusive, more unreliable, more like a gift from the gods.

Through a bramble hedge and there's a small misty field. It's a blank green until you get into the way of seeing and look for the right kind of grass.

Once the eye gets the hang of it, the mushrooms spring out like stars.

Pick one – and there is a slight cough. Nothing offensive, mark you, just a sort of verbal call sign. There's someone else in the field. He carries a plastic bag.

We regard each other for a few moments, then go back to our tasks, each surreptitiously watching the other. He's got the right technique – ignore the little buttons and rotting giants, and pick the nice pink teenagers. Not that a really ripe mushroom isn't tasty if you've a robust palate. Two years ago I knew a field that sprouted huge horse mushrooms and even after I'd taken my shirt off and filled it, I hardly made an impression.

In a few minutes I've got my ration and my solitary co-picker passes me on the way to the stile at the opposite side of the field. We nod. Speech in a mushroom field at half past five on a misty morning is sacrilege.

And back home, pausing twice to leave mushrooms outside the back doors of more favoured neighbours. At this stage a few ink-caps go into the bag – shame to waste them.

And there's happy and sad thoughts. Happy because there's a breakfast of mushrooms and huge knobbly tomatoes. Sad, because somewhere there are mushroom fields I shall never visit and no one knows about – oh, it makes the fingers tingle.

After breakfast the sky's light grey, and some cottage lights are on. Wellington boots clang down the road – someone thinks he's going after mushrooms, and he'll probably look in the local fields, where the farmers use fertilizer out of a bag, and say there's no mushrooms again this year. You've got to look sharp – when the song of the mushrooms drifts out of the night.

Introduction to *The Leaky Establishment* by David Langford

Big Engine, 2001

This says it all, really. We both worked in places where science, engineering and bureaucracy crashed into one another.

As a Press Officer, a man responsible for getting information out in a hurry (sometimes, at any rate), I was forbidden to touch a typewriter. Strictly speaking, I was supposed to write out releases in longhand and send them to the typing pool, from whence they might be returned to me tomorrow. However, by this time the average nuclear reactor can be quite well alight, so I just typed stuff anyway, and no one said anything.

It was, in retrospect, a great life for an SF fan. After Chernobyl it seemed there was no question too weird for the local Nodding Acquaintances of the Earth to plant with willing reporters. Will your nuclear power stations withstand an Ice Age? No? Why not? (Answer: because a two-mile-high glacier scouring the continent down to bedrock puts a crimp in everyone's day.) Isn't it scandalous that there's a fault line running through the power station car park? (Answer: Not really. It's about 200 feet long and hasn't moved for 60,000,000 years . . .)

One of my many strange jobs was escorting TV and movie researchers when they were scouting power station locations for upcoming dramas. I'd take them up to the pile cap (the top of the reactor) and they'd look around in dismay at the total absence of green steam. They never believed me when I told them that green steam is not a normal reactor product. Then they'd bring their own for the shoot. Oh, and big fake panels covered in flashing lights, too, because we didn't have enough. In fact, our power stations were a complete disappointment. They were so unlike the real things.

I had eight years of this. It was a great life, if you held on to your sense of humour.

As far as I'm concerned, The Leaky Establishment *was one step away from being real.*

I hate Dave Langford for writing this book. This was the book I meant to write. God wanted me to write this book.

For a large part of the 1980s I effectively worked (which was definitely not the same as worked effectively) for the civil nuclear industry, or at least that part of it that produced cheap, clean nuclear electricity, if I remember my facts correctly, in South West England.

Reactors hardly ever exploded. I was a Press Officer, so you can trust me on this. But they didn't have to explode. Some little-known component of nuclear radiation made certain that life for anyone involved with the public face of the industry became very weird. And I worked with Dave Langfords all the time. I had to. I knew about words, they knew about uranium. They were a fine body of men, with a refreshingly different view of the universe.

When a member of the public turned up at a nuclear power station and was found to be too radioactive to go near the reactor, they advised me. When I had to deal with the news story about the pixie that shut down a nuclear power station, they advised me again. Scientists with a twisted sense of humour can do wonders for your education, provided you believe only fifty per cent of what they tell you. (Er . . . perhaps thirty per cent, come to think of it – I never did actually use the phrase 'The amount of radiation released was so small that you could hardly see it.')

They'd produce figures to show that the Sun was an illegal emitter of laser light and under Health and Safety regulations no one should be allowed outdoors, or that the natural background radiation in granite areas meant that registered nuclear workers should only be allowed to go on holiday in Cornwall if they wore protective clothing. And I can no longer hear the words 'three completely independent fail-safe systems' without laughing.

The job was also my introduction to the Civil Service. Yes, there really was the man who came round every six months to check that I still had the ancient four-function calculator that I'd signed for on joining, and was probably worth 10p. Yes, some of the Langfords upstairs brought in their own word processors to write their reports and then, because of the regulations, sighed, and sent the printouts down to the typing pool to be re-typed. And then there was the guy who actually went into a nuclear reactor and . . . but I'll save that one, because you'd never believe it. Or the one about the lavatory.

It's no wonder that this clash of mindsets produced something like *The Leaky Establishment* (which of course deals with an entirely different kind of nuclear establishment to the ones I worked in, where things were not actually intended to blow up). The book is practically a documentary. I read it in horror, in between laughing. This man had sat in at exactly the same kind of meetings! He'd dealt with the same kind of people! He'd been at the same Open Days! The sheer reality of it all leaked from every page! It was just like the book I'd been planning to write one day! How could I ever write my book now?

And then I got to the end and . . . well, Dave Langford's garden would probably bear examination by the Health and Safety Executive, that's all I'll say.

I'd rank this book alongside Michael Frayn's *The Tin Men*, another neglected classic. I've wanted for years to see it back in print. It is one of those books you end up buying several copies of, because you just have to lend it to friends. It's very funny. It's very real.

I hope it's as successful as hell, and will happily give up any plans to write my own nuclear book. After all, I'll always have my memories to keep me warm: and, come to think of it, the large, silvery, and curiously heavy mug they presented to me when I left . . .

The Meaning of My Christmas

Western Daily Press (Bristol), 24 December 1997

*Exactly twenty-seven years after my search for frankincense in
Bristol, I tackled Christmas for the* Western Daily Press.
Again.

I am not a member of any religion and I don't believe in any
metaphysical Santa Clauses of any description, and yet, for
all that, I like Christmas.

But it's become confusing. Now it looks as if everyone's
hell-bent on getting hold of Tinky Winky Spice even though
in February you'll be able to pick one up for a fiver.

I've a theory that parents who tramp from shop to shop in
search of the right Teletubby or Action Man are really going
through the old hunter/gatherer ritual again. It calls to something ancient in their bones.

In my latest paperback, *Hogfather*, I looked at the

traditions of a midwinter festival. You have to be a blindly fundamentalist Christian not to understand that there's been a very old tradition of celebrating the rebirth of the sun.

Even now, in our centrally heated homes, where we're separated from the 'great cycle of nature', we still moan about the 'nights drawing in'. We need Christmas.

I'm forty-nine now, and when I was a child Christmas was the time of the big blow-out. It was when you got what you couldn't normally afford, but these days so many people can afford some luxuries through the year that Christmas doesn't figure in quite the same way.

But the Christmas holiday still has a lot going for it. When you're self-employed, like me, for example, it's often hard to stop working. When your office is next to your living space it's so easy to wander over and start writing. Saturdays and Sundays become the easiest days of all to work because the phone doesn't ring as much.

One of the reasons I like Christmas is because it's perfectly socially acceptable not to work for a week. It's a time to take stock.

In some ways, I'd agree that Christmas is too commercial-ized. It can't be good for the country when stuff starts piling up in the shops in early October.

Some retailers stand or fall by Christmas. Take bookshops. They live for Christmas. If they only opened on 1 December and closed on 24 December, it would probably still be worth their while existing. They become shrines to those bookshop saints, St Michael and St Delia.

But the good points outweigh the bad. Charities do very

well at this time of year and, even if you only drop a couple of coins in a collection box in December, surely it's better than never giving at all. And I like the Christmas story. It's a positive one and it isn't shoved down children's throats any more. Schools tend to be very politically correct and teachers can't assume that pupils' parents are Christians.

The fact is that our secular society doesn't offer any alternative celebration or occasion we can enjoy in the depth of winter. Somehow Blair's Day or something similar doesn't give you quite the same gut feeling.

This Christmas our family will do all the usual things – light a huge log fire, cook a turkey and offer a vegetarian option – and I'll enjoy it.

I used to be conned into not enjoying it because it was cool to say that it's over-commercialized and then I thought: 'But it's fun as well.' Now I think, what the hell, I don't have to be cool any more. Anyway, there's always been over-indulgence at the traditional midwinter festival, whether it's been feasting on a hog or an oven-ready turkey.

You can do Christmas your own way if you want to badly enough. And a little bit of commercialism doesn't do anyone any harm. After all, the Wise Men made certain they brought presents, even though the shops were crowded and they had to get hold of some myrrh spice.

Under all the hype people do tend to be a little bit nicer to each other for a while. They lower their defences and get on with people a little bit more. So what if it's only for Christmas? Better once a year than never.

We have a 'non-aggression pact' in my family. We try to

buy each other something small, but which requires a lot of thought.

It's better to ask Santa Claus for a pair of slippers for Christmas rather than peace on earth. You might actually get it.

Big, jolly fat men with beards can't deliver world peace. That's something we have to work at ourselves. And there is no better way at this time of year, than to start with the people next door.

Alien Christmas

1987

[A postprandial speech following 'Christmas Dinner' at Beccon '87 . . . that is, the pre-awards banquet at the 1987 UK Eastercon.]

I'm Dreaming of the Right Christmas . . .
  It's not very subtle, but I reckoned that ten o'clock at a British convention banquet (where you have ALCOHOL) was not the time for Oscar Wilde. I don't know if I delivered this speech, but I must have said something because I got some laughs.

This is a great idea, isn't it? So much nicer to have Christmas at this time of the year instead of at the end of December, when the shops are always so crowded. Reminds me of those clips you used to get in the Queen's Christmas broadcast to the Commonwealth back in the fifties, with the traditional shot of Australians eating chilled prawns, roast turkey, and Christmas pudding on Bondi beach. There was always a Christmas tree planted in the sand. It was decorated with what I now realize was probably vomit.

Last week I got this fortune cookie sort of printout which said Your Role Is Eater. I thought, Fantastic, I like role-playing games, I've never been an Eater before, I wonder how many hit points it has?

And then I saw another printout underneath it which said that at 2200 my role was After Dinner Speaker, which is something you'd expect to find only in the very worst dungeon, a monster lurching around in a white frilly shirt looking for an audience. Three hours later the explorers are found bored rigid, their coffee stone cold, the brick-thick after-dinner mint melted in their hands.

That reminds me why I gave up Dungeons and Dragons. There were too many monsters. Back in the old days you could go around a dungeon without meeting much more than a few orcs and lizard men, but then everyone started inventing monsters and pretty soon it was a case of bugger the magic sword, what you really needed to be the complete adventurer was the Marcus L. Rowland fifteen-volume Guide to Monsters and the ability to read very, very fast, because if you couldn't recognize them from the outside you pretty soon got the chance to try looking at them from the wrong side of their tonsils.

Anyway, this bit of paper said I was to talk about Alien Christmases, which was handy, because I always like to know what subject it is I'm straying away from. I'll give it a try; I've been a lot of bad things in my time although, praise the Lord, I've never been a *Blake's 7* fan.

Not that Christmases aren't pretty alien in any case. It's a funny old thing, but whenever you see pictures of Santa Claus he's always got the same toys in his sack. A teddy, a dolly, a trumpet, and a wooden engine. Always. Sometimes he also has a few red and white striped candy canes. Heaven knows why, you never see them in the shops, and if any kid asks for a wooden engine these days it means he lives at the bottom of a hole on a desert island and has never heard of television, because last Christmas my daughter got a lot of toys, a few cars, a plane, stuff like that, and the thing about them was this. Every single one of them was a robot. Not just a simple robot. I know what robots are supposed to look like, I had a robot when I was a kid. You could tell it was a robot, it had two cogwheels going round in its chest and its eyes lit up when you turned its key, and why not, so would yours. And I had a Magic Robot . . . well, we all had one, didn't we? And when we got fed up with the smug way he spun around on his mirror getting all the right answers, we cut them out and stuck them down differently for the sheer hell of it, gosh, weren't we devils.

But these new robots are subversive. They are robots in disguise.

There's this sort of robot war going on around us. I haven't quite figured it out yet, although the kids seem incredibly well informed on the subject. It appears that you can tell the good robots from the bad robots because the good robots have got human heads, a bit like that scene in *Saturn Three*, you remember, where the robot gets the idea that the best way to look human is hack someone's head off and stick it on your antenna. They all look like an American footballer who's been smashed through a Volkswagen.

They go around saving the universe from another bunch of robots, saving the universe in this case consisting of great laser battles. The universe doesn't look that good by the time they've saved it, but by golly, it's saved.

Anyway, none of her presents looked like it was supposed to. A collection of plastic rocks turned out to be Rock Lords, with exciting rocky names like Boulder and Nugget. Yes, another bunch of bloody robots.

In fact the only Christmassy thing in our house was the crib, and I'm not certain that at a touch of a button it wouldn't transform and the Mary and Josephoids would battle it out with the Three Kingons.

Weirdest of the lot, though, is Kraak, Prince of Darkness. At £14.95 he must be a bargain for a prince of darkness. He's a Zoid, probably from the planet Zoid in the galaxy of Zoid, because while the models are pretty good the storyline behind them is junk, the science fiction equivalent of a McDonald's hamburger. I like old Kraak, though, because it only took the whole of Christmas morning to put him together. He's made of red and grey plastic, an absolute miracle of polystyrene technology, and he looks like a chicken that's been dead for maybe three months. Stuff two batteries up his robot bum and he starts to terrorize the universe as advertised, and he does it like this: what he does is, he walks about nine inches ve-r-ry slowly and painfully, while dozens of little plastic pistons thrash about, and then he falls over.

Kraak has got the kind of instinct for survival that makes a kamikaze pilot look like the Green Cross Code man. I don't know what the terrain is like up there on Zoid, but he finds it pretty difficult to travel over the average living-room carpet. No wonder he terrorizes the universe, it must be pretty frightening, having a thousand tons of war robot collapse on top of you and lie there with its little feet pathetically going round and round. You want to commit suicide in sympathy. Oh, and he's got this other fiendish weapon: his head comes off and rolls under the sofa. Pretty scary, that. We've tested him out with other Zoids, and I'm here to tell you that the technology of robot fighting machines, basically, is trying to fall over in front of your opponent and trip him up. It's a hard job, because the natural instinct of all Zoids is to fall over as soon as you take your hand away.

But even Kraak has problems compared with a robot that was proudly demonstrated to us by the lad next door. A Transformer, I think it was. It isn't just made of one car or plane, it's a whole fleet of vehicles which, when disaster threatens, assemble themselves into one great big fighting machine. That's the theory, anyway. My bet is that at the moment of truth the bloody thing will have to go into battle half-finished because its torso is grounded at Gatwick and its left leg is stuck in a traffic jam outside Luton.

We recently saw *Santa Claus: The Movie*. Anyone else seen it? Pretty dreadful, the only laugh is where they apparently let the reindeer snort coke in order to get them to fly. No wonder Rudolph had a red nose, he spends half the time with a straw stuck up it.

Anyway, you get to see Santa's workshop. Just as I thought. Every damn toy is made of wood, painted in garish primary colours. It might have been possible, in fact I suppose it's probably inevitable, that if you pressed the right switch on the rocking horses and jolly wooden dolls they turned into robots, but I doubt it. I looked very carefully over the whole place and there wasn't a single plastic extrusion machine. Not a single elf looked as though he knew which end to hold a soldering iron. None of the really traditional kids' toys were there – no Rambos, no plastic models of the Karate Kid, none of those weird little spelling and writing machines designed to help your child talk like a NASA launch controller with sinus trouble and a mental age of five.

Now, I've got a theory to account for this. Basically, it is that Father Christmases are planet-specific and we've got the wrong one.

I suspect it was the atom bomb tests in the early fifties that warped the, you know, the fabric of time and space and that. Secret tests at the North Pole opened up this, you know, sort of hole between the dimensions, and all the stuff made by our Father Christmas is somehow diverted to Zoid or wherever and we get all the stuff he makes, and since he's a robot made out of plastic he only makes the things he's good at.

The people it's really tough on are the kids on Zoid. They wake up on Christmas morning, unplug themselves from their recharger units, clank to the end of the bed (pausing only to fall over once or twice) playfully zapping one another with their megadeath lasers, look into their portable pedal extremity enclosures, and what do they find? Not the playful, cuddly death-dealing instruments of mayhem that they have been led to expect, but wooden trains, trumpets, rag dolls, and those curly red and white sugar walking sticks that you never see in real life. Toys that don't need batteries. Toys that you don't have to put together. Toys with varnish on instead of plastic. Alien toys.

And, because of this amazing two-way time warp thingy, our kids get the rest. Weird plastic masters of the universe which are to the imagination what sandpaper is to a tomato. Alien toys. Maybe it's being done on purpose, to turn them all into Zoids. Like the song says – you'd better watch out.

I don't think it will work, though. I took a look into my daughter's dolls'-house. Old Kraak has been hanging out there since his batteries ran out and his mega-cannons fell off. Mr T has been there for a couple of years, ever since she found out he could wear Barbie's clothes, and I see that some plastic cat-woman is living in the bathroom.

I don't know why, but what I saw in there gave me hope. Kraak was having a tea party with a mechanical dog, two Playpeople and three dolls. He wasn't trying to zap anyone. No matter what Santa Claus throws at us, we can beat him . . .

And now your mummies and daddies are turning up to take you home; be sure to pick up your balloons and Party Loot bags, and remember that Father Christmas will soon be along to give presents to all the good boys and girls who've won awards.

2001: The Vision and the Reality

Sunday Times, 24 December 2000

Journalists in the UK, and in my experience practically everywhere else in the world, find it hard to distinguish between fantasy writers and science fiction writers. I'm down in their contacts book as 'guy to talk to about sci-fi'. When possible signs of life were discovered in the famous Martian meteorite ALH84001, I was the person they came to for a comment. Since they had room for a soundbite of about twelve seconds, though, it hardly mattered. Anyone trained as a journalist can be an expert for twelve seconds.

    For similar reasons, I was asked to write this. I could polish it up now, all the tech is hugely or subtly out of date, but that's the trouble with the future. It doesn't stand still for long enough. Anyway, this is journalism, which doesn't have to be true for ever. It just has to be true until tomorrow morning. But I rather enjoyed writing it.

Dah . . . DAH . . . DAAAH! (bing bong bing bong bing bong bing . . . bong. . .)

There had never been a science fiction movie like it. Few have approached it since. You couldn't see the string. Everything looked right. Even the dialogue worked, even though it sounded as though people were softening one another up to sell them life insurance. They didn't say, 'Eat electric death, Emperor Ming!' They said, 'How's that lovely daughter of yours?'

And the science was right. Space wasn't busy and noisy. It was full of dreadful, suffocating silence, and the sound of a human, breathing.

It was glorious, and we were so enthralled we spent several minutes just watching a spaceship dock with a space station. No explosions, no aliens, no guns at all. Just . . . grandeur, and technology turned into a ballet.

Sigh.

I remember that spaceship. We had proper spaceships in those days, not like the sort you get now.

Not that we actually get many now, come to think of it. I grew up expecting to see the first man land on the moon. It never occurred to me that I'd see the last one. We thought there'd be a moonbase. Then . . . onward to Mars!

The future was different back in 1968. Cleaner. Less crowded. And more, well, old-fashioned. We expect the future to be like a huge wave, carrying us forward. We expect to see it coming. Instead, it leaks in around our feet and rises over our heads while we are doing other things. We live in a science fiction world, and we haven't noticed.

Of course we didn't get the moonbase. That was because we realized that the Race for Space had been a mad bout of international willie-waving. So we left the exploration of space to a bunch of flying Lego kits and, instead, filled Earth orbit with dull satellites that do dull things.

Remember the trans-Atlantic phone calls, usually made at Christmas, which were a matter of a vast sum of money and a lot of technical negotiation? And then we spent a lot of time saying, 'It's dark here, is it dark where you are?' and marvelled at the fact that you could have two times at the same time. But recently I rang home while walking through Perth, Australia, to check that the cat was okay. I just dialled the number. It wasn't very exciting. I didn't even ask if it was dark.

The price of a very cheap video recorder now buys us a little GPS device that'll pinpoint us anywhere on the planet. You read *Longitude*? The sheer excitement of humanity trying to find out exactly where it is? A little black box now does the job better than the man with the sextant and the chronometer ever could. It's rather dull. Even my car knows where it is and in a pleasant voice, rather like HAL's sister, can navigate me through Swindon. We don't have to be lost any more.

Remember the weather forecasts? They used to be one step above a lottery, rather than a pretty good description of what's going to happen.

Dull, dull, dull. This stuff is all science fiction that has come true – Arthur C. Clarke is a keen and persuasive salesman for the benefits of satellite technology – and it has come true quietly and it has become humdrum. We hold in our hands a power that emperors dreamed of, and we say, 'It was only £69.95 because Dixons had a sale on.'

What's odd about the movie *2001* now? It's not 'Pan Am' on the side of the spaceship. Companies come and go. It's not Leonard Rossiter wandering around the space station, or the sixties style, all black and white and cerise. It's the lack of keyboards.

Dr Haywood Floyd is important enough to have a moon shuttle all to himself and he uses a pen? Where's the portable computer? Where's the handset? You mean he's not in constant communication? Why isn't he shouting, 'HELLO! I'M ON THE SHUTTLE!'? Why isn't he connected? The Bell videophone he uses in the movie? What? You mean they still have callboxes?

I'd have to stop and think before I could say how many computers we own, but the most amazing thing is that three . . . no, four . . . no, five of them, all miracles of technology by the standards of the sixties, lie unused in cupboards or stripped for parts because they are uselessly out of date. Like many other people, I suspect, I've got a few drawers full of cutting-edge technology that got blunted really quickly. Even I, easily old enough to be a grandfather (I could say to the kids, 'See that moon up there? We used to go there'), used them more or less instinctively. I grew up reading about this stuff. I suffer from the other kind of future shock: I'm shocked that we still don't have reliable voice recognition as good as HAL's, for example.

Science fiction certainly predicted the age of computers. Sooner or later, if you burrow deep enough in the piles of old magazines, you'll find it predicted more or less anything you want; if you fling a thousand darts at the board, some of them will hit the bull. There are even references to something that could be considered as the net. But what took us by surprise was that the people using the computers were not, in fact, shiny new people, but the same dumb old human beings that there have always been. They didn't – much – want to use the technology to get educated. They wanted to look at porn, play games, steal things, and chat.

We're not doing it right. We get handed all this new technology and we're just not up to scratch. And that's just as well, because the dream as sold is pretty suspect, too. It's a worldwide community, provided you use American English. It's a wonderful tool for business, if you're the right kind of business – that is to say, one that doesn't make anything except losses. It brings people together, if your idea of social intercourse is an in-basket full of spam written by people with the social skills of pig dribble. It's a wonderful education tool, if what you want to learn is how to download other people's work straight into your essay.

What we are, in fact, are electronic apemen. We woke up just now in the electronic dawn and there, looming against the brightening sky, is this huge black rectangle. And we're reaching out and touching it and saying, 'Is it WAP enabled? Can we have sex with it? Can you get it in a different colour?

Is it being sold cheap because the Monolith2 is being released next month and has a built-in PDA for the same price? Can we have sex with it? Look, it says here I can "Make $$$ a Month by Sitting on my Butt". Wow, can we use this for smashing pigs over the head? Hey, can we have sex with it?'

And like apemen trying out sticks and stones and fire for the first time, there's a lot of spearing ourselves in the foot, accidentally dropping rocks on the kids, acute problems in trying to have sex with fire, and so on. We have to learn to deal with it.

Where will it all take us? We don't know, because we're back to being apemen again. And if apemen try to second-guess the future, they'll dream of little more than killing bigger pigs.

We don't know what the new wave of technology is going to bring because it's still only up to our knees and we're not used to living in it, so we're trying and discarding ideas very quickly. Reading books off a screen? It doesn't seem to work for us. But electronic paper is already out there. Maybe you'd like just one book on your shelf, that looks and feels just like a book, but which could be any one of a thousand titles chosen from the little keypad on the back? That's still apeman thinking. There's nascent technologies out there that could give us the power of gods – at least, some of the more homely ones.

In the movie, the apeman throws the bone up into the air and it never comes down. Lucky for him. We've been throwing lots of bones into the air and they've been dropping all over the place, often where we can't see them until too late, and too often on other people. The tide is rising – literally, this time. More and more people are trying to occupy less and less ground. We're not killing off the planet. It has recovered from worse catastrophes than us. But the bones are coming back down with a vengeance, and we may not survive being not quite intelligent enough.

Shorn of the spaceships, the message in the movie is as relevant here as it was in that other future: what the apemen really need to do now is learn to become human. It would be a good idea to learn really fast, don't you think?

The God Moment

Mail on Sunday, 22 June 2008, headlined 'I create gods all the time'

I like the small gods. Like Anoia. And I think the Universe has meaning. It has a purpose. It might not be our purpose, but we're part of it.

The vicar when I lived in Penn was a Reverend Muspratt. He was quite posh for a clergyman – I think old ladies gave him a lot of money and a lot of tea. He came in one day through the scullery.* My father had brought back from Burma a bust of the Buddha and my mother really liked it. Reverend Muspratt pointed at it and said, 'That is a pagan icon.'

Even I, at that time, knew enough to know that anyone talking to my mum like that was in trouble. She threw him out on to the step.

---

* We had sculleries in those days. I like them.

I'm a kind of atheist — because, well, you never know. . .

There is a rumour going around that I have found God. I think this is unlikely because I have enough difficulty finding my keys, and there is empirical evidence that *they* exist.

But it is true that in an interview I gave recently I did describe a sudden, distinct feeling I had one hectic day that everything I was doing was right and things were happening as they should. It seemed like the memory of a voice and it came wrapped in its own brief little bubble of tranquillity. I'm not used to this.

As a fantasy writer I create fresh gods and philosophies almost with every new book (I'm rather pleased with Anoia, the goddess of Things That Get Stuck In Drawers, whose temple is hung about with the bent remains of egg whisks and spatulas. She actually appears to work in this world, too). But since contracting Alzheimer's Disease I have spent my long winter walks trying to work out what it is, if anything, that I really believe.

I read the Old Testament all the way through when I was about thirteen and was horrified. A few months afterwards I read *The Origin of Species*, hallucinating very mildly because I was in bed with flu at the time. Despite that or because of that, it all made perfect sense. As soon as I was allowed out again I went and borrowed the sequel and even then it struck me that Darwin had missed a trick with the title. If only a good publicist had pointed out to him that *The Ascent of Man* had more reader appeal, perhaps there wouldn't have been quite as much fuss.

Evolution was far more thrilling to me than the biblical account. Who would not rather be a rising ape than a falling angel? To my juvenile eyes Darwin was proved true every day. It doesn't take much to make us flip back into monkeys again.

The New Testament, now, I quite liked. Jesus had a lot of good things to say and as for his father, he must have been highly thought of by the community to work on wood – a material that couldn't have been widely available in Palestine.

But I could never see the two testaments as one coherent narrative. Besides, by then I was reading mythology for fun, and had run into Sir George Frazer's *Folklore in the Old Testament*, a velvet-gloved hatchet job if ever there was one. By the time I was fourteen I was too smart for my own god.

I could never find the answers, you see. Perhaps I asked the wrong kind of question, or was the wrong kind of kid, even back in primary school.

I was puzzled by the fact that, according to the hymn, there was a green hill far away 'without a city wall'. What was so unusual about a hill not having a wall? If only someone had explained . . . And that is how it went – there was never the explanation.

I asked a teacher what the opposite of a miracle was and she, without thinking, I assume, said it was an act of god. You shouldn't say something like that to the kind of kid who will grow up to be a writer; we have long memories. But I'd asked the question because my mother had told me about two families she knew in the east end of London. They lived in a pair of semi-detached houses. The daughter of one was due to get married to the son of the other and on the night before the wedding a German bomb destroyed all the members of both families who were staying in those houses in one go, except for the sailor brother of the groom who arrived in time to help scrabble through the wreckage with his bare hands. Like many of the stories she told me, this had an enormous effect on me. I thought it was a miracle. It was exactly the same shape as a miracle. It was just . . . reversed.

Did the sailor thank his god that the bomb had missed him? Or did he curse because it had not missed his family? If the sailor had given thanks, wouldn't he be betraying his family? If God saved one, he could have saved the rest, couldn't he? After all, isn't God in charge? Why does he act as if he isn't? Does he want us to act as if he isn't, too? (As a kid I had a very clear image of the Almighty: he had a tail coat and pinstriped trousers, black, slicked-down hair and an aquiline nose. On the whole, I was probably a rather strange child, and I wonder what my life might have been like if I'd met a decent theologian when I was nine.)

About five years ago that child rose up in me again, and I began work on a book, soon to see the light of day as *Nation*. It came to me overnight, in all but the fine detail.

It is set on a world very like this one, at the time of an explosion very like that of Krakatoa, and in the centre of my book, a thirteen-year-old boy, now orphaned, screams at his gods for answers when he hasn't fully understood what the questions are. He hates them too much not to believe. He has had to bury his own family; he is not going to give thanks to *anyone*. And I watched him try to build a new nation and a new philosophy. 'The creator gave us the brains to prove he doesn't exist,' he says as an old man. 'It is better to build a seismograph than to worship the volcano.'

I agree. I don't believe. I never have, not in big beards in the sky. But I was brought up traditionally C of E, which is to say that while churchgoing did not figure in my family's plans for the Sabbath, practically all the ten commandments were obeyed by instinct and a general air of reason, kindness and decency prevailed. Belief was never mentioned at home, but right actions were taught by daily example.

Possibly because of this, I've never *disliked* religion. I think it has some purpose in our evolution. I don't have much truck with the 'religion is the cause of most of our wars' school of thought, because in fact that's manifestly done by mad, manipulative and power-hungry men who cloak their ambition in God.

I number believers of all sorts among my friends. Some of them are praying for me. I'm happy that they wish to do this, I really am, but I think science may be a better bet.

So what shall I make of the voice that spoke to me recently as I was scuttling around getting ready for yet another spell on a chat-show sofa? More accurately it was the memory of a voice in my head, and it told me that everything was okay and things were happening as they should. For a moment, the world had felt at peace. Where did that come from?

Me, actually – the part of all of us that, in my case, caused me to stand in awe the first time I heard Thomas Tallis's *Spem in alium*, and the elation I felt on a walk one day last

February, when the light of the setting sun turned a ploughed field into shocking pink; I believe it's what Abraham felt on the mountain and Einstein did when it turned out that $E=mc^2$. I. It's that moment, that brief epiphany when the universe opens up and shows us something, and in that instant we get just a sense of an order greater than Heaven and, as yet at least, beyond the grasp of Hawking. It doesn't require worship, but, I think, rewards intelligence, observation and enquiring minds. I don't think I've found God but I may have seen where gods come from.

A Genuine Absent-minded Professor

Inaugural Professorial Lecture at Trinity College, Dublin, 4 November 2010

I like Trinity College. I hope to go there again one day, although they have someone new at the top these days, since Professor David Lloyd is now in charge at the University of South Australia – a very long way from Dublin. When they asked me to be a professor I said, 'Are you mad?'

They said, 'Yes. We're Irish.'

Ladies and gentlemen of the University, and distinguished guests.

Much to my astonishment, I find myself addressing you as your latest and most disreputable professor. Only a little while ago I couldn't even spell academic and now I am one.

I greet you as the author of the notorious Discworld series, written over three decades by a man with only one A-level to his name, and since that was for journalism, it probably doesn't count. Although, oddly, I am occasionally presented with evidence that I am the creator of academics; over the years I have received a fairly large number of letters from grateful parents telling me that their son, and it is usually their son, would not pick up a book at all until he found Discworld and suddenly started reading like a demon and is now tearing his way through university, and I get embarrassed, but cheerful when professors tell me that they recall lining up to have me sign a book when they were nineteen. Embarrassed and cheerful, that is, and feeling very, very old.

Tonight may be a very interesting experiment for all of us, because what you have done now, ladies and gentlemen, is gone and got yourselves a genuine absent-minded professor. It is common knowledge, because I took great pains to make it so, that I have a weird form of Alzheimer's called Posterior Cortical Atrophy, which I may describe as a topological version of the traditional disease. In short, I am topologically disadvantaged when it comes to complexities like revolving doors with mirrors, whereat I have to work hard to know if I'm coming or going, although in truth I have spent most of my life not knowing if I was coming or going. Putting on my pants in the morning, too, had also begun to be a problem until I realized that the solution was to turn the situation on its head and look at it from another direction; like all sensible men of my age I wear stout Y-fronts (I hope you're writing this down) but try as I might, the chances of getting them on right first time is 50-50. It's not that I don't know where the legs go, and they never end up on my head, but which way round they are, that's another story. It took some time to realize that there was no point in mucking about with the pants because somehow my eye/brain coordination has difficulty in deconstructing pants. Should the Y therefore be in the wrong place, i.e. back-to-front, just lower the damn things to the ground, walk around them and put them on again from the opposite direction – it works every time. Plus, of course, provides healthy exercise.

I make no apology for telling you this, especially since several elderly gentlemen hearing this confession will be thinking, 'Bloody good idea! I'll give it a try!'

However, I must, for the sake of exactitude, tell you that yesterday, which again started with a healthy stroll around my pants, I walked, correctly aligned in the groinal region, into my office where I worked on the second draft of my next book, and it was goddam literature, so it was, and by now I know when I am on improved form; I was nearly flying.

Usually, if there is no warm body to assist me with my early drafts, I dictate most letters by talking to my computer, something which comes so easily to anybody descended from chattering monkeys. It's not perfect, because Pratchett's First Law of Digital Systems is that when they are sufficiently complex they act very much like analogue systems and get ideas of their own. The situation is like riding a good-but-nervous racehorse: you learn when it's ready to gallop, and when you should slow down a little. Nevertheless, even if my touch-typing ability miraculously came back to me, I would still talk the stories, because stories should be spoken.

While I am here with you in Dublin I will be talking to young people – that is to say, younger than me – who, at the risk of their souls, wish to write for a living, and they all have a wonderful opportunity to find out that my writing, at least for the first draft, is entirely instinctive as I watch the movie in my head and only during the second draft do I close in on what I mean to say.

That reminds me: many years ago I said publicly that I didn't really know how I wrote, and would leave discussion of that (and I quote) 'to the clever buggers in universities', and it has since been quoted back to me by your Dean of Research, a decent guy, but in my opinion not fat enough for the position, with the observation that I was now one of those clever buggers! Officially! I was astonished, and indeed my whole life has been one of astonishment, as I shall now recount. . .

However, there has to be a regrettable caveat. PCA messes with the memory, and also makes it almost impossible to read from a written speech. Doing so means, if the speaker has a hope of holding the audience, that their gaze should flick effortlessly between the painstakingly written text and the audience themselves. I have been robbed of the power to do that. Therefore I shall endeavour to give my speech from memory and assisted by my estimable PA Rob Wilkins, with whom I have agreed that he will occasionally, given that we are all friends here, interject as he sees fit with comments like

'You didn't tell them about the hippopotamus, you daft old fart,' in which case I will have to say, 'Thank you for that but please remember next time that it is in fact "Prof Sir Daft Old Fart OBE, and Blackboard Monitor", thank you so very much.'

And why should I subject you to this charade? It is because it is the truth of the world and the world is growing older, and I am luckier, with my technology, than many others.

Twice, when I have spoken out on subjects like Alzheimer's and assisted dying, helpful Christians have told me that I should try considering my affliction as a gift from God. Now, personally I would have preferred a box of chocolates. Nevertheless, there may be some truth, a curiously convoluted truth, in that because it has made me look at the world, just like my pants, from a new perspective, which, according to G. K. Chesterton, is the role of fantasy anyway. And now I am living in a kind of fantasy, and I have found that growing within me is a steeliness that I never knew was there, a view of the world that might make Bob Dylan look like a man who was only slightly annoyed about the government. Whereas, not so long ago, I used to drift gently through the world, occasionally rebounding softly from the side. I began to open my eyes, which led to a terrible tendency to question authority, because authority that cannot be questioned is tyranny and I will not accept any tyranny, even that of Heaven.

Nevertheless, to question authority is not, in principle, to attack it, although authority always assumes that this is the case since authority must repeatedly establish its right to rule; and if this is done by force, then it turns out that it was a tyranny all along. Good heavens, I can't believe I am preaching this to an audience of Irishmen! Just think about it: a quarter of an hour of rational thinking and an Englishman turns into an Irishman.

Recently, an organization not far from where I live had to make some of its employees redundant. They were called into the office of some functionary who told them that, I quote, 'they were being deleted'. This did make the local news, but the most miraculous thing about it is that nobody, after being dealt with by a cyberman, punched the bastard's lights out and set fire to his desk. I would have stood their bail.

We live in a venal world run largely by men who count numbers and, because they can count people, they think people are numbers. We accept half-truths, we have learned to think that we must do what the government tells us, when in fact the truth of the matter is that the government should do what we tell it. Governments are scared. In England, unlike Ireland, where I gather you punch one another's lights out for fun and entertainment at both weddings and funerals, the government does not like to hold a referendum, because that would mean that stupid people, which is to say people who aren't politicians, would make the decisions which are better left to stupid and, as we learn more and more, dishonest politicians instead. They despise us until an election comes around when they pretend that they do not.

Meanwhile, in the Middle East, three peoples who hold dear to them the same God are at one another's throats. How stupid can one species be? And we will continue to be so stupid until we realize that the Iron Age is over. I write fantasy and I wouldn't have been able to come up with something like that.

It may not surprise you to know that I have some Irishness in my ancestry, but I suspect that everybody has, in the same way that we're all related to Charlemagne.

My mother, sadly no longer with us, had an Irish grandfather who told her stories as a girl and took delight in telling me how she passed them on to me when I was very young. I was too young to remember, but I sometimes suspect that many of those have lurked in the nether regions of my subconscious, waiting to burst out as soon as, to the dismay of the gods of literature, I got my hands on my first word processor. I am pretty certain that one of them surfaced in *Lords and Ladies*, because it has an indefinable Irish construction.

I owe a great deal to my parents. My mother watched me become a Knight, but do you know, she would have been even prouder to talk about 'my son, the professor'. They raised me with kindness and, where appropriate, a side order of brief and effective sternness and – may they be for ever blessed for this final consideration – without any religious upbringing whatsoever. To the best of my knowledge, neither of my parents as an adult ever went into a church with religious aforethought. I know that there was distant Catholicism in my mother's family, but only because once, when I was about six years old, I found a crucifix and, much to her amusement, came up to her holding it and said, 'Mum,

I have found a stick with an acrobat on it!' And although she did indeed never perform an act of worship that I was aware of, the acrobat followed her every house move and after her death I desperately tore my way through her possessions until I found him. He was actually in front of me as I wrote this lecture. I have always considered him an exemplar of mankind, but possibly regrettably *The Origin of Species* hit me before the Bible did.

As a child, I did not read for pleasure. Reading was associated with school and besides, I was always one step behind. A trait that has characterized my life, I feel. Starting with the fact that I was born late! It came as a shock, I can tell you, but not to my mother who had been lying there waiting for me for several hours after the apparently predestined time, or three damn hours as she put it to me some time later.

A few years on, when school days beckoned, the family was still on holiday and I missed my first day. And the First Day, as everybody knows, is the important day. That's when you make your friends and enemies and, more importantly, get your peg on which your raincoat will hang for the next three or four years. I might have got the tank! I could have been a contender for the soldier! I wouldn't have even minded the smiley sun and would have been happy with the purple dog but no, not me, I was left with the two damn cherries. And so I lagged, but you couldn't lag very much with my mum who taught me to read with love, care and affection – and when that didn't work, bribery, at a penny per page read perfectly, which subsequently turned out to be a very wise investment on her part, especially much later when they moved into their new house in quite a posh and sought-after location . . .

However, she made the mistake of educating me above my age. I recall, because it is in fact tattooed on my psyche, the day in the third or fourth form when the teacher asked us where the rain came from. It so happened that my mum had told me about the water cycle and how the seas evaporate gently into the sky and form clouds which are then blown over the land, get cooled down and fall as rain. Of course, all the smart kids, the ones with the pegs not marked by soft fruit, had their hands up and were making 'me miss, me miss' noises, but the teacher's eye lit upon the silly kid, who was the one raising his hand higher than any other child. And upon her surprised nod I triumphantly shouted out, 'The sea, miss!'

The result? The jeering of the class, egged on by the teacher, who hadn't even bothered to ask me why I said so. Even as a bewildered kid I was thinking in some kind of terrified puzzlement, 'Well, surely she can't believe that I don't know that it falls out of the sky, but she asked where it came from and I told her the truth.' There is a circle of Hell for teachers like that, and it's right next to the one set aside for teachers who don't like parents to teach their children to read before they go to school and one furnace away from people who believe that children should only be given books that are suitable for them, and I tell you what, it isn't big enough or indeed low enough. I didn't tell my mother, of course, because you never told your mother, just in case it got you into more trouble, but something began to seethe and grow, I'm sure of it. But still I pressed on. In my school, staff made the decision when you were six, based on your facility with reading, as to whether or not you would pass the old eleven-plus examination, the winners of which would go on to various grammar schools while the losers went to what were called the secondary moderns, where there was a wailing and gnashing of teeth, especially yours.

And because, despite my mother's efforts to teach me to read at all, I didn't pass that staff test, I was put among the goats rather than the sheep and that was the best thing that ever happened in my education, because I was a bright kid, even if a somewhat weird one, and with all the sheep pastured with the teacher who would get them through the examination I, the kid who was always halfway up the class, could suddenly become top with barely an effort. And as you know, when you're on top you want to stay on top, oh my, indeed you do. And so, for the first time, I really worked hard.

Around that time, while I was up in London with my parents an uncle gave me a copy of *The Wind in the Willows*, and I exploded. I'd never heard of books like this. Books were things that the teachers read to you out of, but here was this mole, who had a friend who was a rat, who had a friend who was a badger, and they all had a friend who was a toad, and not just any toad because this toad could drive a car and be mistaken for a washerwoman! And even I was pretty certain that while a washerwoman probably was not a contender for the Miss World contest she was unlikely to be mistaken for a toad.

I couldn't have expressed my feelings at that point, because

I didn't have the language for it, but now I would say that I realized with huge delight that the author was doing a number on us, messing with our minds, twisting the world! Where the hell can I get some more, I thought.

Incidentally, I remembered while writing this, that at the time I was concerned about the horse. Remember? The horse that pulled the canary-coloured caravan in the book? I recalled thinking as a child that all these animals can speak and don't have to go to work for a living, like my dad, whereas the carthorse does all the work, all the time, and doesn't have a voice. The momentary feeling I had then was pure socialism. And that is how I became a Saturday boy at the local public library, feverishly writing out another library ticket to myself every time there was a book I really wanted to read. And I read everything.

There was a sort of chain reaction: one book sends you on to another, and I read it, and went on to the next, without order, method or any plan, except possibly to read them all, and so I was reading Mayhew's *London Labour and the London Poor* at the same time as I was reading Tove Jansson's Moomintroll books and reading both these books in the same, as it were, mental tone of voice.

Some stuff I thought was rubbish, and probably was, but patterns emerged; taking down a book on the Silk Road, simply because it sounded interesting, channelled me on to the history that we didn't learn at school, not because the teachers were bad but because nobody had really thought about what education should be. I remember learning in school about the corn laws, but only vaguely remember what they were; but I do remember that they were a government cock-up to the detriment of the poor. So, no change there then! But the real history – the history that everyone should know – the beginnings of the earth, the dance of the continents, the journeys of mankind, the developments of science – these took little space on the curriculum, but thankfully were in abundance in the library, God bless it.

For me, my education in the library was like putting together a great big jigsaw puzzle of science fiction, history and palaeontology. I read up on them as if they were all part of the same thing which, in a holistic kind of way, they certainly were.

Another breakthrough came when I discovered second-hand bookshops round about the age of twelve; here were the books that no longer turned up on the library shelves, my local library in Beaconsfield being a spanking new library with spanking new books. But my dad told me there was a second-hand bookshop in the village of Penn, a short cycle ride away, although a difficult cycle ride when you're coming back with two full, creaking carrier bags of books hanging off the handlebars. It was a wonderful bookshop, it was where I learned humour.

I did this the easy way, although the easy way is often not at all easy. I read for pleasure every bound copy of the magazine *Punch* between 1840 and the mid 1960s. Why? Well, not to get a master class in humorous writing, but for fun. However, a master class was what I got because I read the best satirists and comic writers of a whole century, including Mark Twain and Jerome K. Jerome, whose laconic styles, it seemed to me, bore a similarity even though they were an ocean apart. Geoffrey Willans and Ronald Searle delighted me by producing the Molesworth series. Surely you know? The very best schoolboy humour in the books *Down with Skool!*, *Whizz for Atoms*, *How to be Topp* and *Back in the Jug Agane*. Then I began to absorb the columnists like Beachcomber, Patrick Campbell, Robert Robinson, and not least, certainly not least, Alan Coren – possibly, as far as observational humour is concerned, the king of them all.

I read all of these when I was, by the standards of the late fifties, still a child, but in doing so for sheer pleasure, I was pressing my foot hard down on the growing up button; I found humour has to be topical and so while reading those musty tomes of *Punch* I picked up, by osmosis, the topics, concerns and even the speech patterns of the millennia, which is money in the bank for a writer. I wasn't looking for ideas, techniques or, that terrible word, tips, I simply absorbed. Writers probably all do this in their separate ways, because it is hard to imagine an author who was not a reader first. I was astonished at the wealth laid out for me. I was learning from the masters and I thought about what I learned. In fact, I did not know it at the time, but a Satanic Mill had started turning in my head and eventually it would turn out a writer, but like every mill, it needed grist. (And if you don't know what grist is, look it up! You're supposed to be academics!)

I was particularly impressed by Alan Coren's grasp of the vocabulary of the average bewildered Englishman, but especially of what we used to call the working class. I know this because my London granny used to take me around the street markets and every single barker, shill, trader, hard bargainer, bus conductor and even my grandmother had a dialogue by Coren. A wonderful man.

I remember having a cheerful argument with my mum after my London granny told me that you could tell where a bus was going to because its name was on the front. My mother had taught me about the Greek myths and had mentioned the first marathon, run by Pheidippides – he ran from Marathon to Athens, as every schoolboy knows, well, used to – and I remember discussing with Mum the valid point that since he was running to Athens he was really running an Athens rather than a Marathon because, quite certainly, this would have been the case had he been employed by London Transport. A point which my mother graciously took without giving me a clip around the ear.

In accordance with the Satanic Mills, to make certain that I was constantly being surprised, the calendar that my mother and father, both working people, had to follow for their summer holidays meant that I also arrived at my secondary school, yes, one day late. And that's the day, if you remember and have been paying attention, they tell you everything important. It's no good coming in on the second day, because the second day is not the first day, and of course that's the day you learn the things you learn on the second day and once again the feeling I had that 'everybody knows something that I don't' reinforced my air, if air can be reinforced, of astonishment.

Obviously on that first day the secret of algebra had been

disseminated. Later on I would dream that I might understand algebra and have mastery of the world, but ten years
ago my friend Ian Stewart, Professor of Mathematics at
Warwick, sat down with me after a university dinner and
scrawled all over the napkins the sheer and obvious under-
standability of the basics of the quadratic equation, with
sweat beading on his brow, to which I sadly reacted with the
philosophical equivalent of the word *duur*. (I had to teach my
speech engine to understand the word duur, you know, yes, I
had to teach a computer to be dumb. A project for a rainy
afternoon.)

And so, once again I settled down to being halfway down
the class, doing enough schoolwork to survive, and no more.
My true education was still coming via the library, and amazingly from the science fiction books I was consuming like
sweets. Bliss it was in that space-age dawn to be alive, but
unfortunately my only reliable source of first-class second-
hand American science fiction magazines was called the
Little Library, and it was in a shack in Frogmoor, a tiny part
of High Wycombe, in which a very nice elderly lady dis-
pensed cheer, the occasional cup of tea and pornography.
However, in order to justify the name and presumably to
have some wares that she could put in the window, she also
sold decent SF and fantasy from second-hand cardboard
boxes, below, how shall I put it, the pinker shelves, which
were not at that time of particular attraction to me. How
could you turn your eyes upwards when there was a Brian
Aldiss that you hadn't read yet, and something by Harry
Harrison, and the third book in James Blish's *Cities in Flight*

trilogy? I consumed, and became such an habitué that I was guaranteed a cup of tea twice every week, after which I would leave with my satchel bulging, possibly to the bewilderment of any regular bystander, who might have been unaware of the SF booty I called my own.

I recall scrabbling around happily one day after school when the door was abruptly pushed open and in came a man who by the look of his efforts not to look like one was clearly, even to me, a plain-clothes policeman. He pointed angrily at me and demanded of my hostess, who was a dear old soul, 'What is he doing in here?'

Gleefully, she brandished a mint copy of Robert Heinlein's *Stranger in a Strange Land*, which I certainly was, and said, 'Honni swarky marley ponce, Geoffrey,' which, astonishingly, he didn't understand but seemingly accepted. And for those of you with little Latin, it broadly translates as 'He who sees any evil in this is a ponce'. Game, set and match to her, I fancy, and she was a decent soul, a nice friend to this kid that she considered was her only legitimate customer. She never encouraged me to become a patron of the pinker shelves, and nor did she offer me any of the slim envelopes which, when she thought I wasn't looking, she handed to the serious and somewhat furtive connoisseurs of the dirty raincoat persuasion, who were always embarrassed by my presence. I think at the time I thought they probably contained mint-condition, and therefore expensive, science fiction. (The penny dropped about a year later, when so did other things . . .)

She was a widow and I don't think I ever knew her name.

In a way she was one of my tutors because the growth of the author requires many varieties of compost and I needed that because I wasn't working at school and school wasn't working for me.

It was a decent school, the teachers were the usual bunch (usual at least in those days): some enthusiasts for their subject, some who could inspire, relics of the war, the needlessly sarcastic and, of course, the madman, the latter a general favourite with every boy in the school.

My fellow pupils, too, were from Central Casting, most with their eyes firmly on their A-levels and a good job, a few who shouldn't really have been there, the bully, the weird kid and the troublemaker, which was me.

It was the worst of times, it was the . . . no, let's stick with what we've got, it was definitely the worst of times, because I was the troublemaker. Picture the scene: the 1960s were moving sluggishly into High Wycombe and, regrettably, my headmaster considered himself a stalwart against sixties behaviour.

As a matter of fact, mostly the kids really just wanted to get their qualifications, just as I did. But when I brought in a copy of *Mad* magazine I was apparently a bad influence. Me! The kid who would spend so much time in the library that he would have to blink before he could get used to daylight again. I was astonished, and I have to say that *Mad* magazine in those days did some remarkably well-observed parodies of Broadway shows, often with a soupçon of harmless political humour and downright comic book fun, but to the headmaster it appeared to be a harbinger of the breakdown of society and indeed his society was under threat. But I just liked the magazine, and then on another occasion I was caught with a copy of *Private Eye*, apparently another crime against society. In fact, I was an amiable if somewhat talkative kid who liked reading anything and didn't even own a Bob Dylan record, making me possibly unique among my peers. In truth, Harry Ward was probably a good teacher, although I don't think that he was a good headmaster, or at least one who understood that adolescents were going to be, well, adolescents and very few of us were really any kind of a problem. We all carried a knife, a penknife, much better than a pencil sharpener if you had to do, as we did, a lot of technical drawing. I can only recall one occasion when one was actually proffered in a fight, and that was by the weird kid, who left shortly afterwards. But Harry made the classic mistake of the tyrant, seeing rebellion in the most innocent transgression, and transgression in the most innocent activity or none at all. I recall a boy I shall call Charles who had the misfortune to be born with an amiable disposition and a face which automatically composed itself into a cheerful grin. Its only other expression, as I recall, was a mild kind of sullen puzzlement when a cheerful grin got him into trouble. And so the suspicious atmosphere of the school meant that he was seen as either a clown or exhibiting dumb insolence. The influence of Harry got him coming and going.

As a natural idiot I was also in permanent trouble with the bully, because I preferred to use my voice in an argument and he preferred his fists, but a friend of mine from those days gleefully recalled to me the day when I lost my rag and ran at the kid down the length of the room, hitting him amidships so hard that he went down and cut his head open on an iron fireplace. After that I became apparently invisible to him; there wasn't any trouble. The schoolboy code was that short of murder you left authority out of it.

Recently a fellow pupil from those days told me that long after I had left (earlier than expected) he spoke as a sixth-former with the headmaster and learned that Harry had been affected by the dreadful scenes he had witnessed during the Second World War, and was sure that this contributed to the man's itchy trigger finger. I can't say.

Knowing now the theatre he had been in, I can sympathize, but how could I have done so then? Besides, I was at worst a clown, and by heavy-handedness the man created what had not been there in the first place. But I thank him *in absentia* for firming up my decision to quit school before taking my A-levels, a previously unthinkable occurrence. I knew I wanted to be a writer. I'd won a prize in a *Punch* competition, and sold two short stories to science fiction magazines. But being the son of my parents, I researched, and realized that the odds of making a living as a writer were, for practical purposes, zero, whereas a newspaper journalist gets paid every week. Still at school, and lined up for the head librarianship, I wrote to the editor of the local newspaper, the *Bucks Free Press*, asking if there was likely to be a vacancy in the following year, and he wrote back instantly saying, 'I don't know about next year, but we have a vacancy right now.'

Thanks to Harry Ward, I went to see him on the

following Saturday and on Monday walked to school and handed back all my school books, and left by the door that could only be used by prefects and visitors, a delightful sensation. The school could be a petty place, and my decision was prompted by the knowledge that Harry was publicly adamant that I could not have the prefectship that tradition-ally went with being the head librarian. I learned this by nefarious means. I had been spending every Thursday evening tidying up the library and repairing books, and this was an act of malice, sheer malice. Having been a prefect looks good on a CV, and might have come in useful; on the other hand, Arthur Church, editor of the *Free Press*, gave me the job right there in the interview. In recollection, he said, 'I like the cut of your jib, young man.' Did he really say that? It would have been in character. But remember, my sub-conscious is that of an author and a former journalist, and probably believes that every quote would benefit from a bit of a polish by an expert. As I believe Douglas Adams once said, sometimes after talking about yourself so often you're not exactly sure how real some things are.

The conditions of a trainee newspaper reporter in the mid-sixties were somewhere just above slavery; you could live at home and not be beaten with chains. On several occasions I worked every day of the week, including most evenings; and certainly Saturdays, especially in the summer, were seldom my own. There was a mystical beast known as the 'day off in lieu'. But it was seldom seen until later in my career. I was an apprentice, a genuine apprentice, my father even had to sign a copy of my indentures, a medieval-looking document. Basically, it sold my soul for three years, in return for which you were taught the rudiments, tricks, dirty jokes, suspicious folklore and clichés of local newspaper journalism. If Johnny Howe was your subeditor, you got all the dirty jokes very quickly, because Johnny was blessed with a wonderfully dirty mind; he needed it, oh yes indeed. A subeditor, on a local newspaper at least, needs a pin-sharp apprehension of every inadvertent double entendre. Did a correspondent once send in a report about a Women's Institute flower, fruit and vegetable show that actually included the bit about the naked man streaking through the marquee, 'causing disarray among the tarts before he was caught by the gooseberries'? Johnny, the spit and image of the late Stubby Kaye, looked me firmly and trustingly in the eye, and almost certainly, I suspect, lied. Any writer needs an eye for the double entendre in the same way that the gamekeeper has to have the mind of a poacher. The deliberate double entendre, on the other hand, is not to be sneezed at; I myself once perpetrated a treble entendre, and I suspect that if sufficient grant money could be made available, the quadruple entendre should not be beyond our grasp.

Whereas Johnny was short and fat, Ken Burroughs (called Bugsy behind his back), the saturnine news editor, was tall and thin, and when the two of them headed off down to the pub at lunchtime it looked like the number 10 going for a walk. Bugsy taught me to get my copy in on time, check my facts, and never to try to put one over on him. George Topley, Chief Reporter, and the best natural journalist I have ever met, taught me the uses of the truth and some useful secrets about human nature. And finally Arthur Church, local boy, editor of the local paper, who took the affairs of High Wycombe very seriously, taught me honesty and self-respect and not, if at all possible, to offend the Methodists. A decent man, the sixties were puzzling him in the same way as they did my recent headmaster, but the sixties were okay with Arthur provided they included High Wycombe. When the first Apollo mission to the moon sent back those glorious pictures of the Earth seen from its satellite, Westminster Press, owners of the paper, got hold of some of these and looked around desperately one Thursday to see which of their papers with colour capability was going to press soonest; and how they must have groaned when they worked out that somebody would have to ring up Arthur Church and tell him to clear the front page and two others at least. Probably, the Chiefs tossed a coin, but us reporters listening at his office door heard his agonized voice as he defended the interests of High Wycombe against those of the universe. And he had a point; every national newspaper next day would carry the pictures of the moon, but only one newspaper would carry the affairs, the important affairs, of High Wycombe, not to mention Marlow, Lacy Green, Loosely Row, West Wycombe and Speen. It was a Chestertonian moment, and there was no doubt that he was right, but although they were asking, he recognized an order in disguise after a fairly lengthy tussle, and we set to work clearing the decks while he walked about grumbling, very nearly in tears. After all, the moon was just a lump of rock, right? And then suddenly the issue was happily resolved in his mind as he beamed and said with good grace, 'Well I suppose the moon shines on High Wycombe just like everywhere else.' We nearly cheered!

Next day the *Bucks Free Press* sold out within minutes, even in Speen, and Arthur's phone was constantly off the hook because local dignitaries were ringing up to congratulate him on his wonderful coup. High Wycombe had approved! He very nearly bought us all a drink, he was so pleased.

The editors of local newspapers were – and probably still are, insofar as they still exist, many having given way to the useless and suspect local government 'information sheets' – often accused of parochialism. But a sense of the parochial is needed for the job. Everybody in the world knows how John F. Kennedy died; somewhat fewer would want to know about the demise of some luckless citizen found dead in his car, in his garage, with a pipe from the exhaust through a partly open window. Murder, probably not, suicide quite likely, but their town or neighbourhood should know the truth and in those days it was conveyed to them by me because I had sat there glumly in the coroner's court taking down the facts of the matter as deduced by the coroner in reasonably good Pitman's. We did not like to do it; people find many and varied ways to end their lives abruptly, and all of them are nasty, especially for those who have to deal with the aftermath – because suicide really needs practice, and there lies the problem. Pierrepoint the executioner knew how to hang a man swiftly, and knew how long the rope should be and where on the neck the knot should lie to ensure a merciful end. Most people don't. And one day, the relative of a particularly gruesome suicide asked the coroner to tell the newspapers not to publish the finding of the inquest. The coroner said, quite correctly, that we were entitled to be there by law, and all would have been well had he not added something on the lines of 'although I sympathize with you and sometimes I myself have wished that the press was at the bottom of the sea'.

Of course, we published that, and Arthur Church, who as I say took local journalism very seriously, wrote an eloquent defence of reporting even the nasty things. The gist of it was this, that it was in the public interest that the truth be known and known because it has been carefully reported and published. Without it, you are relying on the man in the pub, and rumour, possibly malicious rumour. If the local paper does for some reason get it wrong, then this would be known, and an apology and clarification would be made. This was not the best of all worlds, but better than the world of hearsay. Arthur laid this out very carefully and the coroner instantly apologized, handsomely, and honour was satisfied.

Arthur was a stickler for accuracy, and it was not a good day when some angry citizen came up the stairs on a Saturday to complain about some item, at least not if it truly turned out that the luckless reporter had got something wrong; if on the other hand investigation showed that the reporter was accurate, the aggrieved reader was courteously shown the door. And it wasn't only coroner's courts. Along with the other trainee, I travelled on a number of treacherous motorcycles to cover every possible civic event in the area, including the magistrates' courts, where I learned a lifelong cynicism regarding the processes of the justice system. Regrettably, I also learnèd that elderly ladies are sometimes inexorably fond of wearing directoire knickers, the tutor in this case being a magistrate, a lady of the shires, who liked to sit with legs apart, possibly without realizing there was no modesty panel. I sometimes wonder now if she was ever puzzled why people never looked directly at *her*? Indeed, on occasion, it seemed that every man in the courtroom was staring at his shoes, including the lawyers.

Often I have been contacted by internet journalists for an interview or some extended comment and the moment they say that they are a journalist I say, 'Good, tell me the six defences for defamation of character?' I am slightly cheered these days that some know what I am talking about. I am still quite proud of my Pitman's and my indenture.

I was a decent local journalist and well informed and accurate to boot, but when it came to the hurly-burly of the large regional or national newspaper, I just wasn't in contention, I just didn't have the killer instinct, as editor Eric Price perceived when he sacked me from the *Western Daily Press* in Bristol. He was not a happy man if the story as discovered was not the story he wanted, and indeed the *Western Daily Press* appeared on the CVs of many a young journalist that Eric had hired and fired. On the other hand he was kind enough to say much later that I had been the best writer they had. Possibly that was true because I did have, and hopefully still have, the ability to somehow apprehend a topic and write a coherent, informed and readable column about it within half an hour, possibly with the help of one telephone call and a newspaper clipping.

Why am I telling you these disjointed anecdotes? I suppose that it shows how an author is built. Quite a lot of my history found itself scrubbed up, repainted and part of a book. I am pretty certain, for example, that a keen, clever academic bugger could map the wizards of Unseen University to the staff of High Wycombe Technical High School from the late fifties onwards; not all of them got eaten by dragons. Indeed, some of them, including the head of history who I really liked, have been immortalized in print. In the scenery of my books I see the little village where I grew up. Characters speak who remind me of my grandmother and it seems that the mill fondly grinds up every experience, every encounter, and never, ever switches off. And sometimes I detect the influence of my tutors, even if they didn't know who they were. Nevertheless, the grinding mill gives something back.

A few days before I wrote this piece, a friend recounted to me that she had met a brigadier who had discovered the Discworld books in Afghanistan, several in a neat pile. I know about this sort of thing; quite often a squaddie will make contact saying, 'We get told to shift immediately and leave everything inessential', and regrettably it turns out that reading matter counts as a non-essential. But the brigadier taking cover had picked up one of the books and became hooked, I'm pleased to say. Apparently he said to her, 'How does he do it? He hasn't been a soldier, and *Monstrous Regiment* was written by somebody with a deep knowledge of the military, stuff you don't get out of books. So, how does he do it?'

Well, I think I know, because I believe it is the same little discovery which allowed me to win the Amelia Bloomer Award for Feminist Writing in the USA . . . twice. I don't need to explain, because a little thought will bring up the answer.

For the whole of my life since I was nine years old I have enjoyed words, not necessarily words organized, simply some words all by themselves, such as conundrum and onomatopoeia and susurration, words that somehow seemed to speak back. I care for words and their meanings and sometimes stick up for them in a way that the Blessed Lynne Truss would understand, like screaming at the local news on television 'If a policeman "said how he saw the suspect", then he is either describing the position he took in order to observe, or he was giving a very brief lecture on optics.' The word really wanted was 'that'.

Pedantic? Well I am an academic now. And besides, the argument that such bothering about matters of usage is elitist – a view espoused by Stephen Fry, a man with elite written all over him – is a load of dingo's kidneys. Wouldn't you expect a lover of music to wince at a wrong note? Work it out yourself. Words turn us from monkeys into men. We make them, change them, chase them around, eat them and live by them – they are workhorses, carrying any burden, and their usage is the skill of the author's trade, hugely versatile. There are times when the wrong word is the right word, and times when words can be manipulated so that silence shouts. Their care, feeding and indeed breeding is part of the craft of which I am a journeyman.

I will finish by leaving you with a word that I would like to see totally expunged from the English language. Ladies and gentlemen, may I suggest you let fun out of your lives? For it is, brothers and sisters, a mongrel word, an ersatz word, a fast-food bucket of a word! What does it mean? Consider the shameful usage: 'I was doing it for a bit of fun', or 'I thought it would be fun', or 'I was only having fun' and, worst of all, the little bit of white on the top of this chicken dropping, 'Are we having fun yet?'

Why have fun when you could have enjoyment, amusement, entertainment, diversion, relaxation, sport, a bit of a lark, and satisfaction and probably contentment.

Fun pretends to be about enjoyment, but is merely about the attempt. In search of fun, people pull themselves towards places that advertise fun, but they are probably to be avoided, since, in my recollection, fun means trudging around a soaking wet seaside town wearing plastic raincoats that, no matter what you do, always smell of fish. All right, maybe I'm only having fun with you? But these islands of ours have the richest language in the world, mostly because we stole useful words from everybody else, besides frantically inventing new ones ourselves.

So let's have fun with it; you never know, it might be fun!

Thank you, ladies and gentlemen.

Saturdays

'Britain in a Day: Terry Pratchett describes his typical Saturday', *Radio Times*, 12 November 2011

Wake up. This is essential. It's a Saturday, traditionally a day of rest for many people, but for me there are only two types of day: the days when my PA, Rob Wilkins, is in; and those when he isn't.

Generally speaking, I write every day of the week, subject to family considerations, and today I am writing a first draft of a new book, which is fun, and so I lie in bed, cheered by the click of the kettle and ready for the first cup of tea of the day. Then into the bathroom, shower, trim moustache, and sort out the morning' pills, mostly concerned with blood pressure, now quite under control.

Of the other three, one copes with the occasional bout of sciatica and the other two stand between me and the inexorable progress of Alzheimer's.

And since I am a man in his sixties, some of the mental

space at this time of day is directing venom against the drug companies that hermetically package their wares in plastic and metal laminations, which require weightlifter strengths and a safety net to disgorge them, instead of the little pill-boxes that everybody could open without resorting to scissors.

I discuss plans for the day with Lyn, my wife, then attack *The Times* while finishing a bowl of the bowel-scouring muesli that, I am assured, must be doing me some good. Then out to feed the chickens and other creatures on a beautiful late autumn day.

Apart from the vegetable garden, which is sacrosanct, we run the property for the wildlife, by and large, which means we get hedgehogs and, in our barn, barn owls. Everything's a bit scruffy, but it's such a wonderful day that you have to be glad to be born and don't even mind other people having been born either.

And then, as P. G. Wodehouse might have said, it's Ho! for the chapel, the grandiose name for the building that combines my study and library where the computers will get fired up and some writing will ensue.

Oddly enough, Saturdays and Sundays are good days for a writer like me; weekdays are so often punctuated with phone calls it's easy to forget that you are supposed to be working on a book, and even though *Snuff*, my latest book, is out there and in the public domain, there is still some PR activity that I must attend to in the strange, postnatal world that an author slides into when the latest baby is snatched away.

Of course, the cure for this is to start writing something else, but for the sake of my health, and my eyesight, I periodically put on something warm and go outside to chop logs, which is very satisfying, with a nice little curry at lunchtime.

A walk in the afternoon, which is never predictable because here in the countryside you are bound to meet people you know, and the etiquette of the countryside means you should stop and chat.

After that, feed the chickens for the second time, do a bit of gardening while the light allows, possibly back up to the chapel to read the emails (and ignore them! This is the weekend for heaven's sake!) and, eventually, back to the house for the rest of the evening.

We have a vast repository of old DVDs, so, if we're not going out or have other plans, we pick one we haven't played for some time. The absolute rule, however, is that I must always catch the news at 10 p.m. I was a journalist once and the stain never leaves you.

The last act of the day is a kitchen full of cats clamouring to be fed and then upstairs, shower, then bed – a fourposter, sufficiently big that we both have room to stretch out. Wonderful. A quiet day this, with time to think and enjoy life. Nothing much has happened, and sometimes that's a really good thing. I'm glad that there are days like this.

Days of Rage

On Alzheimer's, orangutans, campaigns, controversies, dignified endings and trying to make a lot of things a little better

On Excellence in Schools

Education: what it means to you

Department for Education and Employment,
July 1997

*[Alongside this piece by Terry were contributions from a dozen
other figures – including Trevor McDonald, Keith Waterhouse,
Carol Vorderman, Arthur C. Clarke and Stephen Hawking]*

*Much I learned at school didn't do me any good. They did it in
the wrong way – imagine, for example, giving* Pride and
Prejudice *to teenage boys! There were so many other things they
could have done.*

First, you build a library, then build the school round it. You
make sure that the kids can read adequately, write coherently
if simply, and at least have a good enough grasp of simple

maths to know when a pocket calculator is lying. Then you show them how to use the library, and you *don't* let them loose on the net until they *can* read and write and have grown up enough not to confuse data with information, otherwise they're just monkeys in a banana plantation.

And don't forget workshops and studios. I met a skilled draughtswoman who never had the chance to find out what she was good at until, on a no-hope work experience placement, she ended up making the tea in a drawing office where, one day, she took an interest . . . There must be many like her out there. Tens of thousands of people never find out what their talent is. Where else are they going to find out but at school?

The Orangutans Are Dying

Mail on Sunday Review, 20 February 2000

*This was written a few years ago. How have things changed?
There have been small victories achieved by patience and careful
negotiation, and my hat – all my hats – are off to the people who
have engineered them.*

*Even so, the central facts don't change. The orangutan needs
the forest. A lot of forest. And humans want it, too, both for
what it can make and what's left when it's been felled. You don't
have to be much of a pessimist to wonder about the likely life of
the species as a truly wild creature. A field here, a plantation
there . . . and eventually, the apes will have nowhere to retreat
to except the reserves. That's around the time we'll need a
miracle.*

Maybe half of them went in the last ten years. In another
ten, unless there's a miracle, look for them only in zoos and a

few parks. And this is one of our relatives I'm talking about here. There may be as few as 15,000 of them left. That's the fan base for a third-rate football club.

Forget all that stuff about how much DNA we share. It does not mean a lot; we share quite a lot of DNA with rats, and more with goldfish than you may think. Orangutans are like us. They are intelligent. They use their imagination. They think and solve complex problems. They have personalities. They know how to lie. It's simply that their ancestors stayed in the trees while ours climbed down to tough it out on the plains.

We're going back to the trees now. We're going back with chainsaws. A few years ago all I knew about orangutans was that they were the sad ones sitting with a piece of cardboard on their heads down at the duller end of the primate house. Then, in one of the early books of the Discworld series, I created a librarian who was an orangutan. I did it because I thought it would be mildly amusing. As a piece of creativity it took me all of fifteen seconds. Sorry, but it really did. There was no lifelong fascination, no point to make. It was just a joke. On a different day, the Librarian would have been an aardvark.

The series became inexplicably popular, the Librarian caught the imagination of the readers, one librarian praised me for 'raising the status of the profession' and various organizations started paying me money to go and talk to them. This embarrassed me somewhat, until I heard about the Orangutan Foundation.

I rang them up. I said, 'I seem to be getting all this money, would you like it?' A cautious voice said, 'Yes?'

Then it got serious. I became a Trustee. I sit in at meetings in London in a state of either despair or anger. Sometimes what I hear makes me want to slit my wrists, but often it makes me long to slit someone else's.

The Foundation is a support organization for the work of Dr Birute Galdikas at Camp Leakey in Tanjung Puting. She has spent thirty years studying orangutans in the wild, but increasingly she has had to work to ensure that there are any left to study. When I visited her at the camp six years ago, to do a short film, there was still some optimism, some feeling of bridges built, contacts made, some hope that with goodwill all round there was a way that apes and men could coexist.

I have an affliction peculiar to lifelong journalists. In some circumstances I get detached and go into a sort of 'Record' mode. Then I go and write things down, and the mental film is developed, as if writing things down makes them real.

I remember every detail of my visit like a jewel. I'm damn sure I wouldn't have felt the same about aardvarks. I remember that the eyes of orangutans are the eyes of people, in a way that the eyes of dogs and cats are not, and how the orangutans would pinch the soap and go and wash themselves in the river, and how the camp's motorboat had to be anchored in mid-stream because one young male was taking too intelligent an interest in how to start the engine. I remember the gentle feel of a hand that could have crushed every bone in mine.

And I remember that when I left Borneo there were also long, long rafts of logs floating down the Sekonyer River, and a smell of smoke in the air.

Things have got worse, not better. The orangutans are dying out because the rainforests of Indonesia are being killed.

More than half the timber coming out of Borneo and Sumatra is illegally logged. Even national parks are not safe. A few weeks ago illegal loggers trashed the headquarters at Tanjung Puting National Park. When you're big enough, and powerful enough, and pay the right people, you can do what you like. Greed and corruption are calling the shots.

As they say in Borneo: 'It's illegal – but it's official.'

Oh, there have been successes. They have been achieved by careful and patient negotiation, like tap-dancing on quicksand, and I take off my hat to the people who have done it.

But since my visit and despite all the efforts, the orangutans are still losing. It was hoped that the new Indonesian government could reverse the trend, but nothing in Indonesia is ever straightforward. People like me, who aren't patient, wonder what good a National Park is as a refuge when it is just another source of timber.

The Foundation is even sponsoring additional patrols of local people to support the understaffed park rangers. It is the sort of initiative that was never envisaged when it was set up. It has taken some very delicate negotiation. They cannot be seen to be interfering with the internal affairs of a sovereign country. So no weapons will be involved. In truth, the park is not as uncivilized as, say, some parts of Los Angeles, so not even the bad guys are using guns. But the illegal loggers have quite big machetes and a certain insouciance. The rangers have. . . er . . . well, they have right on their side. Presumably, in a tight corner, they can use harsh language.

This is hardly ideal, but it may help impress on local people that the orangutans are themselves a resource. It is the 'eco-tourism' argument. How much would you pay to see orangutans in the wild, especially if you knew the money was helping to preserve their forest? Currently it's about 12p, the cost of a day ticket into the park, and they throw in the birds and trees for free. There's a bit of scope there, I think.

Unfortunately, what looms is something worse than logging. There has always been logging, legal and illegal. Loggers come and go. The forest can heal, in time.

It's plantations that are now the big and growing problem. Vast tracts of former forest are taken over for agribusiness with the help of foreign investment. They grow palms for palm oil, and a species of acacia to feed new woodpulp mills. This is a profitable business, but it means that the forest can't return. There is nothing for the apes in these barren tree factories.

We benefit, even if we don't realize it. The pulp makes paper, the trees make everything from chipboard to your nice hardwood doors. We can try to shop conscientiously, but that is getting harder to do.

We live in a global economy now and, increasingly, the apes don't. They are being pushed to the edges, and they're running out of edges. I can't crack a joke about that.

We made a big fuss over the possibility of microbes on Mars. If orangutans were Martians we'd cherish them, we'd be so amazed at how they're like us but not like us, they'd be invited to tea and cigars at the White House.

But they're apes, sad in zoos, funny in movies, useful in advertisements and in fantasy books, I'm almost ashamed to say, but at least the Discworld's Librarian has done his bit for the species and caused more than a few bob to flow their way. But the problem, unfortunately, is not money. The problem is lots of money.

A million years ago the orangutans watched Java Man walk into Indonesia. Perhaps there are only a few years left now before we watch the last orangutans ushered into their domes or cages or enclosed parks to live out their lives in a simulacrum of the real world. They will be ghosts, because an orangutan needs the forest like a fish needs the sea.

All this for cheap paper and exotic doors.

Unless, of course, you believe in miracles.

The NHS is Seriously Injured

News of the World, 17 August 2008, headlined
'I'm disgusted. I can get Viagra on NHS,
but not a drug to help my Alzheimer's'

*Initially, my GP told me I didn't have Alzheimer's, but I knew
something was going wrong, so I spoke to her again and she sent
me to a specialist. Then, after I was diagnosed, it turned out
there was something I could take to help, but I was too young to
be given it on the NHS – so that was why I first started kicking
around, and I spoke about what was happening.*

The NHS is seriously injured.

Alzheimer's is a particularly unpleasant and feared
disease. I don't know anyone who's got better from
Alzheimer's.

It strips away our humanity a little bit at a time so you
hardly notice and until you end up a vegetable.

But a drug called Aricept can slow the progress of the disease, and the good news is it costs just £2.50 a day.

The bad news is there are 400,000 Alzheimer's sufferers in the UK so Aricept has been ruled out for NHS use in the mild stages of the disease everywhere except Scotland.

In Scotland Alzheimer's sufferers with the mild form of the disease can actually get the drugs and I think that's a lovely way to run a health service. There is a two-tier NHS, in fact – the Scottish one and the English one. More on that later.

I'm a millionaire so I have no trouble paying, but there are people who can't.

I think it's a sufficiently unpleasant disease to be worth the £2.50 a day Aricept costs.

My wife and PA both noticed real changes in me after two or three months on it. I used to fumble with buttons and needed help with seat belts. Now, I get dressed normally and seat belts slide in first time. Mentally, it's the difference between a sunny day and an overcast day. Ye gods, that's worth it!

I was diagnosed nine months ago. I'm still some way from sixty-five, which makes me 'early onset'.

There are much younger early onset patients than me, and I'm particularly angry on their behalf because, while getting Alzheimer's feels like an insult anyway, the younger you are the more insulting it is. It hits people who may have dependants both younger and older than them, and who are also trying to hold down a job.

I can still work at home and control my environment, and

my rare variant of the disease is not yet a real burden. The novels turn up as they always have – only the typing is hard. There will now be a moment when the letter A, say, vanishes. It's as if the keyboard closes up and the letter A is not there any more. Then I'll blink a few times and concentrate and it comes back.

I've handed in my driving licence – if my brain won't let me see that A, it might not let me see the child on the pedestrian crossing. Unlikely, at this stage, but who would risk it?

I know I am luckier than many others, older and younger, who find paying £1,000 a year a big problem.

And I can afford a voice recognition program for the computer. There's no way I'm going to retire, I'll be writing until I die. It's my passion.

I have other people who can drive me. In the circumstances, I am lucky so far. I didn't think so last November when I was told I had PCA, a rare form of Alzheimer's which affects the back of the brain. I was offered no form of treatment when I was first diagnosed. One local specialist wasn't familiar with PCA so couldn't take me on and I wasn't old enough to go to the other local man who would only deal with patients over sixty-five.

It wasn't their fault, but when I heard this I felt totally exposed and alone.

Hell, I thought, it must be easier to score dope off Fat Charlie behind the bus station than get my hands on Aricept (I made him up, as far as I know).

I didn't have to go that far. For several months I got

Aricept on an ad hoc basis from a private doctor until I wound up with a great specialist in Bath.

And I stood up and said I had Alzheimer's. I didn't expect all the fuss, or my mailbox to melt. Good grief, you write best-sellers for twenty-five years in a kind of welcome obscurity, then you catch one lousy disease and every chat show wants to talk to you.

And I became what they call 'politicized'.

The decisions on who can get which drugs on the NHS are made by the National Institute for Health and Clinical Excellence (NICE), which appraises whether treatments should be considered worthwhile by the NHS.

I would very much like to know the basis on which these decisions are made because some of them don't seem to make very much sense. It is interesting to note I could get Viagra for free. I'm not too certain it's the State's job to provide Viagra.

Even cancer can increasingly, with luck, be survived. For me there is no cure. Alzheimer's is an unstoppable, as yet, process of dying by degrees.

It is not all the fault of NICE, although they have few friends these days. But we have to have a very good look at what has really become a kind of ad hoc NHS which leads, for example, to glaring differences in provision between England and Scotland, and the despicable row over co-payments.

Co-payments, which are banned, are when a patient pays privately for a drug not funded by the NHS but continucs to get the basic NHS care. I would like the NHS to take a serious look at this whole scandal because by banning co-payments they hit at people like my parents, who were frugal and saved and put money by and did all those things that once upon a time were fashionable for people to do.

I see nothing wrong with people purchasing extra medical care. It's really no different from people choosing to buy cars and houses. People decide what to do with their money. It's not fair to punish people who can afford to pay for a non-NHS drug that will help their treatment, but who might not be able to afford to pay for all their medical care.

The NHS was never expected to be what it has become. It was going to give us our glass eyes, our wooden legs and our false teeth and inoculate us against things and then it would just deal with trauma.

We now have cures unthinkable when I was born. Within a generation there will, I believe, be Alzheimer's treatments that put the noble Aricept in deep shade.

They will not be cheap. How will the NHS cope? Our NHS that wants to penalize people who are prepared to pay for drugs the NHS won't give them? It is not even good Soviet thinking. It does not affect the rich, who can rise above it. But it hits at people who saved.

We already have a two-tier NHS service. You can already go to your doctor and then decide to go private for a lot of things. Your NHS dentist, if you have managed to find one, will charge you for various extras.

In the early days of the NHS it was not unknown for those people who had a bit of cash to sort of chip in for their treatment and everyone was very happy. What changed?

Now I know there are all kinds of problems associated with this. The NHS can now refuse to treat you if you pay for your own unilateral treatment. But we're humans not monkeys. We should be able to sort this sort of thing out sensibly.

More and more people are going private when they have a choice. The NHS is great for basic healthcare and emergencies, but can be pretty hopeless in the long haul.

Ah, yes, the long haul. It's a phrase from Australia, that most ferociously egalitarian of countries, where a public/private health system appears to work well.

I really think we have to decide what we want from the NHS – and what it is we're prepared to pay for, and what it is we're prepared to buy for ourselves.

The Baby Boomers, of which I am one, are getting older. They are not going to like old age under the current NHS.

There's a tsunami of patients coming and the NHS isn't prepared. There is going to be a bloody big row. It's starting already.

I'm slipping away a bit at a time
. . . and all I can do is watch
it happen

Daily Mail, 7 October 2008

On the day I was diagnosed with PCA, Rob asked me who we
should tell and I told him that I wanted to tell everyone. I was
angry. And it worked, it really worked. So many people were
writing to me, we couldn't keep up with the deluge.

I wish I could say I've changed things. I suppose I could
modestly say half a yes to that now. At the time I was diagnosed,
if you had Alzheimer's of any kind there was nothing you could
do, no one to ask for help, no golden path. I think after me, some
of that at least got a little better.

Seven hundred thousand people who have dementia in this
country are not heard. I'm fortunate; I can be heard.

Regrettably, it's amazing how people listen if you stand up in public and give away $1million for research into the disease, as I have done.

Why did I do it? I regarded finding I had a form of Alzheimer's as an insult and decided to do my best to marshal any kind of forces I could against this wretched disease.

I have Posterior Cortical Atrophy or PCA. They say, rather ingenuously, that if you have Alzheimer's it's the best form of Alzheimer's to have. This is a moot point, but what it does do, while gradually robbing you of memory, visual acuity and other things you didn't know you had until you miss them, is leave you more or less as fluent and coherent as you always have been.

I spoke to a fellow sufferer recently (or as I prefer to say, 'a person who is thoroughly annoyed with the fact they have dementia') who talked in the tones of a university lecturer and in every respect was quite capable of taking part in an animated conversation.

Nevertheless, he could not see the teacup in front of him. His eyes knew that the cup was there; his brain was not passing along the information. This disease slips you away a little bit at a time and lets you watch it happen.

When I look back now, I suspect there may be some truth in the speculation that dementia (of which Alzheimer's is the most common form) may be present in the body for quite some time before it can be diagnosed.

For me, things came to a head in the late summer of 2007. My typing had been getting progressively worse and my spelling had become erratic. I grew to recognize what I came to call Clapham Junction days when the demands of the office grew too much to deal with.

I was initially diagnosed not with Alzheimer's but with an ischemic change, a simple loss of brain cells due to normal ageing. That satisfied me until the next Clapham Junction day. I went back to my GP and said I knew there was something more going on.

Fortunately, she knew well enough not to bother with the frankly pathetic MMSE test (the thirty-point questionnaire used to determine brain function) and sent me to Addenbrooke's Hospital in Cambridge, where, after examination of my MRI scan and an afternoon of complex tests, I was diagnosed with PCA, an uncommon variant of dementia, which had escaped the eagle eye of the original diagnostician.

When in *Paradise Lost* Milton's Satan stood in the pit of Hell and raged at Heaven, he was merely a trifle miffed compared to how I felt that day. I felt totally alone, with the world receding from me in every direction, and you could have used my anger to weld steel.

Only my family and the fact I had fans in the medical profession, who gave me useful advice, got me through that moment. I feel very sorry for, and angry on behalf of, the people who don't have the easy ride I had.

It is astonishing how long it takes some people to get diagnosed (I know because they write to me). I cannot help but wonder if this is because doctors are sometimes reluctant to give the patient the stigma of dementia since there is no cure.

I was extremely fortunate in my GP. I think she was

amazed to find that of the two specialists in my area, one had no experience of PCA and therefore did not feel he could help me and the other would only take on patients over sixty-five – at fifty-nine I was clearly too young to have Alzheimer's.

I remember on that day of rage thinking that if I'd been diagnosed with cancer of any kind, at least there would have opened in front of me a trodden path.

There would have been specialists, examinations, there would be, in short, some machinery in place.

I was not in the mood for a response that said, more or less, 'Go away and come back in six years.'

My wife said: 'Thank goodness it isn't a brain tumour,' but all I could think then was: 'I know three people who have got better after a brain tumour. I haven't heard of anyone who's got better from Alzheimer's.'

It was my typing and spelling that convinced me the diagnosis was right. They had gone haywire. Other problems I put down to my looming sixtieth birthday.

I thought no one else had noticed the fumbling with seat belts and the several attempts to get clothing on properly, but my wife and PA were worrying. We still have the occasional Clapham Junction days, now understood and dealt with.

I have written forty-seven novels in the past twenty-five years, but now I have to check the spelling of even quite simple words – they just blank on me at random.

I would not dare to write this without the once despised checker, and you would have your work cut out to read it, believe me. On the other hand – and this is very typical of PCA – when the kind lady who periodically checks me out asked me to name as many animals as I can, I started with the rock hyrax, the nearest living relative to the elephant, and thylacine – the probably extinct Tasmanian marsupial wolf.

That's the gift or the curse of our little variant. We have problems handling the physical world but can come pretty close to talking our way out of it so you don't notice. We may have our shirts done up wrong, but might be able to convince you it's a new style.

I felt that all I had was a voice, and I should make it heard. It never occurred to me not to use it. I went on the net and told, well, everyone. I wish I could say it was an act of bravery. It wasn't and I find that suggestion very nearly obscene.

How brave is it to say you have a disease that does not hint of a dissolute youth, riotous living or even terrible eating habits? Anyone can contract dementia; and every day and with a growing momentum, anybody does.

It occurred to me that at one point it was like I had two diseases – one was Alzheimer's and the other was knowing I had Alzheimer's.

There were times when I thought I'd have been much happier not knowing, just accepting that I'd lost brain cells and one day they'd probably grow back or whatever.

It is better to know, though, and better for it to be known, because it has got people talking, which I rather think was what I had in mind. The $1million I pledged to the Alzheimer's Research Trust was just to make them talk louder for a while.

It is a strange life when you 'come out'. People get embarrassed, lower their voices, get lost for words. Part of the report I'm helping to launch today reveals that fifty per cent of Britons think there is a stigma surrounding dementia. Only twenty-five per cent think there is still a stigma associated with cancer.

The stories in the report – of people being told they were too young or intelligent to have dementia; of neighbours crossing the street and friends abandoning them – are like something from a horror novel.

It seems that when you have cancer you are a brave battler against the disease, but when you have Alzheimer's you are an old fart. That's how people see you. It makes you feel quite alone.

It seems to me there's hardly one family in this country that is not touched by the disease somehow. But people don't talk about it because it is so frightening. I swear that people think that if they say the word they're summoning the demon. It used to be the same with cancer.

Journalists, on the other hand – I appreciate that other people living with the disease don't get so much of this – find it hard to talk to me about anything else, and it dominates every interview: Yes, I said I had PCA ten months ago, yes, I still have it, yes, I wish I didn't, no, there is no cure.

I can't really object to all this, but it is strange that a disease that attracts so much attention, awe, fear and super-stition is so underfunded in treatment and research.

We don't know what causes it, and as far as we know the only way to be sure of not developing it is to die young.

Regular exercise and eating sensibly are a good idea, but they don't come with any guarantees. There is no cure.

Researchers are talking about the possibility of a whole palette of treatments or regimes to help those people with dementia to live active and satisfying lives, with the disease kept in reasonably permanent check in very much the same way as treatments now exist for HIV.

Not so much a cure therefore as – we hope – a permanent reprieve. We hope it will come quickly, and be affordable.

In the meantime we hope for Aricept, which is not a cure but acts as a line of sandbags against the rising tide of unknowing. However, it is available free only to those in the moderate stages of the disease; others must pay £1,000 a year, which I do.

Eligibility is determined by the MMSE questionnaire test, and it would be so easy for a patient in the mild stage to cheat their score into the free zone that I take my hat off to those too proud or responsible to do so. I cough up.

NICE says the change it makes at my stage is minimal, but we don't think so in our house, where those little changes make the difference between a dull day and a fine day.

The disease is, after all, about small changes, and it may be that individuals may indeed be individual.

And that is nearly it for hope at the moment.

When my father was in his terminal year, I discussed death with him. I recall very clearly his relief that the cancer that was taking him was at least allowing him 'all his marbles'. Dementia in its varied forms is not like cancer.

Dad saw the cancer in his pancreas as an invader. But

Alzheimer's is me unwinding, losing trust in myself, a butt of my own jokes and on bad days capable of playing hunt the slipper by myself and losing.

You can't battle it, you can't be a plucky 'survivor'. It just steals you from yourself.

And I'm sixty; that's supposed to be the new forty. The Baby Boomers are getting older, and will stay older for longer.

And they will run right into the dementia firing range. How will a society cope?

Especially a society that can't so readily rely on those stable family relationships that traditionally provided the backbone of care.

What is needed is will and determination. The first step is to talk openly about dementia because it's a fact, well enshrined in folklore, that if we are to kill the demon then first we have to say its name.

Once we have recognized the demon, without secrecy or shame, we can find its weaknesses.

Regrettably one of the best swords for killing demons like this is made of gold – lots of gold.

These days we call it funding. I believe the D-Day battle on Alzheimer's will be engaged shortly and a lot of things I've heard from experts, not always formally, strengthen that belief.

It's a physical disease, not some mystic curse; therefore it will fall to a physical cure. There's time to kill the demon before it grows.

Taxworld

What is an author to do when every other word he writes will be written for the Chancellor of the Exchequer?

Letter to *The Times*, 23 May 2009

Sir,

I am very definitely a high-rate taxpayer, although in self-defence I must admit I have become so simply by writing a lot of fairly harmless books over a very long time rather than by, for example, ripping the heart out of the financial system through unbridled greed.

So I am, therefore, somewhat peeved to find that, now, slightly more than every other word I write will be written for the Chancellor of the Exchequer, who will undoubtedly waste the money on computers that don't work and other people's duck shelters.

I have been enormously buoyed up, though, by hearing

from journalists and other pundits that 'the rich won't end up paying the 50 per cent income tax because their smart accountants will find a way around it'. When I put this to my own accountant, a senior member of a reputable London firm, he laughed and said: 'Unless you want to go and live abroad for a very long time, or associate with some extremely unsavoury people, or invest in risky tax schemes, then for someone like you there is really nothing that can be done.'

I assume he knows his stuff and the tax authorities know theirs, so why is this bland assertion repeated so regularly?

Sir Terry Pratchett
Salisbury, Wilts

PS. I have no intention whatsoever of moving to a firm of disreputable accountants.

Point Me to Heaven When the Final Chapter Comes

Mail on Sunday, 2 August 2009

I'm all for assisted death. Of course there are people who are against it, but they come up with the wrong reasons, such as 'God doesn't like it' and so on. Personally, I really don't think God is all that bothered, but I would like to think that my god would be more concerned about unnecessary suffering. Who knows.

We are being stupid. We have been so successful in the past century at the art of living longer and staying alive that we have forgotten how to die. Too often we learn the hard way. As soon as the Baby Boomers pass pensionable age, their lesson will be harsher still. At least, that is what I thought until last week.

Now, however, I live in hope – hope that before the disease in my brain finally wipes it clean, I can jump before I am pushed and drag my evil Nemesis to its doom, like Sherlock Holmes and Moriarty locked in combat as they go over the waterfall.

In any case, such thinking bestows a wonderful feeling of power; the enemy might win but it won't triumph.

Last week a poll revealed that more than three quarters of people in Britain approve of assisted suicide for the terminally ill.

On Thursday, the Law Lords delivered the landmark judgement in a case brought by multiple sclerosis sufferer Debbie Purdy, who feared her husband would be prosecuted if he accompanied her to die abroad.

She wanted the law on assisted dying to be clarified and the Law Lords have now ordered the Director of Public Prosecutions to draw up policy spelling out when prosecutions would and would not be pursued.

It looks as though the Baby Boomers have spoken and some of them, at least, hope they die before they get old – well, too old. Some have seen what happened to their parents or grandparents, and they don't like it. Every day I remember my own father's death. The nurses were kind, but there was something very wrong about it.

The poll result arrived at about the same time as the Royal College of Nursing announced that it was ending its opposition to assisted dying. Other signs indicate that the medical profession as a whole is at least prepared to face the issue.

I hate the term 'assisted suicide'. I have witnessed the aftermath of two suicides, and as a journalist I attended far too many coroners' inquests, where I was amazed and appalled at the many ways that desperate people find to end their lives.

Suicide is fear, shame, despair and grief. It is madness.

Those brave souls lately seeking death abroad seem to me, on the other hand, to be gifted with a furious sanity. They have seen their future, and they don't want to be part of it.

But for me, the scandal has not been solely that innocent people have had the threat of murder charges hanging over their heads for committing a clear act of mercy. It is that people are having to go to another country to die; it should be possible to die with benign assistance here.

You do not have to read much social history, or move in medical circles, to reach the conclusion that the profession has long seen it as part of its remit to help the dying die more comfortably.

Victorians expected to die at home, undoubtedly assisted by the medical profession.

In those days there was no such thing as drug control – just as there was no gun control. Laudanum and opiates were widespread and everyone knew you could get your hands on them. Sherlock Holmes was one of them!

As a young journalist I once listened in awe as a ninety-year-old former nurse told me how she helped a dying cancer patient into the great beyond with the aid of a pillow. In the absence of any better medication in that time and place, and with his wife in hysterics at the pain he was forced to endure, death was going to be a friend; it was life, life gone wild, that was killing him.

'We called it "pointing them to Heaven",' she told me.

Decades later, I mentioned this to another, younger nurse, who gave me a blank look, and then said: 'We used to call it "showing them the way".'

Then she walked off quickly, aware that she had left a hostage to fortune.

I have been told that doctors do not like patients to worry that, theoretically, their GP has the expertise to kill them. Really?

I suspect that even my dentist has the means to kill me. It does not worry me in the slightest, and I imagine that, like many other people, I would be very happy for the medical profession to help me over the step.

I have written a living will to that effect, and indeed this article in the *Mail on Sunday* will be evidence of my determination in this matter. I cannot make the laws but you have no idea how much I hope those in a position to do so will listen.

In the course of the past few years, I have met some delightful people who say they have a passion for caring and I have no reason whatsoever to doubt them. Can they accept, however, that there are some people who have a burning passion not to need to be cared for?

It appears to be an item of faith with many people I have spoken to that both doctors and nurses, at least in hospital, still have 'things they can do' when the patient is in extremis.

I certainly hope this is true, but I wish we could blow away the clouds obscuring the issue and embrace the idea of ending, at their request, the life of a terminally ill person at a time and, if possible, a place of their choosing.

I write this as someone who has, regrettably, become famous for having Alzheimer's. Although being famous is all the rage these days, it's fame I could do without.

I know enough to realize there will not be a cure within my lifetime and I know the later stages of the disease can be very unpleasant. Indeed, it's the most feared disease among the over-65s.

Naturally, I turn my attention to the future. There used to be a term known as 'mercy killing'. I cannot believe it ever had any force in law but it did, and still does, persist in the public consciousness, and in general the public consciousness gets it right.

We would not walk away from a man being attacked by a monster, and if we couldn't get the ravening beast off him we might well conclude that some instant means of less painful death would be preferable before the monster ate him alive.

And certainly we wouldn't tuck it up in bed with him and try to carry on the fight from there, which is a pretty good metaphor for what we do now, particularly with 'old-timer's disease'. (My speech-to-text program persists in transcribing 'Alzheimer's' as 'old-timers'. In fact, I've heard many people absent-mindedly doing the same thing, and as a writer, I cannot help wondering if the perception of the disease might be a little kinder without that sharp, Germanic intonation.)

My father was a man well tuned to the public

consciousness. The day he was diagnosed with pancreatic cancer he told me: 'If you ever see me in a hospital bed with tubes and pipes all over me, then tell them to turn me off.'

There was no chance of that a year later, when medicine's defences had been used up and he was becoming a battle-ground between the cancer and the morphine.

I have no idea what might have been going through his head, but why did we have to go through with this? He had been told he had a year to live, the year was up, and he was a practical man; he knew why he had been taken to the hospice.

Why could we not have had the Victorian finale, perhaps just a week or so earlier, with time for words of love and good advice, and tears just before the end?

It would have made something human and understand-able out of what instead became surreal. It was not the fault of the staff; they were, like us, prisoners of a system.

At least my father's problem was pain, and pain can be controlled right until the end.

But I do not know how you control a sense of loss and the slow slipping of the mind away from the living body – the kind that old-timer's disease causes.

I know my father was the sort of man who didn't make a fuss, and perhaps I would not, either, if pain were the only issue for me. But it isn't.

I am enjoying my life to the full, and hope to continue for quite some time. But I also intend, before the endgame looms, to die sitting in a chair in my own garden with a glass of brandy in my hand and Thomas Tallis on the iPod – the latter because Thomas's music could lift even an atheist a little bit closer to Heaven – and perhaps a second brandy if there is time.

Oh, and since this is England I had better add: 'If wet, in the library.'

Who could say that is bad? Where is the evil here?

But, of course, important points are being made in this debate. Currently, people say they are worried about the possibility of old people being 'urged' by greedy relatives into taking an early death.

If we cannot come up with a means of identifying this, I would be very surprised.

In any case, in my experience it is pretty impossible to get an elderly person to do something they do not wish to do. They tend to know their own mind like the back of their hand, and quite probably would object to this being questioned.

There needs to be, for the safety of all concerned, some kind of gentle tribunal, to make certain that requests for assisted death are bona fide and not perhaps due to gentle persuasion.

It is the sort of thing, in my opinion, coroners could handle well. All the ones I have met have been former lawyers with much experience of the world and of the ways of human nature, people with wisdom, in fact, and that means middle-aged at the very least, and old enough to have some grasp of the world's realities.

I have no way of knowing whether any of them would wish to be involved; this is breaking new ground and we won't know unless we try.

In my early journalistic years, I watched such men deal with the deaths of thalidomide babies and the results of terrible accidents with calm and compassion. If their successors are as caring in their deliberations, I feel this may go some way to meeting the objections that people have.

And I would suggest, too, that Social Services be kept well away from any such arrangement. I don't think they would have much to offer.

In this country we have rather lost faith in the wisdom of ordinary people, among whom my father was a shining example. And it is ordinary people, ultimately, who must make such decisions.

There are those who will object that the care industry can cope. Even if we accept that they are coping now, which most of us will take on trust, in the coming decades they certainly will not be able to without a major reordering of our society.

The numbers tell us this. We already have a situation where elderly people are being cared for at home by people who themselves are of pensionable age. The healthcare system will become messy, and the NHS will struggle to cope.

There are care homes, of course, and they are subject to inspection, and we must take it on trust that the inspection system has teeth, but would you know how to choose one? Would you know what questions to ask?

Would you know, if you suffer from Alzheimer's disease or are representing someone who is, whether the place you would be choosing resorts to 'peg feeding'?

Peg feeding is the forcible feeding of patients who refuse food. I found out about this only recently, and I'm afraid it has entirely coloured my views. These are, after all, innocent people who are on the road to death, and yet someone thinks it is right to subject them to this degrading and painful business.

The Alzheimer's Society says peg feeding is 'not best practice', a rather diplomatic statement. People there that I trust tell me the main problem with the treatment of acute Alzheimer's cases is not a lack of care and goodwill as such, but insufficient numbers of people who are skilled in the special needs of the terminally ill Alzheimer's patient.

I am certain no one sets out to be cruel, but our treatment of the elderly ill seems to have no philosophy to it.

As a society, we should establish whether we have a policy of 'life at any cost'. Apparently there is already such a thing as an official 'quality of life index'; I don't know whether the fact that we have one frightens me more than the possibility that we don't.

In the first book of my Discworld series, published more than twenty-six years ago, I introduced Death as a character; there was nothing particularly new about this – death has featured in art and literature since medieval times, and for centuries we have had a fascination with the Grim Reaper.

But the Death of the Discworld is a little more unusual. He has become popular – after all, as he patiently explains, it is not he who kills. Guns and knives and starvation kill; Death turns up afterwards, to reassure the puzzled arrivals as they begin their journey.

He is kind; after all, he is an angel. And he is fascinated with us, with the way in which we make our little lives so complicated, and our strivings. So am I.

Within a year or two, I started to get letters about Death. They came from people in hospices, and from their relatives and from bereaved individuals, and from young children in leukaemia wards, and the parents of boys who had crashed their motorbikes.

I recall one letter where the writer said the books were of great help to his mother when she was in a hospice. Frequently, the bereaved asked to be allowed to quote some part of the Discworld books in a memorial service.

They all tried to say, in some way, 'thank you', and until I got used to it, the arrival of one of these letters would move me sufficiently to give up writing for the day.

The bravest person I've ever met was a young boy going through massive amounts of treatment for a very rare, complex and unpleasant disease. I last saw him at a Discworld convention, where he chose to take part in a game as an assassin. He died not long afterwards, and I wish I had his fortitude and sense of style.

I would like to think my refusal to go into care towards the end of my life might free up the resources for people such as him.

Let me make this very clear: I do not believe there is any such thing as a 'duty to die'; we should treasure great age as the tangible presence of the past, and honour it as such.

I know that last September Baroness Warnock was quoted, or possibly misquoted, as saying the very elderly sick had a 'duty to die', and I have seen people profess to fear that the existence of a formalized approach to assisted dying could lead to it somehow becoming part of national health policy.

I very much doubt this could be the case. We are a democracy and no democratic government is going to get anywhere with a policy of compulsory or even recommended euthanasia. If we were ever to end up with such a government, we would be in so much trouble that the problem would become the least of our worries.

But neither do I believe in a duty to suffer the worst ravages of terminal illness.

As an author, I've always tended to be known only to a circle of people – quite a large one, I must admit – who read books. I was not prepared for what happened after I 'came out' about having Alzheimer's in December 2007, and appeared on television.

People would stop me in the street to tell me their mother had it, or their father had it. Sometimes, it's both parents, and I look into their eyes and I see a flash of fear.

In London the other day, a beefy man grabbed my arm, smiled at me and said, 'Thanks a lot for what you're doing, my mum died from it,' and disappeared into the crowd.

And, of course, there have been the vast numbers of letters and emails, some of which, I'm ashamed to say, will perhaps never be answered.

People do fear, and not because fear is whipped up, but because they've recalled an unpleasant death in their family history.

Sometimes I find myself involved in strange

conversations, because I am an amiable-looking person who people think they know and, importantly, I am not an authority figure – quite the reverse.

I have met Alzheimer's sufferers who are hoping that another illness takes them away first. Little old ladies confide in me, saying: 'I've been saving up my pills for the end, dear.'

What they are doing, in fact, is buying themselves a feeling of control. I have met retired nurses who have made their own provisions for the future with rather more knowledge-able deliberation.

From personal experience, I believe the recent poll reflects the views of the people in this country. They don't dread death; it's what happens beforehand that worries them.

Life is easy and cheap to make. But the things we add to it, such as pride, self-respect and human dignity, are worthy of preservation, too, and these can be lost in a fetish for life at any cost.

I believe that if the burden gets too great, those who wish to should be allowed to be shown the door.

In my case, in the fullness of time, I hope it will be the one to the garden under an English sky. Or, if wet, the library.

The Richard Dimbleby Lecture: Shaking Hands with Death

Royal Society of Medicine, 1 February 2010
Broadcast on BBC1, with revisions to indicate that Tony
Robinson would be reading the main text.

Firstly I must express my gratitude and grateful thanks to
the Dimbleby family for asking me to give this lecture
today.

I cherish what I suspect is at least part of their reason for
inviting me. I was a young newspaper journalist, still learning
his trade, when Richard Dimbleby died of cancer in late
December 1965. Two pieces of information shook the nation:
one was that he had died and the other was that his family
said that he had died of cancer. At that time it was the
disease whose name was unspoken. People died of 'a long
illness' and as journalists we accepted and connived at this
furtive terminology. However, we all knew what it meant, yet

nobody used the forbidden word. But overnight, people were talking about this, and as a result it seemed to me the war on cancer began in earnest. Before you can kill the monster you have to say its name.

It was the distant echo of that example that prompted me to stand up two years ago and reveal that I had a form of Alzheimer's disease. I remembered the shameful despairing way cancer had been hidden in darkness. That and the Dimbleby family's decision to be open about Richard's death were at the soul and centre of my own decision, which I made because of the sheer impossibility of not doing so. It was not a decision, in fact. It was a determination and a reckoning.

My name is Terry Pratchett and I am the author of a very large number of inexplicably popular fantasy novels.

Contrary to popular belief, fantasy is not about making things up. The world is stuffed full of things. It is almost impossible to invent any more. No, the role of fantasy as defined by G. K. Chesterton is to take what is normal and everyday and usual and unregarded, and turn it around and show it to the audience from a different direction, so that they look at it once again with new eyes.

I intend tonight to talk about Alzheimer's disease, which I am glad to say is no longer in the twilight, but also about another once taboo subject, the nature of our relationship with death.

I have regrettably to point out that the nature of my disease may not allow me to read all the way through this lecture. If this is the case, we have arranged for my friend Tony Robinson, who made a very moving programme about his own mother's struggle with dementia, to step in and be your stunt Terry Pratchett for the evening.

I'm sure you know that, for my sins, which I wish I could remember because they must have been crimson, I am effectively 'Mr Alzheimer's' and I have given more interviews on the subject than I can remember. But there are others, less well known, who have various forms of dementia and go out and about being ambassadors for the Alzheimer's Society in their fight against the wretched disease. It's not just me, by a long way. They are unsung heroes and I salute them.

When I was a young boy, playing on the floor of my grandmother's front room, I glanced up at the television and saw Death, talking to a Knight, and I didn't know very much about death at that point. It was the thing that happened to budgerigars and hamsters. But it was Death, with a scythe and an amiable manner. I didn't know it at the time, of course, but I had just watched a clip from Bergman's *Seventh Seal*, wherein the Knight engages in protracted dialogue, and of course the famous chess game, with the Grim Reaper who, it seemed to me, did not seem so terribly grim.

The image has remained with me ever since and Death as a character appeared in the very first of my Discworld novels. He has evolved in the series to be one of its most popular characters; implacable, because that is his job, he nevertheless appears to have some sneaking regard and compassion for a race of creatures which are to him as ephemeral as mayflies, but which nevertheless spend their brief lives making rules for the universe and counting the stars. He is, in short, a kindly Death, cleaning up the mess that this life leaves, and opening the gate to the next one. Indeed, in some religions he is an angel.

People have written to me about him from convents, ecclesiastical palaces, funeral parlours and, not least, hospices. The letters I've had from people all around the world have sometimes made me give up writing for the day and take a long walk. It is touching, and possibly worrying that people will write, with some difficulty, a six-page letter to an author they have never met, and include in it sentiments that I very much doubt they would share with their doctor.

I have no clear recollection of the death of my grand-parents, but my paternal grandfather died in the ambulance on the way to hospital just after having cooked and eaten his own dinner at the age of ninety-six. (It turned out, when we found his birth certificate, that he was really ninety-four, but he was proud of being ninety-six, so I hope that no celestial being was kind enough to disillusion him.)

He had felt very odd, got a neighbour to ring for the doctor and stepped tidily into the ambulance and out of the world. He died on the way to the hospital – a good death if ever there was one. Except that, according to my father, he did complain to the ambulance men that he hadn't had time to finish his pudding. I am not at all sure about the truth of this, because my father had a finely tuned sense of humour which he was good enough to bequeath to me, presumably to make up for the weak bladder, the short stature and the male-pattern baldness, which regrettably came with the package.

My father's own death was more protracted. He had a year's warning. It was pancreatic cancer. Technology kept him alive, at home and in a state of reasonable comfort and cheerfulness for that year, during which we had those conversations that you have with a dying parent. Perhaps it is when you truly get to know them, when you realize that it is now you marching towards the sound of the guns and you are ready to listen to the advice and reminiscences that life was too crowded for up to that point. He unloaded all the anecdotes that I had heard before, about his time in India during the war, and came up with a few more that I had never heard. As with so many men of his generation, his wartime service was never far from his recollection. Then, at one point, he suddenly looked up and said, 'I can feel the sun of India on my face,' and his face did light up rather magically, brighter and happier than I had seen it at any time in the previous year and if there had been any justice or even narrative sensibility in the universe, he would have died there and then, shading his eyes from the sun of Karachi.

He did not.

On the day he was diagnosed my father told me, and I quote: 'If you ever see me in a hospital bed, full of tubes and pipes and no good to anybody, tell them to switch me off.'

In fact, it took something under a fortnight in the hospice for him to die as a kind of collateral damage in the war between his cancer and the morphine. And in that time he stopped being him and started becoming a corpse, albeit one that moved ever so slightly from time to time.

There wasn't much I could have done, and since the nurses in the Welsh hospice were fine big girls, perhaps that was just as well. I thank them now for the geriatric cat that was allowed to roam the wards and kept me and my mother company as we awaited the outcome. Feline though it was, and also slightly smelly, with a tendency to grumble, it was a touch of humanity in the long reaches of the night.

On the way back home after my father's death I scraped my Jag along a stone wall in Hay-on-Wye. To be fair, it's almost impossible not to scrape Jags along the walls in Hay-on-Wye even if your eyes aren't clouded with tears, but what I didn't know at the time, yet strongly suspect now, was that also playing a part in that little accident was my own disease, subtly making its presence felt. Alzheimer's creeps up very gently over a long period of time, possibly decades, and Baby Boomers like myself know that we are never going to die so always have an explanation ready for life's little hiccups. We say, 'I've had a senior moment. Ha! Ha!' We say, 'Everybody loses their car keys.' We say, 'Oh, I do that, too. I often go upstairs and forget what I have come up for!' We say, 'I often forget someone's name mid sentence,' and thus we are complicit in one another's determination not to be mortal. We like to believe that if all of us are growing old, none of us are growing old.

I have touch-typed since I was thirteen, but now that was going wrong. I got new spectacles. I bought a better keyboard, not such a bad idea since the old one was full of beard hairs and coffee, and finally at the end of self-delusion I went to see my GP. Slightly apologetically she gave me the standard Alzheimer's test, with such taxing questions as 'What day of the week is it?' and then sent me off locally for a scan. The result? I didn't have Alzheimer's. My condition was simply wear and tear on the brain caused by the passage of time that 'happens to everybody'. Old age, in short. I thought, well, I've never been fifty-nine before and so this must be how it is.

So off I went, reassured, about my business; I did a signing tour in Russia, a signing tour in the USA, which included breakfast at the White House (there were lots of other people there, it wasn't as if I handed Mrs Bush the cornflakes or anything), and then I did a signing tour in Italy, where the wife of our Ambassador very diplomatically pointed out that I had made a fist of buttoning up my shirt. Well, I had got up early for the flight, and had dressed in the dark, and so we all had a little chuckle, followed by lunch, and I hoped that everyone but me forgot about it.

Back home my typing was now so full of mistakes that it was simpler for me to dictate to my personal assistant. I went to see my GP again and she sent me to Addenbrooke's Hospital in Cambridge. I have never discussed the interview with her, but either by luck or prescience I ended up in front of Dr Peter Nestor, one of the few specialists in the country, or maybe the world, who would recognize Posterior Cortical Atrophy, the rare variant of my disease. He and his colleagues put me through a battery of tests, and he looked again at my scans, this time, importantly, in a different place. When he gave me the news that I had a rare form of Alzheimer's disease I quite genuinely saw him outlined in a rectangle of flaming red lines. We had a little bit of a discussion, and then, because the facility was closing for the day, I went home, passing another doctor putting on his bicycle clips – this was Cambridge, after all – and such was my state of mind that he too was outlined in red fire. The whole world had changed.

I was lucky in several ways. PCA is sufficiently different from 'classic' Alzheimer's that I have met fellow sufferers from it who dislike it being linked with that disease, even though the pathology and the endgame are ultimately the same. The journey, however, is different. PCA manifests itself through sight problems, and difficulty with topological tasks, such as buttoning up a shirt. I have the opposite of a superpower; sometimes, I cannot see what is there. I see the teacup with my eyes, but my brain refuses to send me the teacup message. It's very Zen. First there is no teacup and then, because I know there is a teacup, the teacup will appear the next time I look. I have little work-arounds to deal with this sort of thing – people with PCA live in a world of work-arounds. A glass revolving door is a potential Waterloo; I have a work-around for that now, too. In short, if you did not know there was anything wrong with me, you would not know there is anything wrong with me. People who have spoken to me for half an hour or so ask me if I am sure I have the illness. Yes, it's certainly there, but cunning and subterfuge get me through. So does money. The first draft of this speech was dictated using TalkingPoint on my computer which, while not perfect, produces a result that is marvellously better than anything I could tap out on the keyboard. From the inside, the disease makes me believe that I am constantly being followed by an invisible moron who moves things, steals things, hides things that I have put down a second before and, in general, sometimes causes me to yell with frustration. You see, the disease moves slowly, but you know it's there. Imagine that you're in a very, very slow motion car crash. Nothing much seems to be happening. There's an occasional little bang, a crunch, a screw pops out and spins across the dashboard as if we're in Apollo 13. But the radio is still playing, the heater is on and it doesn't seem all that bad, except for the certain knowledge that sooner or later you will be definitely going head first through the windscreen.

My first call when I got back from Cambridge was to my GP. I wanted to know what was going to happen next. In fact, it became clear that nothing at all was going to happen next unless we made it happen; there was no specialist anywhere local to me prepared to take on an early onset patient with PCA, and therefore nobody who could legitimately write me a prescription for the only palliative Alzheimer's drug on the market. When I learned this I was filled with a rage, a rage that is with me still, but by now tempered and harnessed to practical purposes. I felt alone. A cancer sufferer, just diagnosed, can at least have some map showing the way the future might, hopefully, go. And I don't seek to minimize how dreadful that disease would be, but there would be appointments, there would be specialists, there would be tests. Hopefully, you would receive sympathy, and hopefully you would have hope.

But at that time the Alzheimer's patient was more or less told to go home. Indeed, I have been contacted by patients who were in effect told just that, with not even the suggestion that they might talk to, for example, the Alzheimer's Society. I will say in another aside, I'm not the sort of person who goes to groups, but much later, I was persuaded to go to a PCA meeting in London, hosted by Professor Rosser of the National Hospital for Neurology and Neurosurgery. I remember the smiles when I started talking about the symptoms and it was hugely refreshing to be among people who understood without having to be told. But I had seen the bicycle clips of fire; I would have thrown a brick through a pharmacy window late at night for the medication I needed, and come to think of it, that might have made a damn good photo opportunity, but friends and contacts of mine who cared about my liberty helped me deal with the situation in the way that people deal with such situations in stupid hidebound bureaucracies. We bent things, just a tiny little bit. It wasn't as though I was stealing. I still had to pay for the damn drugs.

But then it was time to decide who I was going to tell, and for the reasons given earlier, I decided to tell everybody. After that, my life ceased to be my own. I have had so much mail that not all of it can be answered in my lifetime. And I cannot remember how many interviews I have given. They must run into three figures easily. We did the BAFTA Award-winning documentary, in which I demonstrated to the world the impossibility of my tying a tie (funnily enough, I can tie my shoe laces, presumably because I have known how to do that for longer). I have also been able to write two more books, which my PA insists I tell you were best-sellers, had a stone bridge built over the stream in my garden, have been kissed by Joanna Lumley, and after being, astonishingly, knighted, subsequently made, with the help of knowledge-able friends, a sword – doing it the hard way, by first digging the iron ore out of the ground and smelting it in the garden. Of course, I shall never be able to take it out on the street, because such is the decay of our society that not even Knights can carry their swords in public. But who could ask for any-thing more? Except for, maybe, another kiss from Joanna Lumley.

But most of all in the last couple of years I have been listening. As a journalist, I learned to listen. It is amazing how much people will tell you if you listen in the right way. Rob, my PA, says that I can listen like a vacuum cleaner. Always beware of somebody who is a really good listener.

I have heard it said that some people feel that they are being avoided once the news gets around that they have Alzheimer's. For me it has been just the reverse. People want to talk to me, on city streets, in theatre queues, on aeroplanes over the Atlantic, even on country walks. They want to tell me about their mother, their husband, their grandmother. Sometimes it is clear to me that they are extremely frightened. And increasingly, they want to talk about what I prefer to call 'assisted death', but which is still called, wrongly in my opinion, 'assisted suicide'.

I will digress slightly at this point to talk about the baggage that words carry. Let us start with suicide. As a pallid and nervous young journalist I got to know about suicide. Oh, didn't I just. It was part of my regular tasks to sit in at the coroner's court, where I learned all the manifold ways the disturbed human brain can devise to die. High bridges and trains were, I suspect, the most traumatic instruments for all concerned, especially those who had to deal with the aftermath. Newspapers were a little more kindly in those days, and we tended not to go into too much detail, but I had to listen to it. And I remember that coroners never used the word 'insanity'. They preferred the more compassionate verdict that the subject had 'taken his life while the balance of his mind was disturbed'. There was ambivalence to the phrase, a suggestion of the winds of fate and overwhelming circumstance. No need to go into the horrible details that the coroner's officer, always a policeman, mentioned to me after the case. In fact, by now, I have reached the conclusion that a person may make a decision to die because the balance of their mind is level, realistic, pragmatic, stoic and sharp. And that is why I dislike the term 'assisted suicide' applied to the carefully thought out and weighed up process of having one's life ended by gentle medical means.

The people who thus far have made the harrowing trip to Dignitas in Switzerland to die seemed to me to be very firm and methodical of purpose, with a clear prima facie case for wanting their death to be on their own terms. In short, their mind may well be in better balance than the world around them.

I'll return again to my father's request to me, that I was unable to fulfil. In the course of the past year or so I have talked amiably about the issues of assisted dying to people of all sorts, because they have broached the subject. A lot of them get nervy about the term 'assisted death' and seriously nervous about 'assisted suicide', but when I mention my father's mantra about not wishing to go on living supported by the pipes and tubes they brighten up and say, 'Oh, yes, I don't have any problem with that.' That was the problem reduced from a sterile title into the wishes of a real person in whom, perhaps, they could see themselves.

When I began to draft this speech, the so-called debate on assisted dying was like a snowball fight in the dark. Now, it seems to be occupying so much space in the media that I wonder whether it is something in the air, an idea whose time is really coming. Very recently an impassioned outburst by Martin Amis in an interview he gave to the *Sunday Times* called for euthanasia booths on every street corner. I firmly believe it was there to trap the hard of irony, and I note that it has done so – he was, after all, a novelist talking about a new book. Did it get publicity? It surely did. Apart from being tasteless, the idea is impractical, especially if there happens to be a photo booth next door. But his anger and grief at the way elderly relatives, friends and colleagues have died is clearly genuine and shared by a great many. The post-war generation have seen what's happened to their elders and are determined that it should not happen to them.

Even more recently, the British Social Attitude Survey

found that 71 per cent of religious people and 92 per cent of non-religious people were in favour of medically assisted dying for patients with incurable illnesses if they should request it.

Insofar as there are sides in this debate, they tend to polarize around the Dignity in Dying organization, who favour assisted death in special circumstances, and the Care Not Killing Alliance whose position, in a nutshell, appears to be that care will cope.

And once again I remember my father. He did not want to die a curious kind of living death. He wasn't that kind of person. He wanted to say goodbye to me, and, knowing him, he would probably have finished with a joke of some sort. And if the nurses had put the relevant syringe in the cannula, I would have pressed it, and felt it was my duty. There would have been tears, of course there would: tears would be appropriate and unsuppressable.

But of course, this did not happen because I, my father and the nurses were locked in the aspic of the law. But he actually had a good death in the arms of morphia and I envy him.

I got involved in the debate surrounding 'assisted death' by accident after taking a long and, yes, informed look at my future as someone with Alzheimer's and subsequently writing an article about my conclusions. As a result of my 'coming out' about the disease I now have contacts in medical research industries all over the world, and I have no reason to believe that a 'cure' is imminent. I do think, on their good advice, that there may be some very interesting developments in the next couple of years and I'm not the only one to hope for some kind of 'stepping stone' – a treatment that will keep me going long enough for a better treatment to be developed.

I said earlier that PCA at the endgame is effectively the same as Alzheimer's and that it is the most feared disease among the elderly. I was diagnosed when I was fifty-nine, but it has struck adults in their thirties. I enjoy my life, and wish to continue it for as long as I am still myself, knowing who I am and recognizing my nearest and dearest. But I know enough about the endgame to be fearful of it, despite the fact that as a wealthy man I could probably shield myself from the worst; even the wealthy, whatever they may do, have their appointment in Samarra. For younger members of the audience, I should say that the fable 'Appointment in Samarra' is probably one of the oldest stories in the world and has been recast many times; its central point is that you can run and you can hide, but every man has his inevitable appointment with death. It's worth a Google.

Back in my early reporting days I was told something that surprised me at the time: nobody has to do what the doctor tells them. I learned this when the Chief Reporter, George Topley, slung my copy back at me and said, 'Never say that a patient has been released from hospital unless you are talking about someone who is being detained on mental grounds. The proper word is "discharged", and even though the staff would like you to believe that you can't just walk out until they say so, you damn well can. Although, generally speaking, it's best not to be dragging a portable life support system down the steps with you.' George was a remarkable journalist who as a fiery young man would have fought fascism in the Spanish Civil War were it not for the fact that he stowed away on the wrong boat and ended up in Hull.

And I remembered what George said and vowed that rather than let Alzheimer's take me, I would take it. I would live my life as ever to the full and die, before the disease mounted its last attack, in my own home, in a chair on the lawn, with a brandy in my hand to wash down whatever modern version of the 'Brompton Cocktail' (a potent mixture of painkillers and brandy) some helpful medic could supply. And with Thomas Tallis on my iPod, I would shake hands with Death.

I have made my position publicly clear; it seems to me quite a reasonable and sensible decision, for someone with a serious, incurable and debilitating disease to elect for a medically assisted death by appointment.

These days non-traumatic deaths – not the best word, but you will know what I mean – which is to say, deaths that don't, for example, involve several cars, a tanker and a patch of ice on the M4 – largely take place in hospitals and hospices. Not so long ago death took place in your own bed. The Victorians knew how to die. They saw a lot of death. And Victorian and Edwardian London was awash with what we would call recreational drugs, which were seen as a boon and a blessing to all. Departing on schedule with the help of a friendly doctor was quite usual and there is every reason to believe that the medical profession considered that part of its duty was to help the stricken patient on their way.

Does that still apply? It would seem so. Did the Victorians fear death? As Death says in one of my own books, most men don't fear death, they fear those things – the knife, the shipwreck, the illness, the bomb – which precede, by micro-seconds if you're lucky, and many years if you're not, the moment of death.

And this brings us into the whole care or killing argument.

The Care Not Killing Alliance, as they phrase themselves, assure us that no one need consider a voluntary death of any sort since care is always available. This is questionable. Medicine is keeping more and more people alive, all requiring more and more care. Alzheimer's and other dementias place a huge care burden on the country, a burden which falls initially on the next of kin who may even be elderly and, indeed, be in need of some sort of care themselves. The number is climbing as the Baby Boomers get older, but in addition the percentage of cases of dementia among the population is also growing. We then have to consider the quality of whatever care there may be, not just for dementia but for all long-term conditions. I will not go into the horror stories, this is not the place and maybe I should leave the field open to Sir Michael Parkinson who, as the government's dignity ambassador, describes incidents that are, and I quote, 'absolutely barmy and cruel beyond belief' and care homes as little more than 'waiting rooms for death'.

It appears that care is a lottery and there are those of us who don't wish to be cared for and who do not want to spend their time in anyone's waiting room, who want to have the right not to do what you are told by a nurse, not to obey the doctor. A right, in my case, to demand here and now the power of attorney over the fate of the Terry Pratchett that, at some future date, I will become. People exercise themselves in wondering what their nearest and dearest would really want. Well, my nearest and dearest know. So do you.

A major objection frequently flourished by opponents of 'assisted dying' is that elderly people might be illegally persuaded into 'asking' for assisted death. Could be, but the *Journal of Medical Ethics* reported in 2007 that there was no evidence of abuse of vulnerable patients in Oregon where assisted dying is currently legal. I don't see why things should be any different here. I'm sure nobody considers death flippantly; the idea that people would persuade themselves to die just because some hypothetical Acme One-Stop Death shop has opened down the road is fantastical. But I can easily envisage that a person, elderly or otherwise, weighed down with medical problems and understandably fearful of the future, and dreading what is hopefully called care, might consider the 'Victorian-style' death, gently assisted by a medical professional, at home, a more dignified way to go.

Last year, the government finally published guidelines on dealing with assisted death. They did not appear to satisfy anybody. It seems that those wishing to assist a friend or relative to die would have to meet quite a large number of criteria in order to escape the chance of prosecution for murder. We should be thankful that some possibility that they might not be prosecuted is in theory possible, but as laid out, the best anyone can do is keep within the rules and hope for the best.

That's why I and others have suggested some kind of strictly non-aggressive tribunal that would establish the facts of the case well before the assisted death takes place. This might make some people, including me, a little uneasy as it suggests the government has the power to tell you whether you can live or die. But that said, the government cannot sidestep the responsibility to ensure the protection of the vulnerable and we must respect that. It grieves me that those against assisted death seem to assume, as a matter of course, that those of us who support it have not thought long and hard about this very issue and know that it is of fundamental importance. It is, in fact, at the soul and centre of my argument.

The members of the tribunal would be acting for the good of society as well as that of the applicant, horrible word, and ensure they are of sound and informed mind, firm in their purpose, suffering from a life-threatening and incurable disease and not under the influence of a third party. It would need wiser heads than mine, though heaven knows they should be easy enough to find, to determine how such tribunals are constituted. But I would suggest there should be a lawyer, one with expertise in dynastic family affairs who has become good at recognizing what somebody really means and, indeed, whether there is outside pressure. And a medical practitioner experienced in dealing with the complexities of serious long-term illnesses.

Those opposing 'assisted death' say that the vulnerable

must be protected, as if that would not have occurred to anyone else. As a matter of fact there is no evidence – and evidence has been sought – of the sick or elderly being cajoled into assisted death by relatives anywhere in the world where assisted dying is practised, and I see no reason why that would be the case here. Doctors tell me that, to the contrary, family members more often beg them to keep Granny alive even when Granny is indeed, by all medical standards, at the end of her natural life. Importantly, the tribunal would also serve to prevent, as far as humanly possible, any abuses.

I would also suggest that all those on the tribunal are over forty-five years old, by which time they may have acquired the rare gift of wisdom, because wisdom and compassion should in this tribunal stand side by side with the law. The tribunal would also have to be a check on those seeking death for reasons that reasonable people may consider trivial or transient distress. I dare say that quite a few people have contemplated death for reasons that much later seemed to them to be quite minor. If we are to live in a world where a socially acceptable 'early death' can be allowed, it must be allowed as a result of careful consideration.

Let us consider me as a test case. As I have said, I would like to die peacefully with Thomas Tallis on my iPod before the disease takes me over and I hope that will not be for quite some time to come, because if I knew that I could die at any time I wanted, then suddenly every day would be as precious as a million pounds. If I knew that I could die, I would live. My life, my death, my choice.

There has been no evidence in those areas where assisted

dying is currently practised that it leads to any kind of 'slippery slope'. It seems to be an item of faith among those opposed to assisted dying that it will open the door to abuses all the way up to the culling of the elderly sick. This is a nightmare and only a nightmare. This cannot be envisaged in any democracy unless we find ourselves under a tyranny, that is to say a tyranny that is far more aggressive than the mild one currently operated by the Health and Safety Executive. Frankly, that objection is a bogeyman.

It has been suggested that people would not trust their doctor if they knew that he or she had the power to kill them. Why should this be? A doctor has an awful lot to lose by killing a patient. Indeed, it seems to me that asking a medical practitioner who is fully aware of your situation to bring your life to an end is placing the utmost trust in them.

The saying 'Thou shalt not kill; but needst not strive officiously to keep alive' has never been formal advice to the medical profession. Given that it was made up by Arthur Hugh Clough, who was in a similar profession to me, that is not surprising. But, ever since the birth of medicine, doctors have understood its meaning. They have striven, oh how they have striven. In the past two centuries we have improved the length of our lives and the quality of said lives to the point where we feel somewhat uneasy if anyone dies as early as the biblical age of seventy. But there comes a time when technology outpaces sense, when a blip on an oscilloscope is confused with life, and humanity unravels into a state of mere existence.

Observation, conversation and some careful deduction

lead me to believe that the majority of doctors who support the right to die are those who are most closely involved day to day with patients, while support appears to tail off as you reach those heights where politics and medicine merge. It would be interesting to speculate how many doctors would 'come out' were it not for the baleful glare of the BMA. Anyone who has any long-term friendships, acquaintances or professional dealings within the medical profession, let alone knows anything about the social history of medicine, knows that down the ages doctors and nurses have seen it as part of their duty to allow those beyond hope and skill to depart in peace. I can recall the metaphors that have been used: 'helping them over the step', 'showing them the way', 'helping them find the door', 'pointing them to Heaven'. But never, ever 'killing them', because in their minds they were not killing and in their minds they were right.

In fact, I have not found any reputable information from those places where assisted death is allowed that shows any deleterious effect on the community. I certainly do not expect or assume that every GP or hospital practitioner would be prepared to assist death by arrangement, even in the face of overwhelming medical evidence. That is their choice. Choice is very important in this matter. But there will be some, probably older, probably wiser, who will understand. It seems sensible to me that we should look to the medical profession, that over the centuries has helped us to live longer and healthier lives, to help us die peacefully among our loved ones in our own home without a long stay in God's waiting room.

And finally there is the God argument, which I think these days appears to have been subsumed into concern for the innocent who may suffer if assisted dying were allowed. The problem with the God argument is that it only works if you believe in God, more specifically, Jehovah, which I do not. Spinoza, Darwin and Carl Sagan have found in my imagination places which God has never found. Therefore I am a humanist and would rather believe that we are a rising ape, not a falling angel. Nevertheless, I have a sneaking regard for the Church of England and those I disagree with. We should always debate ideas that appear to strike at the centre of our humanity. Ideas and proposals should be tested. I believe that consensual 'assisted death' for those that ask for it is quite hard to oppose, especially by those that have some compassion. But we do need in this world people to remind us that we are all human, and that humanity is precious.

It's that much heralded thing the quality of life that is important. How you live your life, what you get out of it, what you put into it and what you leave behind after it. We should aim for a good and rich life well lived, and at the end of it, in the comfort of our own home, in the company of those who love us, have a death worth dying for.

At last we have real compassion in assisted-dying guidelines

The DPP's new guidelines are good. People, not the diseases, need to be in control

The Times, 26 February 2010

It's a scene right out of *Trading Places*. We're all waiting for the crop reports, although this turns out to be my fevered imagination, as I didn't sleep much last night.

We are watching the clock, waiting for Keir Starmer, Director of Public Prosecutions, to formally present the new guidelines on assisted suicide. And then suddenly it's eleven o'clock and we're all in Millbank, where you can't shake a stick without hitting two reporters, or three if you're lucky.

For Debbie Purdy and me, the race is on. We pass each other endlessly in lifts and in corridors. It's like a high-tech slave auction. You stagger around from one TV interview to another and end up not remembering anything about it.

We're talking about assisted dying. I find out what I think by listening to what I say. And it seems to me that the guidelines presented are about as good as we can expect without a change in the law. I hated the provisional guidelines released in September last year. They seemed to be about ticking boxes. They seemed to be about bureaucracy.

But the word 'compassion' catches my eye. And as I read on, it seems to me that this streamlined policy is more about what goes through the hearts and minds of people than exactly which hoops to jump through. I might dare to believe that someone who, out of compassion and love, helps another human who is not physically able to do it themselves to leave behind an unbearable life, would have little to fear from the authorities.

Nevertheless, I believe that a tribunal, proposed by me and others, should definitely come into existence through a change in the law. It would establish the facts of a case well before the assisted death takes place. But it is also vitally important that the limited freedoms suggested by these guidelines are not used to mask abuse. I believe it is essential that, for the safety of all concerned, the proposed actions and the reasons behind them are discussed in the non-aggressive atmosphere of the tribunal, which may advise, warn or, should it be suspicious, refuse.

The enlightened US state of Oregon is one of three that at the moment allow assisted suicide. In Oregon, after consultation with two doctors, the terminally ill patient is given a prescription that will end their life.

But here is the interesting bit: forty per cent of those who have the prescription to hand die without using it. They've known that they can, and every day they have decided not to. They know that, if they choose, it is they who are in control, not the disease. That is power. That is triumph. That is how a human being should die.

Assisted Dying: It's time the government gave us the right to end our lives

New Humanist, July/August 2011

A short time ago I had to insist to a not very youthful journalist that during my early lifetime anyone who attempted to commit suicide and failed would face a criminal charge and be locked up, presumably to show them life was wonderful and thoroughly worth living.

It would be nice to think that in the not too distant future someone will be incredulous when told that a British citizen stricken with a debilitating and ultimately fatal disease, and yet nevertheless still quite compos mentis, would have to go all the way to another country to die. They would ask for an explanation, and I'd be damned if I could think of one. Three decent, sedate and civilized European countries already allow physician-assisted suicide and yet, despite the fact that every indication is that British people understand and are in favour of assisted dying, if properly conducted, the government consistently turns its back on it. A year ago I was told by a cabinet minister that it would never happen in Britain and I suggested that this was a strange thing to say in a democracy and got a black look for my pains.

Initially, I thought the opposition was largely due to a certain amount of curdled Christianity; despite the fact that there is no scriptural objection, the prohibition came about in the fourteenth century when, because of religious wars and the Black Death, people were committing suicide on the basis that, well, since this world was now so dreadfully unpleasant then maybe it would be a good idea to make an attempt on heaven. Authority thought otherwise and objected. Who would milk the cows? Who would fight the wars? People couldn't be allowed to slope off like that. They had to stay and face their just punishment for being born.

Even now I detect some echoes of that frame of mind: that affliction is somehow a penance for an unknown transgression. To hell with that! Every time the question of assisted dying is broached in this country there is a choreographed outcry, at suggested overtones of Nazism and, of course, the murder of grandmothers for their money. And the perpetrators get away with it because the British have a certain tradition of bullying from the top down. 'The common people are stupid and we who know better must make the decisions for them.'

Well, the common people are not stupid. They might

watch god-awfully stupid reality TV and make a lot of noise in football grounds and they don't understand, perhaps, the politics of Trident, but they are very clever about the politics of blood and bone and pain and suffering. They understand about compassion and, like my father, they are nothing if not practical about these things. He was incurably ill and saw no reason, given the absence of the hope of any cure, that he shouldn't forgo any more suffering and head straight for the door.

And people also understand that, especially if you don't have much money, long-term care in the UK can be somewhat problematical at best. And yet the government sits there like an ancient Pope, hoping that it will all go away.

Death Knocked and
We Let Him In

Sunday Times, 12 June 2011

[The title Terry gave this piece was 'Visiting Switzerland']

Just before Christmas I saw a man die; Peter Smedley and his wife Christine had travelled to the Dignitas clinic in Switzerland, because Peter felt that only there could he find what he wanted, which was a neat, tidy and timely death. And I went with him to watch. The mind does indeed boggle. I once read that you should judge the length of the journey by the things you learn along the way. If that is true, then my road to Switzerland, and back home again, was a marathon.

Late last year the BBC, who had transmitted my Dimbleby Lecture on assisted dying much earlier in the year, asked me

to learn something about assisted dying as practised elsewhere in Europe, and also to speak to Britons who had
signed up with Dignitas, the Swiss organization which is
your last resort if you live in Europe and your country does
not allow you an assisted death. Of course, I said yes.

Three years ago I was diagnosed with Alzheimer's disease.
I will not go into the reasons here why I may wish to be able
to choose to end my life before the disease takes hold – I
have spoken about and investigated dementia at length. As a
writer I am blessed and cursed with an overactive
imagination.

But would I still think this was such a good idea if I went
to witness it first hand?

In the UK assisted dying is illegal and anyone who dares
assist a stricken friend or relative at their request is liable to
end up in court, possibly on a charge of murder. There is
some fine detail around this and it appears that some
leniency could be afforded in the case of those who help out
of compassion or love, which is why, so far, the judges have
been extremely understanding; in short, here in Britain,
amateurs are allowed to help other amateurs to die. It is a
nonsense but it is the only nonsense we have got.

In Belgium, Holland and Switzerland citizens stricken
with a debilitating and incurable disease can choose to die at
the kindly hands of a physician who would have the skills
and the legal framework on which to depend. These
countries are amiable, decent democracies, not known for
excitability or stupidity. Usually their churches treat this with
some dismay, but generally the position seems to be that it is

entirely up to the conscience of the individual concerned.

I followed two men to Dignitas, Peter Smedley and Andrew Colgan, two entirely different men from entirely different backgrounds with entirely different diseases and one steadfast intent which was not to spend any more time in the jaws of the beast and go straight to the last act.

I first met Peter Smedley and his wife Christine at their large and beautiful home. The Smedleys have a wonderful talent of getting on with everybody they meet in a very English way. Christine would have rather Peter stayed at home to be cared for and, indeed, could have afforded the very best of care, but in the little world of this marriage an accord had been reached and Christine was on her husband's side and to hell with what the law might say.

I must admit that I entertained a brief vision of what might happen if Christine Smedley was sent to prison for the dreadful crime of helping her husband to travel to another country, and concluded she would certainly shake the place up to its general improvement and probably end up taking tea with the Warden. As it was, she and Peter went off on a holiday before Christmas to see friends in Switzerland.

Later, in the vicious early winter weather, I met Andrew Colgan, forty-two with multiple sclerosis. Like Peter, he had no further interest in receiving care. I must report that both men had nothing bad at all to say about the care of the seriously ill in this country. In fact, they had very little to say about care at all except that they were resolute in not wanting to be cared for.

Andrew looked younger than his age, wiry, all sinews, and

at first you would think, 'Well, nothing much wrong with him,' until you saw the strain in his face. He was a science fiction fan, and the director had several times to scold us for neglecting the purpose of the interview to indulge in such weighty debates as 'Was *Blake's Seven* really as pants as it seems in memory, or what?' But it was when we were back on track that I found the anger welling up. Andrew was going to die in Switzerland earlier than he might have needed to because, like Peter, he did not want to put any member of his family in jeopardy of the law for assisting him to travel. In truth, I wondered if his fears were essentially groundless, and given that the Director of Public Prosecutions is surely not a vindictive or cruel man and also that the judiciary is noticeably sensible in cases like this I may well be right.

However, sometimes authority gets a rush of blood to its head and prefers to punish the lamb that strays more harshly than the wolf that ravages. Besides, who would choose to see their mother in a court of law, however benign? So he was going alone, and I was thinking, 'Why couldn't he have a physician-assisted death here in England?' And, who knows, if he'd known that he could die when he chose to then perhaps he would have hung on for longer; there is some evidence that this might have been the case, to judge by experience elsewhere.

But, when I talked to him, he was adamant, picking up my hesitant counter suggestions and detecting them for what they were with the speed of Russian over-the-horizon radar. He had been through all that, did not want to be cared for and, like Sherlock Holmes, wanted to take his enemy with him.

We met Andrew in Switzerland for a drink. And I think it was at that point that my head gently started to spin. I have been to wakes, but never one where the principal performer was going to be raising a glass. The way you deal with a situation like this is with humour and so we laughed and joked and, for a blessed while, found ourselves in a happy place. I know this because I was fortunate enough to have with my father, in the months before his death, those conversations that you would wish to have with a parent in those circumstances and we found that somehow humour always got through.

I once heard an opponent of assisted dying in general and Dignitas in particular say, 'People get killed in an industrial estate!', clearly hoping to conjure up images of cybermen on the march. In fact it is an industrial estate where you will find the small blue house with a little garden about which one can best say that someone has tried very hard. It has to be in an industrial area, because it would not be acceptable in a residential area. There was a field of pumpkins on the other side of the narrow road, no traffic to speak of and no sounds at all emanating from the other buildings, which seemed quite benign; perhaps the cybermen were off on their holidays.

I knew that Christine Smedley was going to sit with her husband and, thinking that a knighthood must have some purpose, I had earlier asked her if she would like a fellow Brit there as well, and she was grateful for the offer. Peter wanted our director to film his death, and to include it in the documentary, because he wanted his death to count for something.

I have seen dead bodies before, one of them exceedingly, horribly dead, and I reckoned that the death of a stricken man who sincerely wished to die would not be too stressful. As it happened I was wrong, but for all the wrong reasons.

According to my watch his death took about twenty-five minutes. As the organs and chambers of his body yielded, I heard occasional sounds not too dissimilar to those made by my father as he gradually succumbed to pancreatic cancer and morphine. My mother believed he was trying to say something. I didn't. Outside of actual trauma it takes quite some time for a body to die, treacherously hanging on despite the wishes of the brain.

Peter's wife was holding his hand and frankly, as a bystander, I can't be sure of the point where he departed this world for the next. A kind Swiss lady called Erika, not wearing any kind of official uniform, but gently in charge all the same, knelt beside him while outside the picture window of the little house in which we were gathered the snow fell gently. Everything was silent and on the veranda outside, Erika's husband Horst, who looked like your favourite grandfather, smoked his, yes, incredibly big and curly pipe, the smoke gently mixing with the falling snow. He was outside because, you see, although assisted dying is legal in Switzerland it would appear that smoking indoors is now the last taboo. No wonder the whole experience was for me so memorably surreal.

And Christine? She leaned over to ask me if I was all right. I am not a natural or promiscuous hugger but I hugged that day.

The police arrived shortly after, to check that what had happened was within the law. They were not unpleasant but neither were they friendly; they were just, well, the police, doing their job. As we waited, one of them came up to us and simply said 'BBC?' and took our mumbled word for it, the BBC of course being internationally known as the body who would not be party to any hanky-panky. And in my mind, I waved a little Union Jack.

I am in no doubt that the BBC will be criticized for showing the death of the good man who was Peter Smedley, who died between his wife and an attentive nurse while the snow fell slowly outside. After the Dimbleby Lecture I gave last year where I first put forth my support for assisted dying in theory, a cross-party collection of MPs proposed a vote of censure against the BBC, clearly being unaware that, in a democracy, it is not against the law to argue peacefully for a change in the law. But the fact is that Peter and Andrew dragged themselves to Switzerland to die with the dignity they feared that they would not get in Britain. More have gone since then, often at great cost.

Politicians, fearful of full in-trays from the ultra religious, mutter phrases like 'the sanctity of life' without defining what they mean, or why. They murmur 'It's all very complicated', when it is in essence very simple; my father understood it and so did my mother and really, I suspect, so do most people in this country.

States in the USA and sensible, stable countries here in Europe have found ways of creating a sensible way of allowing assisted dying for those that request it without any collateral damage to the society as a whole. The templates are there, even though I think we could do better.

A year ago a senior Tory shrugged me off on this subject with 'That sort of thing should be left to doctors.' Perhaps by now he knows that it *is* left to doctors in Holland and Belgium and Switzerland and, indeed, parts of the USA. France and Italy do not have any formal system of assisted dying, probably because of too much religion, while Germany does not, very emphatically does not, because of too much history. But why not here? And the answer had better be more sophisticated than 'God won't like it' or 'It's very difficult' or 'How do you protect the vulnerable?' The answer to that is: quite easily, with a little thought and a little willingness and some cognizance of the term 'the freedom of the individual', a concept coming under some strain here in Britain. The same old arguments against will be rolled out by those that repeatedly pose the questions and then don't listen to the answers and, I fear, men and women in some distress, and certainly at some cost, will continue to make their way to Switzerland to the embarrassment of the Swiss and the shame of the British.

Will I be one of them? I certainly hope not. I suspect that I am just like you, and like Peter and Andrew, in wanting to die peacefully at home, surrounded by my loved ones. I do not think that it is too much to demand.

A Week in the Death of Terry Pratchett

The best-selling author and Alzheimer's sufferer reflects on the days following his controversial right-to-die documentary

✫ ✫ ✫ ✫ ✫

Independent, Saturday, 18 June 2011

Monday

D-Day; that's Documentary Day on the calendar here in our office. We spend the morning piling into the ever-present workload until it's time to head off to watch the documentary with the director, Charlie Russell, and his family and friends.

There is just enough time for a drink and a nibble before we're on air. Absolute silence in the room except for the occasional muffled sob as the story of Peter and Andrew unfolds and, at the end, the release and the discussion. I am glad there was a discussion, because there was a lot to be discussed.

A short break and then a BBC *Newsnight* special with Jeremy Paxman, David Aaronovitch, Liz Carr, Dinah Rose QC, Debbie Purdy, the Rt Revd Michael Langrish, the Bishop of Exeter (who was at least open to arguments, unlike some bishops), and also, I was glad to see, Erika Preisig whom I met and admired in Switzerland.

I was surprised to hear from Erika that a Roman Catholic priest had come to Dignitas and had spoken to her, had agreed that it wasn't his time, had told her she was doing a good thing, and came back later and did indeed go through with his assisted death. I have a lot of time for Dr Preisig. She is a Christian, but understands those who beg for an assisted death; like me she has been appalled at some of the terrible outcomes of 'traditional' suicides.

Tuesday

The documentary was not made to encourage, dismay or condone, it was made to see. I was also hoping that it would lead to discussion and it certainly has done so.

And under Jeremy Paxman's tactful arbitration, views were aired and discussed in a reasonably civilized way. With a sigh of relief, my assistant Rob and I hurtled into the city to grab what rest we could, getting, in my case, no more than two hours' sleep before heading to the sofa in the BBC *Breakfast* studio. Rob, sitting next to me in the cab, was trying to keep up with the tweets and reported that they were coming in at a rate of more than one a second with an approval/

disapproval rating of 99.9 per cent. One of the objections being against Rob's Russian naval officer's hat, which he thinks is rather spiffy, but there is no accounting for taste. Other online discussions seemed positive too, with objections being more about the running of Dignitas than whether assisted dying should be available here in the UK.

As I feel I have to keep saying, I don't want to be a publicist for Dignitas, but the unfortunate fact is that for a Briton who wants an assisted death, Dignitas represents the only choice and five more of our citizens have quietly made their way there since the documentary was filmed.

Then we stagger into another couple of interviews before again meeting the director to learn that there had been 1,219 complaints to the BBC and 301 calls in favour, making it one of the top ten programmes this year for appreciation. We were also told the complaints showed some evidence of lobbying; I just bet they did. The good people at the Care Not Killing Alliance certainly know how to use a telephone.

Then it's back home to catch up on sleep and to find that Michael Nazir-Ali, the former Bishop of Rochester, wishes to tell me that real life is not like science fiction. Actually, sir, it is. I live in a science fiction world and so does he; the stents in my heart are science fiction and so are the little pills that go some way to make my Alzheimer's bearable.

A very large number of things which we take for granted were science fiction once, and some others were never science fiction because not even science fiction writers had imagined them. The bishop ought to respect science fiction;

he's living in it.

And once again he triumphantly delivers the ever-present question: how, if assisted dying is allowed in the UK, do you safeguard the vulnerable? This is without fail trotted out by all those against the idea and is delivered as if it is the killer argument.

As the documentary says, there are four countries in Europe that practise some form of assisted dying and recently the Swiss voted in a referendum to maintain the practice. They even voted in favour of continuing to allow the so-called death tourism for those unfortunates, like the British, who make their way to Dignitas.

This does not sound like people who are living in a world where innocent citizens are being killed against their will, does it?

Wednesday

We start trawling through the interminable number of emails that had arrived while we were asleep and we find that many viewers had been touched and impressed by the testimony of Veerla Claus-De Wit, whose husband Hugo was granted his request for an assisted death by sympathetic and caring doctors. He had the same disease as I have and I certainly took that one to heart.

There are those that would never accept the concept of assisted dying, it seems, and yet it does appear, sitting here looking at the emails still coming in, that this country, if not our government, is thinking constructively. Sniping is, of course, going on from various newspapers that we are picking up. However, there are thoughtful columns as well, but I must say that Alex Hardy's inconsiderate sneer in *The Times* at Christine Smedley, a woman endeavouring to put a brave face on the death of her husband, was execrable.

I wouldn't have expected that even from the *Daily Mail*.

Thursday

Right now we are sitting in the Chapel, which is covered with stacks of books that must be signed and sent to New Orleans post haste, and still the emails and letters are coming in and we are getting requests from countries around the world to talk about the documentary.

Not quite sure about that.

I would like to see carefully controlled assisted dying available in the UK, which is why I helped fund a commission of the great and the good who have an open mind on the subject and a working knowledge of the mechanics and expectations of this country, to see whether sensible arrangements should be put in place that would be acceptable to the population at large, so that in the fullness of time stricken people who do not wish to be prisoners of their disease can at least die with dignity in their own country.

But when the British government is unresponsive, then individual citizens must try to move things along and, for now, we are going to write a book, and it's not about death.

Friday

Last night the BBC's *Question Time* was held in Scotland and, of course, the issue came up. Not so long ago I recall another BBC *Question Time* in Scotland, where the issue was raised and got some very short shrift.

This time the panel, while not all on side, spoke carefully and thoughtfully to a very respectful audience which seemed, for the most part, to be open-minded on the subject. The world changes, but slowly.

And finally . . .

Terry Pratchett's Wild Unattached Footnotes to Life

Space (at the) Bar. A Compute for Charity *magazine.*
Compiled by Octarine Science Fiction and
Fantasy Humour Appreciation Society.
Hull, 1 July 1990

ANTIPASTA (inspired by seeing it on an Italian menu)
Possibly the greatest, and certainly the most expensive, food in the world. You need a massive particle accelerator and enough electricity to power Greater London just to make one plateful of antipasta because, like all antimatter, it *travels backwards through time*. Normal pasta is made several hours before you eat it; antipasta is made several hours *after* you've eaten it. If correctly timed, both can be made to appear on your fork at the same moment, resulting in the inevitable taste explosion. In fact, most of the expense involved in the creation of antipasta is due to the cost

of cleaning all the tomato sauce off the walls afterwards.

Sir Thomas Crapper

Everyone knows that Sir Thomas Crapper invented the first practical, efficient flush lavatory (star of the Great Exhibition of 1851) and thus gave his name to the device and, eventually, the verb and associated noun. The strange thing is that what everyone knows is *wrong*. 'Crap' and its various derivations date back to the sixteenth century (one name for a privy was a 'crapping castle'). So it follows that if Thomas Crapper existed, he must have had a really bad time of it at school, and realized that he had no alternative but to enter hydraulic engineering and at least make sure that crappers were efficient. Strange but true.

Beau Trap (early nineteenth-century slang, probably originating in Bath)

Now, at last, a word for something that really needs a name. Almost every street in these Thatcherite days has, somewhere along its length, a paving stone which has come loose so that rainwater can get underneath. And when you tread on it, tips up and pumps half a litre of rainwater up your trouser. This is a beau trap.

Things to Order Loudly in Restaurants

1) Liver with bigger tubes
2) Whitebait with extra eyes
3) Smorgasbord with the tops on

BARRY NORMAL'S GUIDE TO STRANGE JOBS
IN HOLLYWOOD

#1. The man who reverses big lorries out of side streets during the big car-chase scene (you know . . . usually the hero manages to steer round it and the villains hilariously have the tops of their heads removed as their car goes under it).

It was not realized until 1988 that this is not only the same lorry but the same driver on the same delivery round.

''S not my fault,' said Hiram Kaputnik, 47. 'Some of the places they want I should deliver to, there's no way I can three-point turn there. I got commendations for careful driving. It's just that I back out and two cars come down the next alley at 90 mph, what am I supposed to do? If I've had the underseal redone once, it's been done fifty times.'

Strangely enough, Mr Kaputnik's father and uncle spent a lot of time in Hollywood during the 1920s trying to deliver one sheet of plate glass by hand. And why not?

A Blink of the Screen

Collected shorter fiction

**Terry Pratchett
With a foreword by A.S. Byatt**

In the four decades since his books first appeared in print, Terry Pratchett became one of the world's best-selling and best-loved authors. *A Blink of the Screen* collects the best of his short fiction into one volume, and charts the course of Pratchett's long writing career: from his schooldays through to his first writing job on the *Bucks Free Press*, and the origins of his debut novel, *The Carpet People*; and on again to his phenomenally successful Discworld series.

Here are characters both familiar and yet to be discovered; abandoned worlds and others still expanding; adventure, chickens, death, disco and, actually, some quite disturbing ideas about Christmas, all of it shot through with his inimitable brand of humour. With an introduction by Booker Prize-winning author A.S. Byatt, illustrations by the late Josh Kirby and drawings by the author himself, this is a book to treasure.

'Clever, neatly constructed and funny . . . Pratchett is one of the great comic writers and storytellers of our time'
GUARDIAN

Raising Steam

A Discworld® Novel

Terry Pratchett

It's all change for Moist von Lipwig, swindler, conman, and (naturally) head of the Royal Bank and Post Office.

A steaming, clanging new invention, driven by Dick Simnel, the man with t'flat cap and t'sliding rule, is drawing astonished crowds – including a few particularly keen young men armed with notepads and very sensible rainwear – and suddenly it's a matter of national importance that the trains run on time.

Moist does not enjoy hard work. His . . . *vital* input at the bank and post office consists mainly of words, which are not that heavy. Or greasy. And it certainly doesn't involve rickety bridges, runaway cheeses or a fat controller with knuckledusters. What he does enjoy is being alive, which may not be a perk of running the new railway. Because, of course, some people have OBJECTIONS, and they'll go to extremes to stop locomotion in its tracks.

'British fiction's most brilliant satire on contemporary life'
TELEGRAPH

Visit

www.**terrypratchett**.co.uk

to discover everything you need to know
about Terry Pratchett and his writing, plus all
manner of other things you may find interesting, such as
videos, competitions, character profiles and games.

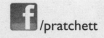 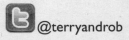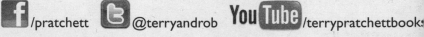